God and Modernity

God and Modernity is a really distinctive contribution to the question of how religious discourse is to find its way and its place in the fragmenting political world we inhabit.

Rowan Williams, Bishop of Monmouth

It is not often one reads an original manuscript, but this is one ... Shanks is a consummate exegete – one of the best I have ever come across ... The book contains genuine insights and a genuine alternative to previous ways of doing theology.

Linda Woodhead, Lancaster University

God and Modernity boldly pioneers a new genre of theology. Andrew Shanks goes beyond the theological debate that has dominated the past four centuries: between, on the one hand, those seeking to reconcile Christian tradition with the spirit of the Enlightenment and, on the other, those who are more critical of that spirit.

Shanks argues that God is most present in a culture where public debate over ethical issues flourishes best. In recent years, new social movements have emerged, no longer confined to a particular confessional religious identity, and unfettered by the constraints of party-politics – feminist movements, peace movements and green movements, for example.

Each of these social movements has already made its own individual impact on theology. But what would a theology look like which systematically aimed to reconcile the old truths of liberalism and neo-orthodoxy with a new loyalty to such movements' common ethos? That is the basic question addressed here.

Anyone wishing to entertain the possibility of 'a new and better way to do theology' will welcome this ground-breaking book.

Andrew Shanks is a priest in the Church of England, currently working for the diocese of York. He is also the author of *Hegel's Political Theology* and *Civil Society, Civil Religion*.

God and Modernity

A new and better way to do theology

Andrew Shanks

London and New York

First published 2000
by Routledge
11 New Fetter Lane, London EC4P 4EE

Simultaneously published in the USA and Canada
by Routledge
29 West 35th Street, New York, NY 10001

Routledge is an imprint of the Taylor & Francis Group

Typeset in Times by Taylor & Francis Books Ltd
Printed and bound in Great Britain by Biddles Ltd, Guildford and
King's Lynn

British Library Cataloguing in Publication Data
A catalogue record for this book is available from the British Library

Library of Congress Cataloguing in Publication Data
A catalogue record for this book has been requested

ISBN 0–415–22188–9 (hbk)
ISBN 0–415–22189–7 (pbk)

For Dian,

an elaborately encoded token of my admiration

Contents

Preface

Who reads books of theology? On the one hand, university students and academics. On the other hand, churchpeople. Especially those who are both.

Who writes books of theology? For by far the greater part, the same. I myself for instance am a priest of the Church of England, and have worked both in parishes and as a university lecturer.

Some forms of nineteenth- and twentieth-century theology – the sort usually called 'liberal' – are more loyal than others to the distinctive ethos of the university. Some are more loyal to the ethos of the church: the 'neo-orthodox' sort. But in any case, all contemporary theology belongs in one way or another to the buffeting interplay between these two dominant institutions: the university and the church.

Yet theology is also meant to be a testimony to divine transcendence. And not least in this sense, surely: *that it calls for a form of thinking which transcends the inherent limitations of both these contexts.* Or so I want to argue.

The university ethos, in the most general terms, is clearly one which tends to privilege neutral, objective observation and research. But theology springs from religious faith. It is not only a matter of neutral, objective observation of – and research into – the history and current consequences of faith. To be sure, it does require a good deal of such observation and research. And yet, at the same time, it is essentially premissed on the actual having of faith; it is the scholarly self-expression of faith. This is what differentiates it from those other closely related disciplines, which belong so much more easily to the university ethos: 'religious studies', 'sociology of religion', 'philosophy of religion'. Theology has a much more complex (I would say a much more interestingly critical) relationship to the university ethos. It partly inhabits that ethos. But it also transcends it – largely thanks to the countervailing gravitational pull to which it is exposed from all that is un-academic in the faith-based ethos of the church.

Behind the church ethos, though, is a set of institutions with their own very distinct forms of ideological self-interest. And, to that extent, this ethos clearly needs transcending too. Good theology must be something more than just the mere articulation of church ideology. In order to flourish as that 'something more', again it needs to be both part of, and yet at the same time set apart from, the larger ethos of the institutional church which sponsors it.

Up to a point, its participation in the university world helps supply that necessary inner independence. However, I have to say, I very much doubt if that – on its own – is enough.

I want to argue for something more.

Thus, there is after all yet another set of loyalties which has increasingly begun to impinge on theology over the past few decades: namely, loyalties to various sorts of 'new social movement'. So, for instance, one encounters such phenomena as 'feminist theology', 'green theology', 'black theology' and 'peace movement theology'.

But what, I want to ask, if one were now, in a much more general fashion, to take this other sort of loyalty – a loyalty to the underlying ethos of these movements, considered here as a collectivity – and explore what it might mean *systematically to prioritize that loyalty* as a basis for theology, in essentially the same way that liberal theology has in the past been founded on a relative prioritization of loyalty to the university ethos and neo-orthodox theology has been founded on a counter-emphasis on loyalty to the ethos of the institutional church?

That is what I am advocating in this book: a whole other approach to theology, in short; equidistant from traditional liberalism and traditional neo-orthodoxy, because drawing fundamentally, and not only in single-issue terms, on a whole other area of experience, in addition to those of the university and the church.

It is a matter, one might say, of trying to grasp something of the sheer aliveness of the living God, in the public realm. All theology is by definition a response to 'revelation'. Conventional theology however, in both its neo-orthodox and to a large extent also its liberal forms, has always tended to focus primarily if not exclusively on revelation in biblical and church history, as such. But here I am concerned with revelation in the *entirety* of history – and above all with what new things we might possibly learn about God by pondering on the general record of the twentieth century. 'New social movements', on the whole, seem to me to be by far the most sensitive communities when it comes to registering the major moral lessons of the age – both as regards its promise and its various nightmares – in pre-theological terms. And what therefore preoccupies me is the question of how that pre-theological insight of theirs is to be interpreted theologically.

By way of a provisional answer, I have constructed an argument covering the following topics:

1 To begin with, the opening chapters are an attempt to spell out what it might basically mean to speak of a general 'new social movement' ethos, as a potential grounding for theology. Amongst other things, the resultant discussion connects up with ongoing sociological debates about 'civil society' and 'civil religion'.

2   More importantly, this discussion also suggests a new theological angle on the interrelationship between 'modernity' and 'postmodernity' – considered here with particular reference to the thought of Jean-François Lyotard. What I am advocating might, I think, very well be described as a 'post-postmodern' approach to theology.

3   Such theology will at the same time be neither confessionally Christian nor anti-Christian, but 'trans-confessional', in the same way that 'new social movements' tend to be trans-confessional in character. I seek to explore the nature of this trans-confessionality (a) in its philosophical aspect, as anticipated perhaps most poetically in the thought of Martin Heidegger, and (b) with regard to what is commonly (if somewhat misleadingly) referred to as 'inter-faith dialogue'.

4   Then I turn to consider the major historical precedents for a theology of revelation in world-history as a whole. The most notable of these is undoubtedly provided by Hegel. In a sense, I am simply trying to do for today something like what Hegel did for the early nineteenth century. (Francis Fukuyama has recently also attempted a systematic reapplication of Hegelian historicism to the present. Only, his is a completely de-theologized Hegelianism. I think Fukuyama is wrong, and I try to show why.)

5   On the basis of the position thereby established, there follows a critical consideration of some of the, to my mind, most interesting current developments in English-speaking theology: (a) the renewed neo-orthodoxy represented on the one hand by Oliver O'Donovan, and on the other hand by John Milbank; and (b) the hyper-liberalism of Mark C. Taylor.

6   Having looked at some of the obstacles to an acceptance of what I am advocating within the Christian world, I also go on to consider the rather different obstacles that exist in the Islamic world.

7   Finally, I try to address the scepticism of the non-theologically minded amongst those who sympathize with the 'new social movement' ethos. Amongst whom Jürgen Habermas, for instance, is clearly one very significant representative figure.

In order to establish a new approach at this level one has to provide a synoptic overview of how it applies over quite a large territory; and the argument therefore has to move quite fast. Nor is it possible entirely to avoid new technical terminology. All of which makes for difficulty. And yet – precisely because of its mixed responsibilities – theology perhaps more than any other discipline, by its very nature, requires to be made as accessible as possible.

I can only say that I have tried to write as accessibly as I can.

My claim is that the approach I am experimenting with represents 'a new and better way' to do theology. It is certainly new. I am not aware of anyone else (as yet!) attempting anything similar. And this, of course, makes it all the more presumptuous of me to suggest that it might be 'better'. Let me immediately therefore concede that I do not think that it is better in every respect – theology will no doubt always continue to thrive from the interplay of a multiplicity of different approaches. Both liberal theology and neo-orthodox theology also have their own special modes of access to truth. I am by no means suggesting that they will ever be altogether superceded.

But what chiefly concerns me is *the distinctive theological truth of the present historical moment – in all its novelty*. And what I think I am on the track of is just the most promising way of making sense of that.

Andrew Shanks
Old Byland, 1999

1 The promise of new social movements

Once upon a time there was a greengrocer. Václav Havel tells this tale – it is a sort of parable.

A Czech greengrocer. In the 1970s. Havel's essay 'The Power of the Powerless', in which the parable appears, is actually dated 1978. This greengrocer was thus the citizen of an officially Communist country; the manager of a state-owned store.

Yet the Czechoslovak regime of the 1970s was one which was quite lacking in real popular support. In 1968 the Russians had invaded, to suppress the Czechs' brief experiment with a new sort of politics: 'socialism with a human face'. And thereafter the government installed by the invaders set about what they themselves called 'normalization'. No one believed their propaganda any longer, not even the most dedicated Communist Party loyalists. They ruled by fear, and by fear alone. True, this was nothing like the rampant terror of Stalinist times. But, even so, it was generally enough. Enough, that is, to inspire a pervasive blank hopelessness.

The action of the story is very simple: the greengrocer does just two things. First, he puts up a poster in his shop window. And then, some time later – without being instructed to – he takes it down again. Everything hangs on the symbolic meaning of these two little acts.

On the poster there is a slogan. It is the ringing call at the conclusion of Karl Marx's *Communist Manifesto*: 'Workers of the world, unite!' Well and good. But why in actual fact, Havel asks, does the greengrocer install this slogan among his onions and carrots?

> What is he trying to communicate to the world? Is his enthusiasm so great that he feels an irrepressible impulse to acquaint the public with his ideals? Has he really given more than a moment's thought to how such a unification might occur and what it would mean?[1]

Surely not. Far more likely, at this stage, that he is just doing the done thing. The enterprise headquarters sent him the poster, along with a delivery of vegetables. And so he put it up automatically.

This is not to say that the sign is altogether meaningless. Only, the point is, it does not really mean what it says. It is, first and foremost, a message addressed to the greengrocer's superiors. As Havel translates it, its real meaning is: 'I, the greengrocer XY, live here and I know what I must do. I behave in the manner expected of me. I can be depended upon and am above reproach. I am obedient and therefore I have the right to be left in peace.' Or, in summary: 'I am afraid and therefore unquestioningly obedient.'[2] That indeed is the underlying truth of the matter. But of course the authorities are not going to ask anyone to put up a poster explicitly admitting, in so many words, 'I am afraid'. It would be too humiliating. They do not want to make the greengrocer unnecessarily resentful. The system requires that he should signal his submission in the most anaes-thetized way possible – and Karl Marx's noble words serve the purpose perfectly. 'After all', the greengrocer can always say to himself, 'I have no great objection to the workers of the world uniting. What conceivable harm could there be in that?'

And, besides, it is such an insignificant little act. No one will take much notice of it. Havel imagines, for instance, asking a woman who had stopped for a moment in front of the shop what she remembers seeing in the window. It is most unlikely that she will mention the poster. The fact is, all that concerned her was whether or not he had any tomatoes in today worth buying.

Well, yes – but then why is it that a poster like this is so easily ignored? It is because posters of that sort are everywhere. 'They form part of the panorama of everyday life.'[3] The woman we just talked to: no more than an hour ago, as it happens, she herself was busy hanging up a similar slogan in the office where she works, for much the same sort of reason as the green-grocer. The whole city is a panorama full of these subliminal messages, reminding its citizens of who they are and what the system demands of them – so many little acts of ignoble fear, all of them artfully disguised as affirma-tions of the noblest endeavour.

> Individuals need not believe these mystifications, but they must behave as though they did, or they must at least tolerate them in silence, or get along well with those who work with them. For this reason, however, they must *live within a lie*. They need not accept the lie. It is enough for them to have accepted their life with it and in it. For by this very fact, individuals confirm the system, fulfil the system, make the system, *are* the system.[4]

All it requires is for enough people to behave as the greengrocer behaves, in our first sight of him, putting up his 'decoration'.

Before – that is – the fateful moment when, at long last, something in him finally snaps ...

Let us note, here, that this parable derives its special power from Havel's evocation of a very particular sort of society. The mass-fervour of the earlier 'totalitarian' period having long since departed, his own term for it is 'post-totalitarian'. What he presents us with is a world in which there is absolutely no escaping the all-pervasive pressure of 'the lie'. Yet at the same time there can be no mistaking either, by anyone, that it *is* a lie. No one here needs disillusioning. That is not the issue. It is not, in the end, disillusionment which drives the greengrocer to his decisive change of heart.

No, he simply opts to '*live within the truth*'.

Let the window, therefore, be cleared of empty slogans! That is the first step, signalling the change. And other deeds will no doubt follow. The greengrocer is well aware of what the likely penalties are, for perceived disloyalty:

> He will be relieved of his post as manager of the shop and transferred to the warehouse. His pay will be reduced. His hopes for a holiday in Bulgaria will evaporate. His children's access to higher education will be threatened. His superiors will harass him and his fellow workers will wonder about him.[5]

Nevertheless, he is determined now to persist.

The parables of the New Testament are framed as statements concerning 'the kingdom of God'. Havel's essay makes no special reference to God; but – even so – it is not difficult to recast the tale in New Testament form:

> To what shall I liken the kingdom of God?
>
> Truly I tell you, it is like a Czech greengrocer of some twenty years ago or more who one fine day, unbidden, took down the sign that said 'Workers of the world, unite!' from among the onions and carrots in his shop window.
>
> Those who have ears to hear, let them hear.

'The solidarity of the shaken'

When Havel wrote the essay in which the greengrocer appears he did so as one of the chief spokespeople of a burgeoning dissident movement in Czechoslovakia: Charter 77.

The original Charter text is dated 1 January 1977. For the most part a rather dryly legalistic document, it starts out as follows:

> In the Czechoslovak Collection of Laws, no. 120 of 13 October 1976, texts were published of the International Covenant on Civil and Political Rights, and of the International Covenant on Economic, Social and Cultural Rights, which were signed on behalf of our Republic in 1968, were confirmed at Helsinki in 1975 and came into force in our country on 23 March 1976. From that date our citizens have the right, and our state the duty, to abide by them.[6]

There then follows a whole list of different ways in which these human-rights provisions are nevertheless, in actual practice, regularly being violated by the Czech authorities. (Along with the other Communist bloc governments the Czechs had, after all, only ratified them as a token gesture – in exchange for various diplomatic trade-offs with the West.) And, in conclusion, the signatories pledge themselves to campaign for more effective implementation in future.

The argument is framed in very general terms. But the original stimulus to the movement actually came from the arrest and imprisonment, in 1976, of a number of young rock musicians – from two hitherto quite obscure 'underground' groups, entitled Plastic People Of The Universe and DG 307 – for the allegedly anti-social 'vulgarity' of their songs. There were in the first instance 240 signatories, most of them intellectuals. By 1980 the number had swollen to over a thousand, from all walks of life – except for actual Party functionaries or members of the security forces.

The government responded with a savage mass-media campaign of slander and character assassination, against the movement's leading figures. Their houses were raided and searched; they were harassed, arrested, subjected to continual surveillance. Still, the movement continued to hang together and to flourish. Leadership was exercised by a small team of consensually accepted spokespeople; as soon as one spokesperson was arrested, or resigned, another was smoothly appointed. Without access even to photocopiers, communications were assured by teams of typists, through the *samizdat* method, producing several carbon copies at a time. Before long, the movement had generated a whole *samizdat* publishing industry of its own: issuing a spate of pamphlets, magazines, books of every sort. Seminars were established for young people politically excluded from university education, on the model of the dissident Flying University in Poland. Chartist music festivals were organized, Chartist theatrical performances, Chartist art shows.

The parable of the greengrocer belongs in this context. Havel's essay is an attempt to articulate the underlying ethos of Charter 77, as – quite simply – a corporate turning away from life lived 'within a lie' to life lived 'within the truth'.

It was possible to present the Charter project in such elementary moral terms essentially because it was a *pre*-political project. As the founding document said:

> Charter 77 is not an organisation; it has no rules, permanent bodies or formal membership. It embraces everyone who agrees with its ideas, participates in its work, and supports it. It does not form the basis for any oppositional political activity. Like many similar citizen initiatives in various countries, East and West, it seeks to promote the general public interest. It does not aim, then, to set out its own programmes for political or social reforms or changes, but within its own sphere of

activity it wishes to conduct a constructive dialogue with the political and state authorities.[7]

It was not, in the strict sense, a political movement because in the Czechoslovakia of those days there was just no room for any political movement apart from the Communist Party. That is to say, no room for any properly *living* political movement at all. Rather than itself being a political movement, Charter 77 was thus a movement dedicated to re-establishing the *conditions for the possibility* of such movements in general, by re-creating the sort of social space – above all, the freedom of speech – which they require if they are to thrive.

Hence, the Charter drew together people of widely differing convictions. Catholics, Protestants, atheists and agnostics: all were equally welcome. There were reform-minded ex-Communists in the movement, anarchists, social democrats, liberals and conservatives. They were almost all Czechs, along with a handful of Slovaks. But Charter 77 was by no means an ideological expression of Czech nationalism. Besides their shared experience as Czechs of the post-1968 period, the one and only other thing which united its participants was their shared longing for an open public environment in which to converse with one another, freely airing their differences.

The senior figure among the original leaders of the movement was, in fact, the philosopher Jan Patočka. Tragically, Patočka's direct contribution to Chartist thinking was cut short when, during his interrogation by the security police in March 1977 – an elderly and frail man – he suffered a cerebral haemorrhage and died. Still, his earlier writings do already provide some indication of the particular form of ethical idealism inspiring his final stand; notably, the closing pages of his *Heretical Essays on the Philosophy of History*.[8] Here he speaks of what he calls 'the solidarity of the shaken'.

By 'the shaken' Patočka means: those who have been shaken, especially by the experience of great historic trauma, out of life 'within a lie' – or, in general, out of the unquestioned prejudices of their culture – into a genuinely open-minded thoughtfulness. This is not the thoughtfulness of scholarly expertise; but, rather, that other sort of thoughtfulness (to be found at all different levels of scholarly sophistication or articulacy) which may also be described as a fundamental openness to transcendence. To be among the shaken is to have responded to grimly disturbing experiences, not by retreating into mental anaesthesia, but on the contrary by a determined attempt to rethink one's whole moral attitude to the world, as it is called into question by those experiences, and to reconstruct one's life accordingly. 'Participants in Charter 77', Patočka wrote,

> do not take upon themselves any political rights or functions, nor do they want to be a moral authority or 'the conscience' of society; they do not raise themselves above anyone or pass judgement on anyone; their

effort is aimed exclusively at cleansing and reinforcing the awareness that *a higher authority does exist* ...[9]

A 'higher authority': the authority, namely, to which all shakenness – *shakenness in whatever circumstances or whatever form* – bears witness; the more shaken, the more urgently. And to which, moreover, *nothing else, except shakenness*, bears witness. The authority of that-which-shakes.

One might indeed well say that Charter 77 was in many ways a remarkably pure embodiment of the solidarity of the shaken.[10]

A process of conversation

In 1989 the cause of Charter 77 triumphed – with a sudden decisiveness no one could seriously have anticipated twelve years earlier – as the old regime collapsed. And the movement's *raison d'être* therefore disappeared.

Around the same time I personally became involved in the process of dialogue then underway between Western European peace movement activists and human rights campaigners from all over Communist Eastern/Central Europe, including the Czechs. In the church context this process was largely co-ordinated by that truly formidable enterprise, the Dutch Inter-Church Peace Council (IKV). I also spent some time in Prague interviewing a number of church-related people who had been active in Charter 77; as well as others who, in order to try and safeguard the institutional church, had opted for collaboration with the regime instead. Time and again I found myself thinking, 'These people have already had a real foretaste of the Day of Judgement, such as we in the West have never had.' When one is faced with a secret police, demanding that one betray the confidential affairs of one's friends and colleagues – or else pay the consequences, oneself and one's whole family – moral choice becomes a cruel thing. And if then the old regime is swept away and the archives of the secret police are thrown open, revealing all the ugly details of who betrayed whom – this is not easy, either.

The experience of the Western European peace movement was obviously very different from that of movements like Charter 77. And it was perhaps only natural that these differences should have issued in a certain degree of mutual mistrust. Havel, in particular, set out to explain to the Westerners why it was that the Central/Eastern Europeans were often rather hesitant about responding to their overtures. Anxious that the two groups should be able to co-operate as effectively as possible, he was also concerned that there should be no misunderstanding between them.[11]

The Western European peace movement of the 1980s arose in response to the sheer corporate moral and political idiocy of the NATO alliance, as manifested most immediately in the 1979 decision to station Pershing II and cruise medium-range nuclear missiles on European soil. Whereas the problem in the Communist world was one of grotesquely excessive government interference in every sphere of life, here by contrast the problem was government passivity: politicians unreflectively surrendering to the natural inertia of their military-industrial complex, which was motivated by the huge profits it was making from the Cold War. Unlike Charter 77 and its equivalents, the peace movement was able to mobilize mass demonstrations. Its appeal was partly to a sense of high-minded moral outrage, at the prospect of being involved in genocidal aggression – this tended to be of prime importance to its most committed participants. But, at the same time, it owed its ability to mobilize such large crowds to a widespread eruption of apocalyptic panic. When its participants went to prison, this was because they had positively invited arrest by theatrical acts of civil disobedience. And, although for the most part it remained independent of party politics, there were numerous attempts to co-opt it for party-political ends. Which, again, was not a problem which Central/Eastern European dissidents had to face.

At the level of the issues at stake, the logic of the Cold War actually tended to put Western European peace movement activists and Central/Eastern European human rights campaigners into opposing camps. For how could peace and nuclear disarmament be primary campaigning issues in the Communist context? Before one can even begin to tackle such issues at all effectively one first needs free speech. And, besides, the propaganda-machines of the Communist world were for ever celebrating the Western peace movement – as if its actions were a straightforward extension of their own policy. Night after night the television showed peace movement demonstrations in Western cities, with commentaries revelling in the Western world's discomfiture. The Communist regimes each ran their own puppet 'peace movements' at home; they endlessly proclaimed themselves to be the true friends of 'peace', so that many human rights campaigners developed something of an allergy to the very word itself – an allergy which was, moreover, further intensified when they saw, or thought they saw, elements in the Western peace movement succumbing to the flattery.

Yet, at another level, the two groups were nevertheless natural partners.

For suppose the situation had been reversed. It seems clear to me that these dissident human rights campaigners were precisely those who, in the sort of circumstances prevailing in the West, would have tended to become the most dedicated peace activists. And vice versa. Deep down, at any rate for the most part, both sides *were surely just the same people.*

No doubt there was a certain element of truth in the Easterners' suspicions about the peace movement: above all that – as it was so easy to belong to – it sometimes functioned as little more, in effect, than a fashionable means of letting off moralistic steam. No mass movement is ever going to be, in all its enterprises, consistently thoughtful; there will always be some lapses, into the merely propagandistic, even in the best justified of movements. But (as Havel himself acknowledges)[12] the real undergirding strength of the peace movement lay in what it *shared* with Charter 77. Thus, as

Charter 77 expressed the solidarity of the shaken in Czech terms, so the peace movement flourished above all by virtue of its also expressing, in the very different terms demanded by its context, the same.

And, certainly, the solidarity which developed in and through the dialogue between the two groups was pre-eminently of this quality. In short, 'the solidarity of the shaken' is essentially a name for that deeper level of solidarity which was able to flourish even here, between two groups with such altogether opposite political perspectives.

What I mean by 'new social movements'

This is a book about 'new social movements', by which I basically mean *every sort of campaigning organization, or set of organizations, insofar as it approximates to the ideal of the most radical solidarity of the shaken, purely and simply as such.*

Note what that excludes. It means, in the first place, that these cannot be the sorts of movement which offer, or claim to offer, attractive *answers* to life's problems. The movements I am talking about do not cater to any form of the lust for certainty. Nor do they primarily seek to gain followers by supplying remedies for personal grief, either through a discipline of spiritual detachment in this life or through hope for post-mortem rewards. Herein lies their basic difference from that older type of movement, the missionary enterprise, which sets out to convert new adherents to a particular form of confessional identity: Christian, Muslim, Buddhist or whatever. To affirm the solidarity of the shaken is to affirm the value – not of any one partic-ular, 'correct' mode of thinking – but of thoughtfulness, as such. And, moreover, it is to affirm thoughtfulness strictly for its own sake; not to affirm a particular mode of thinking, merely as a means to some other promised end.

Secondly, these are movements whose essential aim is, so far as possible, to open up the public space for unhindered conversation among the shaken. Insofar as they seek to transform the general conduct of public affairs, it is through the consciousness-raising impact of such conversations. They are not, in the first instance, concerned with the deployment of governmental coercion, to enact reform from above. Rather, they work from below. And so they do not aim at any direct share in government. They are, in that regard, deliberately self-limiting movements – the better to preserve their proper freedom of action, in testimony to shakenness, undistorted by any pressures of immediate political expediency.

Another way of putting this is to say that they belong very much to *civil society*. I am actually thinking here in terms of a three-fold distinction: between 'civil society', 'political society' and 'economic society'.[13] Thus, whatever modes of social organization derive, in essence, from the elemen-tary imperatives of physical survival, or from a drive to accumulate wealth, may be said to belong to 'economic society'. To 'political society' there then belongs whatever is constituted, on the one hand, by projects for the gaining or preserving of governmental power and, on the other hand, by activities which the government has initiated, with a view to serving the particular interests of those in office. But organizations belong to 'civil society' insofar as they develop social bonds for the sake of the good that is *intrinsic* to those bonds; not in any way allowing them to be instrumentalized, either in pursuit of economic or political gain.

Clubs and mutual aid associations of every kind, charities, the communications media, artistic and educational institutions, religious communities: to the extent that they are both, in principle, committed to permanent independence from government and, at the same time, inspired by something more than just the profit motive, all such organizations are also part of 'civil society' as I would use the term. New social movements are simply those elements of civil society which are most decisively shaped by the solidarity of the shaken.

Where *economic* society generates its own collective ethos, independently from political and civil society, the adherents of that ethos tend to evaluate the public domain, first and foremost, as an environment for all sorts of business enterprise: what matters most is just that there should be a stable framework of law and order for the protection of property, and minimal other interference from the political authorities. If a form of *political* society starts to set its own moral agenda – with only incidental regard to the claims of economic society and none at all to the claims of civil society – it turns *itself* into a single mighty enterprise. So it aspires to the ruthless building-up of an empire, or a war-machine, or a utopia; or perhaps, as in the case of the great totalitarian regimes, all three at once. The corporate ethos of a comparably autonomous *civil* society will be quite different from either of those other two – and, on the whole, altogether more thoughtful.[14] Like the ethos of purely economic society, it will look to a plurality of spontaneous enterprises. Only, here we are concerned with intellectual or spiritual enterprises. The burning question, for its adherents, must surely be: what will best enhance the general quality of public conversation? The fundamental test is, to what extent the culture in question is genuinely open to the widest possible range of contributions – different voices representing different groups, with different traditions and different experiences of the world – such that no relevant voice on any issue, even if it be the least articulate of voices, is ever suppressed or ignored. This is the primary challenge to which new social movements, shaken into an enquiring attentiveness, are responding – as they speak up on behalf of those who would otherwise not be heard: the poor, the oppressed, or (in the case of peace and ecology groups) the not yet born.

An autonomous civil society is what totalitarian regimes, by definition, essentially seek to annihilate. And the 'post-totalitarian' regime of pre-1989 Czechoslovakia still had the same aspirations. Charter 77 was thus a movement driven, by force of circumstance, to act as the explicit advocate of Czech civil society as a whole. When in December 1989 all the old placards, like the greengrocer's, disappeared, and the streets of Prague were suddenly instead festooned with signs saying '*Havel na hrad*' – 'Havel to the castle' – this was therefore a most paradoxical development. Havel was swept to the pinnacle of political society, as President of his liberated country, precisely due to his role as the symbolic champion, hitherto, of everything most actively '*anti*-political'.

And so then there came a moment of decision: should he now make the full transition to become an active player in the new, liberalized political society? Should he found his own political party? In fact, he decided not to. Had he done so – with all the backing of his extraordinary prestige at that vital moment – the resulting party would no doubt very soon have developed into a major force; and he has been criticized for his reluctance by some who think that it would probably have been a much better party than any of those which, in the event, did emerge. Yet he decided not to, out of a persisting loyalty to the very different ethos of critical civil society.

It is surely quite wrong to expect political parties to act as pioneers in the cultivation of a community's public conscience. They have a different sort of moral vocation. Indeed, it is a distinctive characteristic of *totalitarian* parties that they want to transform the moral character of those they claim to represent, by coercive means – therein lies the ultimate source of all their mischief. Far better if party politicians content themselves with the more modest task they have as representatives: gently guiding and restraining public opinion perhaps, where necessary; but only gently.

The non-coercive cultivation of a public conscience demands quite another sort of politics. Which nowadays, I think – in every modern culture – must pre-eminently mean the conscientious anti-politics of the 'new social movements'.

The 'newness' of new social movements

The actual term, 'new social movements', first began to enter the general currency of sociological debate in the 1970s.[15] In its original context, it referred essentially to a set of developments deriving from the 1960s. The perceived newness of what were called 'new social movements', in this period, consisted partly in their general calling into question of cultural conservatism; but partly, also, in their departure from the older 'progressivism' of the immediately preceding decades – which in retrospect appears to have been far more heavily dominated by party-political ideology. Thus, by contrast, the old progressivism is the progressivism associated with the original rise of political parties: the progressivism of movements for the extension of the right to vote, nationalist movements, fascist movements, free trade movements (in mid-Victorian Britain classically the great campaign against the Corn Laws, for instance) and movements associated with the self-assertion of the organized working class. The new social movements of the 1960s and after are different in that they have had other sorts of agenda, which established political parties may to some extent latch on to, but which are no longer so essentially formative of distinctive party-political identities.

The establishment and defence of free speech is clearly the most elementary requirement for the flourishing of social movements, of any sort. That was Charter 77's basic demand; and the founding of Amnesty International in 1961 was also a key moment in the evolution of the new ethos, globally. Where freedom of speech in itself has been less problematic, other non-party political progressivist movements have of course proliferated over the past few decades. New-wave feminism is one prime example. The movement for gay and lesbian liberation is another. The civil rights movement in the United States, the international solidarity movement in the struggle against apartheid in South Africa – plus a whole range of other civil-society anti-racist movements – also belong to the same category. So do various sorts of contemporary anti-poverty consciousness-raising movements, child-protection movements and anti-corruption movements. Then there have been the peace movements: campaigns in solidarity with 'Third World' liberation struggles, against superpower domination; campaigns for nuclear disarmament; campaigns for the effective extension of international law. And the same period has also witnessed the many-stranded rise of the ecological movement, with green political parties representing an often rather uneasy hybrid between the new and the old – in that, whilst they are political parties, many of their members nevertheless have serious misgivings about the whole party-political process.

Plainly, not all of these movements consistently conform to my ideal definition of 'new social movements', above. They are by no means always, in all their actions, exemplary expressions of the solidarity of the shaken. And yet it does seem to me to be at any rate their general tendency to clear the space for such solidarity.

I have no interest in exaggerating their novelty. Such movements typically differ from older forms of progressivism in their common inclination to mistrust large-scale hierarchical structures. They tend to favour small informal affinity groups instead, allowing a maximum of direct, spontaneous participation in the decision-making process by all concerned. Their detachment from political society helps render this possible: because they are not aiming at immediate political power, but rather to shift public opinion towards a deeper thoughtfulness, they can readily dispense with the type of disciplinary constraints which belong to party politics. The anti-politics of civil society can, in that sense, be far more radically 'personalized'. But this is by no means an altogether new invention of the late twentieth century: one finds much the same approach already, especially amongst groups representing the anarchist wing of old-style working-class progressivism, say; or in certain forms of Protestant religious nonconformity.

As for the post-1960 new social movements' campaigning methods, these are for the most part just the same as those of all other movements within a mass democracy. The one area in which they undoubtedly have, in some cases, shown a particular inventiveness is in their use of symbolic non-violent direct action, or civil disobedience – but even here the great original pioneer was Gandhi's Congress Party, in its campaign for Indian independence from the 1920s onwards: a classic instance of an *old* social movement.

Many of the 'new' social movements of the present can trace their roots directly back to the nineteenth century, or even beyond. The first stirrings of a movement demanding equal rights for women, for example, can be traced all the way back to pre-revolutionary France; it was the French Revolution which produced its first popular initiatives, in the period 1789–93.[16] And the second half of the nineteenth century witnessed the rise of feminist mass movements in a number of countries – most notably the USA. The campaign for women's suffrage, inaugurated by the Seneca Falls Women's Rights Convention of 1848, was just one aspect of this; at the same time it significantly overlapped with several other campaigns, such as that of the temperance movement.[17]

Or again, the first large-scale peace movement was that which was initiated by the League of Universal Brotherhood, in Britain and the USA, in the late 1840s, culminating in the series of mostly British-organized international peace congresses in Brussels (1848), Paris (1849), Frankfurt (1850) and London (1851). The Quakers played a leading role in this, and there had indeed been a largely, although not exclusively, Quaker-run Peace Society in existence in London ever since 1816, which had emerged out of the earlier resistance to the Napoleonic wars, as well as several in America.[18] Along with evangelicals, Quakers played a major role, as well, in the anti-slavery movement on both sides of the Atlantic, from the 1780s to the 1860s. But here too – insofar as it was a simple concern with the issue itself, rather than any sort of associated sectarian confessionalism, which provided the effective basis for solidarity – we have another very notable forerunner of the late twentieth century new social movement ethos.[19] And there was then a vigorous British peace movement arising out of the First World War.[20]

So what has the late twentieth century really added, in this regard?

I would say, above all, a greatly accentuated sense of elemental *danger*. On the one hand there is a new awareness of the dangers of runaway technological developments, inspiring the nuclear disarmament movement, the green movement more generally, and those strands of feminism which are particularly related to this. And on the other hand, in all those movements which appeal to 'human rights', there is now a traumatic sense of the potential dangers of totalitarianism.

The new social movements of the present day are movements – after Hiroshima, after Auschwitz – haunted, deep down, by new nightmare fears. They are, at their most thoughtful, the self-expression of those most profoundly shaken by those memories; those rendered most acutely suspicious, therefore, of the growth of unaccountable bureaucracies, the unscrupulous propaganda methods employed by governments and political parties, or any resort whatever to the politics of scapegoating.

The actual movements themselves come in all shapes and sizes. They may die; they may mutate; after seeming to die, they may suddenly be reborn. Within them, individual organizations come and go, swell and shrink and sometimes swell again. It is a very fluid scene. The various movements pursue all sorts of different strategic aims. But herein lies their underlying common identity: an ethically principled commitment to trans-confessional solidarity-building within a civil-society context – plus a radically shaken sense of danger to inspire it. That is what constitutes the scene in question as the coherent scene it is; a set of possibilities, at least, which – now that they have been discovered – will henceforth always be with us. And this is a book about that whole scene, considered in terms of its philosophico-theological implications. It is an attempt to situate a certain claim about the proper significance of that scene, within the general context of the Western philosophical and theological tradition.

New social movements, I think, are theologically interesting by virtue of the sheer *pioneering directness* with which they embody the solidarity of the shaken. But their obvious weakness is their ephemerality.

On the other hand, the solidarity of the shaken may also be embodied – albeit less directly, more ambiguously – in the more deep-rooted and more stable communities of popular religion. My search here is just for the proper resources to mediate between these two embodiments: both so as to help open up the world of popular religion to the fresh inspiration of such movements, and to draw out what I would see as their deeper religious implications.

2 'Theology'

What follows is, as I have said, in one sense a philosophico-theological argument; both philosophical and theological.

But, in another sense, I am inclined to say that it is *primarily* theological. Only, not in the conventional meaning of that word. And to say that it is at the same time also 'philosophical' is, really, just to signal this fundamental element of unconventionality.

Thus, let us begin by defining 'theology'.

In terms of its Greek etymology, 'theology' simply means discourse (*logos*) about God (*theos*). However, it is by no means obvious that all discourse about God should automatically be termed 'theology'. Philosophers, surely, may speak about God without being theologians, in discussing the intrinsic logic of theistic ideas; as may sociologists, psychologists, anthropologists or historians, in discussing the attitudes towards God of other people. Theology is different just because it implies a direct personal *commitment*, to God, on the part of the thinker. Which, in turn, then takes shape in and through a range of further commitments: social, cultural and political.

In the first instance, one might therefore say that to do theology is – at that particular level which is marked out by a discourse about God – to set about analysing the provenance, and the implications, of one's own loyalties. Abstracting from the particularity of the actual social, cultural, (anti-?) political struggles which the loyalties in question serve to inform, theology attempts to provide a frame for those struggles, of the most universal possible validity.

Hence, it has three basic interconnected tasks:

(a) to define a set of key loyalty-focusing concepts, as such;
(b) to unfold those concepts into a set of paradigmatic narratives, for the interpretation of current struggles; and
(c) to help shape a suitable strategy of ritual practice, understood as the worship of God, for the public appropriation of both concepts and narratives.

In the broadest sense of the term, *any* form of thinking which performs these three tasks together may surely be classed as 'theology'.

But then everything depends on what specific *type* of loyalty the theologian is concerned with. Of course, most theology in Western culture is confessionally Christian: seeking to articulate the solidarity of Christians with Christians, as Christians. And yet I want to argue that there are also other possibilities even for the most loyal sort of Christian (amongst whom I count myself). Indeed, I consider it vitally necessary, not least for the sake of Christian faith itself, that a Christian believer's primary loyalty to Christ should be mediated through something more than just a narrow confessionalism.

The basic question that I am interested in exploring here is: *what might it mean to do theology, quite directly, on the basis of the solidarity of the shaken?*

What happens, theologically, when one starts out first and foremost from an apprehension of God as the animating spirit of this most purely thoughtful form of solidarity? In fact, it seems to me to be vital for the authenticity of *any* theology that it should include at least some infusion of the solidarity of the shaken amongst its various ingredients. But what if that is made the real core-element?

Amongst the shaken, some believe in God, some do not. At one level, both have the same stories to tell, of cultural shake-up – this is the level that sociologists and historians operate on. At another level, the theologian tells the same story, only now as a story about God: God as the one who shakes. Here the story is being shaped for the purposes of community-building commemorative ritual. And the sort of theology I envisage would simply be a systematic attempt to transform the pure solidarity of the shaken, which is otherwise just a negative reaction to oppression, into a constructive, ritually-focused community-tradition.

As such it would, in the first instance, be a form of trans-confessional theology: not exclusively grounded in the authority of any one particular set of sacred scriptures. This is by no means to say that it would be *anti*-confessional. On the contrary – I want to be both a trans-confessional and a confessional theologian, in alternation. All theology is anyhow a process of mediation between diverse intellectual cultures. It is the most responsible of the sciences – in that it has to respond not only to the demands of the academic community, in its scholarly integrity, but also to the spiritual needs of another, more populist moral community. In the case of Christian-confessional theology that more populist community is the church; in the case of trans-confessional theology, of the sort I am proposing, it would be the emergent world of new social movements. But there is nothing necessarily incompatible about these two.

Let me immediately concede that, of course, confessional theology will always have certain major advantages over trans-confessional theology: it is answerable to a far more stable and coherent community, in which intellectuals tend to be altogether more closely mixed with all sorts of non-intellectuals, possessing an aesthetic and spiritual tradition far richer in accumulated historic resonances. (I will come back to this: see Chapter 13, below.) But if it is the solidarity of the shaken that one values – and if one is therefore inclined to identify divine revelation with the very deepest shaking-power of cultural shake-ups *in general* – then there are at the same time also some rather obvious disadvantages in an exclusively confessional approach. The solidarity of the shaken is a radically trans-confessional ideal. And, at any rate in a culture which is *de facto* religiously pluralistic, it therefore seems to me that the real need is for a thinking which systematically oscillates between the confessional and the trans-confessional.

There are thus three loyalties at work here: a loyalty to the community of academic scholarship, a loyalty to the traditional religion of the church, and a loyalty to the general new social movement ethos. I want to think through their potential convergence.

As regards the specific relationship of the solidarity of the shaken to the Christian gospel, take for example those familiar words of Jesus, the Beatitudes, set by Matthew at the beginning of the sermon on the mount. This is the New English Bible translation, with variant readings suggested in brackets:

> When he saw the crowds Jesus went up the hill. There he took his seat, and when his disciples had gathered round him he began to address them. And this is the teaching he gave:
>
> 'How blest are those who know their need of God [literally the 'poor in spirit', those infinitely unsettled by an authentic visionary grasp of better things that might be]; the kingdom of Heaven is theirs.
>
> How blest are the sorrowful [or the mourners, that is, whoever is unsettled by their own personal experience of affliction]; they shall find consolation.
>
> How blest are those of a gentle spirit [that is, those rendered receptively attentive by their 'poverty in spirit' and their chastening experiences of sorrow]; they shall have the earth for their possession.
>
> How blest are those who hunger and thirst to see right prevail [or to do what is right]; they shall be satisfied.
>
> How blest are those who show mercy [that is, those whose judgement of what is right is undistorted by any impulse of resentment]; mercy shall be shown to them.
>
> How blest are those whose hearts are pure; they shall see God.
>
> How blest are the peacemakers [that is, those who actively challenge the unrighteousness of the war-makers]; God shall call them his sons.
>
> How blest are those who have suffered persecution for the cause of right; the kingdom of Heaven is theirs.'

Is this not exactly a description of people like Havel's repentant green-grocer? One might well read it as eight different ways of saying, 'how blest are the shaken' – and indeed the whole of Jesus' original teaching appears to have been conceived in very much that spirit.

The sort of trans-confessional theology I envisage would essentially be an attempt to re-articulate the same spirit, and explore its implications for today, in the most unambiguous terms possible. Thus, in this case, the three-fold theological challenge is: first, to clarify the concepts necessary for the further explication – and vindication – of the solidarity of the shaken; second, to explore the historical emergence of the actual conditions for the possibility of a thinking explicitly oriented towards such solidarity, as a primary goal; and, third, to devise an effective strategy for the incorporation of that thinking into the very richest possible culture of actual 'civil religious' practice. Beyond the particular already-established single-issue contributions of 'feminist theology', 'green theology', 'black theology', 'peace movement theology' and so forth, what I think we need now is an altogether more comprehensive sort of new social movement theology, in this sense.

3 Three stages of modernity?

So let us begin. We need, first of all, some general conceptual framework within which to juxtapose the new possibilities of trans-confessional theology with all the old wealth of confessional tradition: how are we, in fact, to characterize the full flowering of the new social movement ethos, as an historic moment of potential new insight?

Are we, for instance, to say that its newness finally transcends '*modernity*'?

Is it – at its most authentic, as an expression of the solidarity of the shaken – something '*post*modern'? Or is it, on the contrary, essentially still a variant of 'modernity' – only, 'modernity' now in a new mode?

I am using these two terms, 'modern' and 'postmodern', more or less in the particular sense pioneered by Jean-François Lyotard. For Lyotard's thinking, in this regard, is all about the proper sources of solidarity. He is an advocate of 'postmodernism' essentially as a species of solidarity-project, opposed to the solidarity-projects of 'modernity'.

Postmodernism, according to Lyotard's definition, is a species of solidarity-project founded on 'incredulity towards *grand narratives*'.[1] Modernity is that which is constituted by 'grand narratives', as a basis for solidarity. Postmodernity, on this understanding, is not a period coming after modernity. Rather, it is a counter-current of disillusionment with those narratives – almost as old as modernity itself.[2]

A 'grand narrative' here may perhaps be best defined as a multi-layered narrative about vocations:

- it outlines the origins and development of a certain ideal trans-culturally unifying ethos, participation in which is supposed to be the ultimate vocation of humanity as a whole;
- it traces the struggles of a particular community, or set of communities, called to be the missionary carrier of that ethos to all others;
- it teaches individuals, generally, to identify their own personal vocation in life with a maximum solidarity-commitment to the historic hopes of that carrier-community, or those carrier-communities.

What Lyotard calls 'postmodern' thinking mistrusts grand narratives for their evident potential usefulness to those seeking a theoretical justification for cultural imperialism. Rejecting the entire genre, it therefore turns instead to more modest forms of solidarity, preferring all manner of piecemeal local alliance-brokering, purged of such 'grandeur'.

But, after all, I am not so sure.

The solidarity of the shaken, as the ideal corporate ethos of new social movements, certainly does imply an acute mistrust of any sort of glorified cultural imperialism: the grand narrative which vindicates an attitude of mere disdain towards the unfamiliar – as being outside the true historical mainstream – tends to reinforce just the sort of mental rigidity which is most alien to this ethos.[3] And yet, at the same time, the solidarity of the shaken surely is an ethos which in its own way aspires to universal moral hegemony. The 'shaken' are shaken not only out of the imperialism of their own cultures, but also – and no less decisively – out of those cultures' particularism. Shakenness is not tied to any particular ethnic, civic or confessional identity – it is precisely the condition of being, to some extent, *un*-tied from the constraints of those identities. An ethos celebratory of shakenness is necessarily therefore an ethos for all. It can scarcely escape from grand narrative thinking; for, in its origins, grand narrative is just what springs from the experience of being systematically shaken out of the social compartmentedness of the pre-modern.

As I see it, the basic trouble with Lyotardian dogmatic postmodernism is that it is an over-generalizing reaction to the moral bankruptcy of a certain mode of grand narrative, which falsely identifies that hitherto dominant mode with the genre as a whole. The point is: if we are to define 'modernity', in a broad sense, as whatever is constituted by grand narratives, then there are surely as many different basic types of modernity as there are potential different types of carrier-community for such narrative.

What we more conventionally call 'modernity' – i.e. the dominant modernity of the past four centuries or so – may be said to be that particular type which has had as its carrier-communities various sorts of groups all belonging to *secular political society*. Sometimes the grand narrative has emerged as part of a bid for the patronage of secular-minded governments on the part of progressive intellectuals – organized at first in learned societies and Masonic lodges, or around publishing houses; later, in universities. Here we have the modernity of the Enlightenment. At other times it has entered into the propaganda of factions and parties aspiring to have executive control over the government of secular states. Here we have the modernity of liberalism, revolutionary socialism and messianic nationalism.

But, either way, this species of secularizing grand narrative essentially originates in Western Europe as a counter-blast to another, earlier species – that of Christendom. The advocates of secularizing politics have been impelled to enter the terrain of grand narrative essentially because that was the terrain already occupied by their opponents.

The grand narrative of Christendom is, thus, one form of what might be termed '*first modernity*': a category in which I would include any grand narrative ethos carried by a particular confessional community, acting on its own; either *pre-* or *anti-*secular. Whereas, set over against this, I propose to call what starts with the Enlightenment '*second modernity*'.

In a sense, first modernity begins with the universalist vision in Isaiah 2: 1–4/Micah 4: 1–4, of all the nations streaming together in pilgrimage to Zion. Only, there is still no actual missionary strategy at this point to help get the process going. Or, as an organized missionary enterprise, it is inaugurated by the 'descent' of the Holy Spirit at Pentecost.[4] Its main carriers have been the Christian church and the Islamic *umma*.[5] Virtually all the most creative developments in theology over the past three centuries or so have, in one way or another, arisen as a direct response to the clash between first and second modernity; upholding one against the other, or attempting to make peace between them.

What happens, though, if and when new social movements become the carrier-communities for modernist hope – that is, the whole community of such movements in general? In that they are on the one hand intrinsically trans-confessional, and on the other hand part of civil society not political society, such movements elude both of the previous two categories.

Here, therefore, we are confronted by something else again: this, surely, is nothing less than a *third modernity*.

Lyotardian postmodernism arises as a response to the perceived collapse of the once-inspiring ideals of second modernity, on the part of thinkers with no interest in trying to revitalize first modernity as an alternative. Lyotard himself is an ex-Marxist. Of all the various strands of second modernity, Marxism was perhaps the most dynamic, but also the one most painfully in recession over the past few decades. Lyotard's radical rejection of modernist hope in general is a generalizing of his disillusionment with Marxism: if that particular form of modernist hope will not do, he will have no other.

Where second modernity ultimately falls short, on this analysis, is in its capacity to cope with *corporate trauma*. Much of the moral authority of Lyotard's thought derives from the way it is so pervasively haunted, above all, by the memory of the Holocaust. His thinking is, in general, a struggle to liberate what he calls the 'figural' quality of traumatic memory – at the public level – from its Babylonian captivity to the conceptual 'discourse' of definitive texts, incorporating the trauma into some fixed and stable general world-view. By 'the figural' he means that which appears, at its purest, in dreams: a sheer excess of meaning, radically resistant to final interpretation; or appears in the raw shaking-power of memory. And for him the primary 'figure' is always the nightmare of Auschwitz.[6]

His repudiation of grand narrative is largely a sort of second-order response to that trauma. A second-order response – for Nazi ideology is very far from being a straightforward example of the grand narrative genre.

On the contrary, Nazi racism is in the first instance very much a reaction against it: inasmuch as, fundamentally, the true subject of any grand narrative must always be humanity as a whole, or some principle working through the whole of humanity; not a single race. Yet there is also a sense in which (as he puts it) Nazi propaganda is not just saying, 'Let us become what we are – Aryans', but 'Let the whole of humanity be Aryan, or purified by the exercise of Aryan power'.[7] It was, after all, out of the world shaped by second modernity that Nazism rose. And the essential thrust of the Lyotardian argument is well encapsulated in his striking designation for the shaken: as 'the jews'.[8] Not all 'jews' are Jews, not all Jews are 'jews'. The 'jews' include all manner of thoughtful outsider. But the point is: the Nazi genocide of the Jews is just the most extreme outcome of, and symbolic representation for, modernity's age-old failure to welcome properly its 'jews', without making them abandon their 'jewishness'; the failure of the hitherto dominant grand narratives ever to do adequate justice to the nonconformity of their perspectives; and orthodox modernist ideologues' persistent inclination to devalue, if not suppress, those perspectives.

Lyotard rejects the grand narrative form, finally, because of the way he sees it constraining the free play of imagination in the therapeutic 'working through' of unresolved trauma. This idea of 'working through' ('*Durcharbeiten*') he derives – loosely – from Freud: specifically from Freud's opposition between 'working through' and 'repetition' – a contrast which, however, he expands with the addition of a separate third category, simply called 'remembering'.[9]

'Repetition', here, is the name of the problem: neurosis represents a certain enslavement to the past, inasmuch as the past supplies a set of behaviour patterns which the neurotic compulsively repeats. The notion of fate in mythical world-views, where human life is envisaged as being continuously subject to the compelling intervention of the gods, is a straightforward symbolic projection of the same. In its broadest sense 'repetition' is thus a comprehensive term for everything that belongs to human culture at its least reflective, that is, at the level of a mere concatenation of shared habits.[10] It is the sum of all artificial obstacles to genuine thought.

But, Lyotard argues, there are then two quite opposite ways of tackling it. One way is that of 'remembering'. By this he means something like the construction – by individuals or communities – of an official story, or repertoire of stories, to live by; as a way in which they publicly define their identities, and their conventional wisdom. This is what, at the macro-cultural level, grand narrative does. 'Working through', though, is different: it is a much less wilful, more modest mode of continuously 'rewriting' the past. The psychoanalytic method of 'free association' is one example of 'working through' – as a relaxed procedure of circling around what Freud calls 'primary repression', the residues of trauma. Great art, insofar as it is an effective evocation of the sublime – that is, the ultimate inexpressibility or 'figural' quality of that which matters most – is another. As opposed to 'working through', the discipline of 'remembering', when applied to cultural history, becomes a matter of prescribed technique: one follows certain given rules; truth is identified with the systematic results of applying those rules. And the grand narrative is the modern way of defining them. 'Working through', by contrast, is not a technique but an art, or a family of arts – the arts of *anamnesis*, not-forgetting. Rather than following given rules, it makes up its rules along the way. It can afford to be freely experimental because, as a thinking of 'the figural', its desire is not for universally valid answers; it does not start out with a set of theoretical puzzles, to be resolved. But, rather, its whole desire is for an intensified sensibility – precisely, to the element of singularity in the particular events it recalls. Its aim is not so much to interpret trauma theoretically, as to stay with it; just to be honest in communicating it.

In the terms of my argument here, one might say that the true 'working through' of corporate trauma is a process of absolute shakenness. In other words: a decisive exposure to trauma – purged of any distraction. But the political parties of mature second modernity are hooked on every sort of distraction. They are distracted, in the first place, by the games and manœuvrings which constitute the necessary infrastructure of political society. And then their whole life is one of reaching out to the masses, as the masses, to gain their votes. Hence they necessarily tend to participate in all the distractions of the mass-mind, as well. Even where some serious engagement with trauma is inescapable, they are inevitably inclined to exploit it for merely propagandistic purposes. Consider for example the party politics of Israel – or, in another register, those of contemporary Germany – in relation to the Holocaust. Nothing, in short, could be less favourable to the sort of 'working through' Lyotard has in mind than the culture of party politics.

The particular grand narratives Lyotard appears to have chiefly in mind, in denouncing the genre, are those which inform the identity of political parties; or those which originally helped prepare the secularized social space within which political parties have arisen. And so far as these go he surely has a point.

However, new social movements are something else.

Whilst they clearly cannot exclude manipulative intrigue, the fact is that their primarily consciousness-raising organizations offer far less by way of potential reward for it than political parties do. Or, indeed, than the great confessional institutions of first modernity do, or did. No doubt they offer something to careerists; but not much. Unlike political parties, moreover, they are not immediately in search of votes in a mass democracy; and are therefore not so absolutely obliged to address the masses on the masses' own terms. They may use propaganda techniques on occasion – but at least those techniques tend not to be quite so integral to their thinking as in the case of political parties. With neither the strategic pressures of political society nor the mental constraints of a rigid confessionalism to impede them, their way of remembering the past is far more readily attuned to a proper 'working through' of corporate trauma than is the case with any of the movements of second or first modernity. And, by the same token, they are far more immediately a potential channel for the insights of the thoughtful outsider; in Lyotard's terms, 'the jew'.

Third modernity is at present only a possibility. It would only become an actuality to the extent that the participants in new social movements actually started to think in the sort of grand narrative fashion I am advocating.

Nor am I making any predictions as to how *likely* that is to happen. Who can tell? There are indeed plenty of arguments for pessimism, and some of them very strong. What I am seeking to articulate here is a set of more or less defiant hopes, rather than any very confident expectations.

My claim is just that history has now brought us to the point where a new potential vision of the possible future has started to emerge which, for good reason, could never previously have been envisaged. Maybe that vision will in fact be snuffed out before it attains its full modernist potential. That this too is perfectly possible I do not deny. All I am saying is that it would be a shame if it were. For by 'third modernity' I mean: an unprecedented new potential clarity as to the proper nature of the solidarity of the shaken.

All three forms of modernity, in their contrasting ways, may thus be said to originate as a solidarity-building affirmation of shakenness. But in the case of first modernity that affirmation is obviously complicated by the self-interest of the institutional church, or its Islamic equivalents; whilst in the case of second modernity it is complicated by the self-interest especially of political parties. What is most significantly new about the possibility of third modernity is just that it represents the solidarity of the shaken as mediated through groups with a relatively far smaller degree of distorting self-interest.

The weakness of the Lyotardian position (it seems to me) is that, whilst it embodies a powerful advocacy of shakenness, it in effect takes the impulse to solidarity for granted. A grand narrative is a framework for, and a stimulus to, solidarity-building. The solidarity of the shaken is the most *un*natural form of solidarity. The natural forms of solidarity, which scarcely need any argument to undergird them, are those deriving from family or tribal bonds; from participation in an embattled linguistic community or a common loyalty to endangered folk-customs; and from shared economic needs and aspirations. But the solidarity of the shaken belongs to the order of grace not nature.[11] It transcends all these natural bonds – and is therefore absolutely dependent upon the power of argument. Grand narratives supply such argument. That is their basic virtue.

Over the past four centuries virtually every creative new development in theology has arisen, in one way or another, out of the struggle between first and second modernity; my project here, however, is to start to explore something of another order altogether. Namely: the new grand-narrative theological possibilities inherent in the idea of a third modernity. How to reconcile this new grand narrative with a proper 'working through' of those corporate traumas which have tended to shake people's confidence in earlier grand narratives remains a central problem. But I am, at all events, still hopeful that such a reconciliation is achievable.

4   A second Axial Period?

No doubt the most urgent particular challenge which new social movements pose to traditional theology, as such, consists in their trans-confessionalism: the new opportunities they provide for active principled collaboration between people from differing religious cultures.

The secularized political order of second modernity prepares the way, in that it supplies a framework for the guaranteeing of mutual toleration – with narrowly confessional enterprises, henceforth, tending to limit themselves to the sphere of civil society alone. But that, on its own, does not yet demand a fully trans-confessional approach to theology. Only when agencies imbued with a spirit of serious trans-confessionalism begin to emerge right within civil society itself does the basic issue with regard to theological methodology finally become inescapable. It is a relatively simple matter to think through the de-confessionalizing of the state; but to extend the principle further, as the trans-confessional ethos of these civil-society movements invites us to do – that is something else.

And it seems to me in fact that this development marks a major step forward, towards the true fulfilment of historically-minded, or faith-inspired, religion in general.

In order to elucidate this further claim, however, I first of all need to clarify just exactly what I mean by the word 'religion'.

'Religion' is, of course, a very slippery term. But I am writing here as a theologian, so I want to deploy it in the most helpful possible way for the special purposes of theology – and it is a distinguishing feature of theology, as an intellectual discipline, that it requires concepts which refer back, already in their very definition, to certain particular historic moments of revelation.

Theology deals in loyalty-defining stories. Therefore a good theological concept has got to be, as sharply as possible, *story-focused*: its usefulness depends upon its having, intrinsically encapsulated within it, some distinctive story, or limited set of stories, waiting to be retold in endless variation. From this point of view, just to name a general category of universal human experience can never be enough. To think of 'religion' in the way, for instance, that Durkheimian 'sociology of religion' defines it – as naming a perennial aspect of all society, in the sense that all society depends upon some sort of ritual underpinning to its moral coherence – is at once to render the concept quite un-theological. I am not using the term in that sense.

Certain confessional theologians, on the other hand, are inclined to speak of 'religion' in a derogatory fashion. The prime examples of this are *Karl Barth* and *Dietrich Bonhoeffer*. Here, of course, the defining narrative element is the Christian gospel-story. 'Religion', for Barth, is a name for all those pre-existing types of authority-claim (domestic, tribal or civic norms) which are essentially superseded by the revolutionary advent of Christian faith; in the sense that – whilst they may not be entirely discredited – from then on they only retain their authority to the extent that they have been redeemed and transformed by absolute submission to the gospel's higher claim.[1] Whereas for Bonhoeffer, 'religion' is everything which is superseded by the gospel, in the much stronger sense of still needing to be positively purged away from the distorted self-understanding of the church itself.[2]

Given, though, that the term still has a primary function of designating points of similarity between Christian practice and the prayer-traditions of other cultures, there is an obvious danger in loading it with these negative connotations. The risk is that such a devaluation will merely serve to reinforce a certain sort of confessional chauvinism: as if the one and only thing ever wrong with Christianity was that it failed to go deep enough in its hostility to other 'religious' traditions!

I am not suggesting that either Barth or Bonhoeffer actually meant to say anything quite so crudely one-sided as this. Nevertheless, the ambiguity remains. And a bridge-building trans-confessional theology must, therefore, tend to make the exactly opposite move to theirs. It is more or less bound, I think, to speak of 'religion' rather as – *a transcendent ideal.*

In the present context, then, let us take 'religion' as a term precisely for *the ideal solidarity-reinforcing ritual expression – and transmission-process – of shakenness.*

And let us, accordingly, insist upon the radical otherness of authentic religion from any mere 'sacred ideology', or practice of 'magic', whereby shakenness is, on the contrary, suppressed.

To put it in the narrative terms required by theology, one might say that the long-term movement towards religion in this ideal sense begins with what Karl Jaspers called 'the Axial Period' of human history.[3] Namely the band of time, extending from about the eighth to the second century before Christ, which witnessed the early flowering of the Zoroastrian tradition; the literature, on the one hand, of Israelite prophecy and, on the other hand, of the Upanishads; the birth of the Buddhist, Confucian and Taoist traditions; and classical Greek philosophy. My proposal is that we put it this way: before the Axial Period there was no religion, only magic. And outside the various cultures stemming from these transformations there is still only magic.

As with 'religion', it will be apparent that I am also using the term 'magic' here in a rather different sense from Durkheim's. He confines it to rituals provided as a specialist service to private clients. But what I mean is any sort of ritual – including the community-bonding sort – insofar as it continues to cater, primarily, to people's basic anxieties about their material interests. The point is: only with the Axial Period does another, properly 'religious' species of ritual begin to emerge, in the sense of affirming *infinite* ethical demands, quite regardless of such interests. And hence post-Axial cultures essentially differ from pre-Axial ones in their pressing religious concern with 'salvation' or liberation – from whatever would obscure those demands.

Notwithstanding the immense diversity of post-Axial traditions, they all have at any rate this much elementarily in common. In pre-Axial cultures the trans-mundane – that is, the realm of gods and spirits – tends to be envisaged as a more or less shadowy extension of the mundane order, organized along not dissimilar lines. Post-Axial cultures, however, tend to posit a sharp contrast between two opposing orders of reality; metaphysically reflecting the existential contrast between ordinary this-worldliness and the way of liberation. Pre-Axial ritual, insofar as it is a public affair, belongs quite straightforwardly to the natural life-processes of society as a coherent whole. But the Axial Period generates new sorts of intellectual or clerical élite; sharply differentiated from other, rival élites in their role as the self-professed announcers of, and guides to, liberation. And the resulting power-struggles then provide an opening for the malign influence of the *libido dominandi* (in English, 'the addictive lust for domination')[4] to muscle in, converting what once were religious movements into its own ideological instruments. So that, in this scheme of things, 'religion' and 'ideology' are two fundamentally opposing spirits, battling one another for control of the same post-Axial 'liberation'-heritage.

The various streams flowing from the Axial Period have all contained aspirations to authentic religion, more or less mixed with residues of magic and accretions of ideology.

By 'residues of magic' I mean not only the persistence of superstition, but also every invocation of the sacred primarily intended just to console; and, indeed, every trespass of theologians into the proper domain of natural science, even if intended as apologetic back-up to the most sublime spirituality. In the rather broad sense meant here, 'magic' is what serves to make life easier, whether through the hope of changing things through the use of spells or through the promise of other-worldly consolation. Whereas true 'religion', on the contrary, makes life more difficult. Magic offers explanations, consonant with its impulse to make life easier; religion offers only challenges, to an ever more radical self-critique.

By 'accretions of ideology', on the other hand, I mean the twisting of those challenges into a strategy of mere manipulation.

Hitherto, the various streams of post-Axial thought – each containing its own mix of competing impulses – have for the most part flowed separately;

either in mutual ignorance or else in limited contact with just one or two others.[5] But now they are all beginning to flow together into a single, global conversation-process. It is just this process of confluence which for the first time renders it possible for us in retrospect to conceive of the original Axial Period synoptically, as such. And might it not in fact also, quite significantly, help re-open the issue of the fundamental otherness of true religion from magic or ideology? For everything, surely, is going to be called into question as a result.

So momentous is the potential transformation that Jaspers himself toys with the idea of its leading us into a *'second'* Axial Period.[6] Writing as he was in the immediate gloomy aftermath of the Second World War, he insists primarily on the immense distance still to be travelled. Nevertheless, he does at least glimpse the prospect.

And what are the chief obstacles to the flourishing of the new conversation-process? They surely derive from the two basic sorts of ideology: both the confessional-exclusivist sort belonging to the corruption of first modernity and – in more or less equal measure, I think – the merely de-traditionalising overreaction to that first sort in the ideologies of a corrupt second modernity. Whereas, conversely, the chief positive stimuli to the process are nothing other than the intermingling critical passions of an emergent cosmopolitan postmodernity/third modernity.

The solidarity of the shaken has, on the one hand, its general (anti-)political merits which require religious celebration: that is to say, its merits as a strategy for the restraint of corrupted rule. But then, on the other hand, it also has this more immediately religious merit, that it represents the best possible context for the development of intercultural conversation, between the adherents of different post-Axial traditions. In what follows I want to think through both of these two aspects of the matter together.

5   Arguments for calendar-reform

Against this background, the potential religious fulfilment that I am advocating would in the first instance demand an extensive process of actual liturgical experimentation.

Clearly, the shape of any culture's ritual calendar not only reflects that culture's sense of corporate moral identity; it also (inasmuch as all self-appropriated identity comes from reflection) makes a substantial contribution to actually forming the identity it reflects. At all events, modernity in each of its stages has always made calendar-reform a central feature of its strategy.

First modernity gave our years their numbers; and decisively superimposed upon their older festive ordering, derived from the cycle of nature, a new ordering derived from the requirements of historical commemoration. The calendrical deposits of second modernity, overlying those of first modernity, admittedly tend to form a somewhat thinner layer – with all the privileges of state sponsorship, already almost from the outset, second modernity always had a wealth of other means also at its disposal to promote its values. The new social movements of third modernity however, which lack those advantages, are just for that reason, surely, all the more in need of this sort of religious backing.

The religion of first modernity is by definition exclusively confessional: it is simply a matter of Christians working through, and inwardly appropriating, their corporate identity as Christians; or Muslims, their corporate identity as Muslims. The liturgy of both second and third modernity differs, in that it is essentially a form of *civil* religion. That is to say, it has primarily to do with the worshippers' other, civil identities.

In some cases civil religion may indeed appear as a direct rival to confessional religion. It was Jean-Jacques Rousseau who first coined the actual term, 'civil religion'; and what Rousseau was proposing, under this heading, was very much a Deist alternative, designed to supplant church-religion.[1] Thus, whereas church-religion was the establishment of a rival organization to that of the state, Rousseauian civil religion was intended simply as a form of social cement, helping to unify the state by giving sacred authority to republican law. The great Jacobin religious festivals, masterminded by the artist Jacques-Louis David at the time of the French Revolutionary Terror, were also conceived in that Rousseauian spirit. And one might further include the public rituals of Communism in the same category.

In other cases, however, civil and confessional religion are able quite peaceably to overlap with one another: as, for example, when American churchpeople devoutly observe such festivals as Memorial Day, the Fourth of July, the birthdays of George Washington and Abraham Lincoln, or now Martin Luther King Day. Or when British churchpeople devoutly observe Remembrance Sunday. The observance of these occasions may involve cere- monies in church – and yet they are civil religious events, inasmuch as the stories they commemorate are not so much about what it means to be a church-member, but rather about what it means to be an American or British citizen. They are festivals which churchpeople share, as equal part- ners, with their non-Christian neighbours.

One may well have some misgivings about these precedents. Civil religion, in general, may serve so very many different purposes. To consider simply the American phenomena, partly these are a religious celebration of American democratic liberty, as such; partly, they have the same sort of elementary social-cement function as Rousseauian civil religion. And no doubt they very often, also, tend towards a rather questionable ideological reinforcement of American superpower nationalism.

Nevertheless – even in spite of all these ambiguities in what has hitherto been developed – the basic ongoing need for civil religious experimentation seems clear enough to me. For, after all, every individual has numerous interlocking social identities. And how can we suppose that, when it comes to the Day of Judgement, God will only be concerned with how we have dealt with the confessional one? Why not also how we have dealt with our citizenship identities, our ethnic identities, our class identities, our gender identities? Do we not, as a matter of general principle, equally need to set time aside for a prayerful pondering of the stories which serve to define these other identities – even where those stories transcend the given frame of confessional narrative, as in secularized societies they increasingly do? At all events, the chief prophetic advocate of 'American civil religion', Robert Bellah, is by no means wanting to defend it in any ideological sense.[2] Bellah develops his civil theology around a structuring of American history in terms of 'three times of trial': the great moral shake-up of the Revolution, the great moral shake-up of the Civil War, and the great moral shake-ups of the later twentieth century, resulting from the new demands of superpower status. But in each 'time of trial' the fundamental issue, as he sees it, has always been the same. The test has been, precisely, to what extent the conduct of American public debate could be raised above the level of mere combat between self-serving party-ideologies.

And besides, all the examples given above belong to the civil religion of second modernity. What Rousseau advocated, what David organized, the rituals of Communism, 'American civil religion', Remembrance Sunday in

Britain: all of these are, in one way or another, rites associated with the upholding of the secularized state. They are all actively promoted by the state authorities. The scarcely yet-developed civil religion of *third* modernity, associated more with the consciousness-raising work of new social movements, must look very different.

These counter-cultural observances will not be imposed from above; if they ever establish themselves, it will be more likely as a result of having sprung up spontaneously from below. As commemorations, they will be focused on the key historic memories underlying the emergence of new social movements: the decisive traumas marking the progressive collapse of the hopes of second modernity; the first stirrings of an alternative civil society ethos. They will be, precisely, liturgical processes of 'working through' – in the Lyotardian sense – all the most pressing 'figural' memories of our culture; sacramental celebrations of the very purest solidarity of the shaken, as such.

Here and there, such experiments are in fact already underway. The closest I myself have ever come to a direct experience of the possibility of a second Axial Period, for example, is in the context of a regular trans-confessional observance of 6 August as Hiroshima Day, in Leeds; a series of gatherings initiated, in the 1980s, under the aegis of the anti-nuclear peace movement. For here was a coming-together of people from all the major religious traditions nowadays to be found in a British city – Christians of sundry denominations, Jews, Muslims, Sikhs, Hindus, Buddhists – each group in turn offering up prayers and meditation after its own fashion, yet all at least for the moment brought together in a common concern for peace. A colourful, somewhat chaotic experiment – nothing very spectacular, in itself. But was not this (I now wonder in retrospect) a rather apt symbol for the new situation which theology has to confront, and think through?

And then there are clearly a great number of other possibilities.

As the date on which the Berlin Wall was breached in 1989, 9 November might for example be a time for commemorating the whole history of totalitarianism, and of the resistance to it. Particular aspects of that history have a special relevance to particular communities. (When will the Christian churches of Europe start setting liturgical time aside to reflect upon their own complicity, over so many centuries, in the history of anti-Semitism, culminating in the Nazi genocide?) But we surely also ought to ponder the significance of totalitarianism in itself, even those of us who have always lived safe in liberal democracies; not least because of its character as *a spiritual twin-phenomenon* to liberal democracy itself. For totalitarian regimes exhibit in an extreme form at least two features which are, in fact, common to all industrialized cultures: in the first place, they dramatize for us the destructive potential inherent in any culture of mass-propaganda; and second, they highlight the moral-anaesthetic potential inherent in any system of bureaucracy. It is easy enough to see the differences between totalitarianism and liberal democracy, and it is not to devalue those differences to say that they scarcely require much spiritual 'working through'. But the underlying resemblances do, just because they are so much more troubling in their implications.

Or again – since we continue to live with the long-term consequences of the trans-Atlantic slave trade, ought we not to set some time aside for the meditative 'working through', black and white together, of that history? I think that the Rastafarians have a point when they accuse their parents' church-Christianity of still being implicated in the 'Babylonian' heritage of that trade. In taking up the biblical story of the Jewish people's enslavement and exile in Babylon, and applying it to themselves, the Rastas are looking for a form of religion which puts centre-stage that great unmastered memory which still continues, more than any other, to define their ethnic community's historic identity. And is this not, at least in part, the proper job of religion? Whatever its virtues, their parents' Christianity has not done that job; it has tended to remain the purely confessional affair which the white missionaries brought.

The only trouble is, the Rastafarian protest is then caught up in an ideology of racial separatism – represented by the worship of a 'black' God, as such. There is, it seems to me, always a special danger when the commemoration of a painful past is left to a victim-community, on its own. The truly shaking experience, after all, is the sense of oneself as an accomplice, not victim. And, whilst victims may very well also be accomplices in their own oppression, everything here depends upon oppressor-communities, so far as possible, honestly sharing the burden of remembrance with them. It is always too heavy a burden for victim-communities to carry alone.

Likewise, the same principle applies for instance to the conflict in Ireland: when will British churches start to set serious liturgical time aside to reflect on their own Britishness, in the context of Irish history? For an ex-imperial people like the British (the English especially) history holds no great pain. We happily leave it in the hands of the Heritage industry, to sell it back to us then as so much material for nostalgia; and find it hard to understand how it might mean anything much more than that to others. Remembrance Sunday is, in principle, one attempt to achieve a different sort of relationship to the past. But it is still relatively easy for us – forgetting the sheer futility of 1914–18 – to celebrate the courageous exploits of a war against Nazism. Whereas the most valuable initiatives in such corporate memory-work are always the more difficult ones.

The chief agencies in our world attempting to keep shaking-memory alive, at its most shaking, are the new social movements. This is not to say that they always get it right. They do not – and it is, to a large extent, in order to help remedy matters that a suitable theology is needed, by way of critique. But subversive commemoration nevertheless remains a major aspect of their general consciousness-raising vocation. Each new social movement has its own distinctive calendar-contributions to make. In each different context, there are a different set of observances. Indeed. one could go on multiplying potential examples for ever.

Let me reiterate: the necessary consensus underlying these observances cannot be restricted to any particular code of 'political correctness', in the sense of setting dogmatic limits on what may legitimately be thought or said. God forbid! It can no more be restricted in that way than it can be restricted to any one set of metaphysical opinions, however loose. If there is any new theological truth in the emergent ethos of new social movements, as I believe there is, then it consists in their potential to embrace the solidarity of the shaken; which however – far from distinguishing between what may and may not be thought, in metaphysical or political terms – demands only that whatever is thought should proceed from the most fundamental calling into question of all given assumptions.

A meditative celebration of the solidarity of the shaken will therefore, so far as possible, seek to stimulate thought religiously; without in any way channelling it ideologically. Granted, the channelling impulse is a perpetual temptation. But the movement-theologian's essential task is, by every means available, to work towards new observances which resist it.

6　Beyond 'metaphysics'

There are in fact two distinct levels on which one might discuss the potential religious implications of this (utopian?) dream of a third modernity. One level is that of theology: with a focus on all that needs to go into the solidarity-building aspect of the solidarity of the shaken. But, complementary to the theological and undergirding it, there is also a *pre*-theological level. By which I mean a thinking strictly focused on the identification of the most radical shakenness, in itself, as a matter of sheer inwardness; a direct registering of the initial impact of God, so to speak, prior to the solidarity-building process out of which theology proper comes.

Amongst twentieth-century thinkers one of the most interesting in this latter regard is perhaps Martin Heidegger. Certainly, Heidegger is a key influence on Patočka's thinking, and hence on Havel's also. At the same time, he is a major source for philosophical postmodernism generally; a persistently haunting presence in the background to Lyotard's work, in particular. And one can well see why.

As it happens, Heidegger is a thinker who thinks on both levels: both the 'pre-theological' and, in my sense of the term, the 'theological'. It is true that he uses the actual term 'theology' rather differently, confining it to specifically confessional doctrine; and in that sense seeks only ever to get beyond it.[1] But if one allows the possibility of there being such a thing as trans-confessional theology, then he is clearly also a trans-confessional theologian.

However, of these two aspects of his thought his pre-theology is surely very much the stronger. Debate of course rages, book after book of it, on the subject of Heidegger's notorious support for, and active although short-lived collaboration with, the Nazi revolution of 1933. His thinking would in any case be one of the most thought-provoking contributions to twentieth century intellectual life, by virtue of its extraordinarily rich poetic suggestiveness and startling originality; the embarrassment of his having also been, for however short a period, an active Nazi naturally adds to the provocation in another way. But it seems to me that all the problems here belong to what I have called the 'theological' level of his thought. This is intriguing and instructive; it also remains profoundly ambivalent.

His pre-theology, on the other hand, is quite another matter.

Das Ereignis – in general

At the pre-theological level, Heidegger may I think be very well described as being, essentially, an explorer of the intrinsic truth of shakenness. Not that this is his term. In his own terminology, he is a thinker of 'Being'. But – in the decisive distinction he draws between that true, sublimely concrete plenitude, 'Being' (*das Sein*), and the mere abstract concept of 'being' (*das Seiende*) – 'Being' in effect becomes, precisely, his term for the sheer shaking-power which belongs to whatever the shaken are shaken by. It is the primal 'other' to thinking, the inexhaustible lure to it; beyond any given framework of ideas – that which, shakingly, just *is*.

Heidegger himself does not speak of 'shakenness', as such. The closest equivalent in his thinking is the concept of '*Angst*' ('anxiety'/'dread'), as analysed in *Being and Time*. Here *Angst* is counterposed, in the first instance, to fear. Like fear, *Angst* comes with a loss of security. But it nevertheless differs from fear in not being focused on any one particular danger. Rather, it is a direct response to the shaking-power – his own term is '*die Unheimlichkeit*' ('the uncanniness') – of Being, generally. It is the definitive indication of a direct encounter with Being.

After *Being and Time* the actual concept of *Angst* drops out of Heidegger's thinking. In his later writings, with their turn towards the poetic, *Angst* is evoked rather than self-consciously discussed. It becomes an implicit presence: there in the menacing darkness round the metaphoric 'clearing' where Being is said to be made manifest, or in the faintly sinister rustlings alongside the lonely 'forest trails' of his thought – imagery rich in Germanic resonance.

However, when he speaks of breaking free of the limitations of 'metaphysics', what he means by 'metaphysics' (I think one may say) is simply any philosophical thought-project whatsoever – to the extent that it falls short of an absolute focus on the demands of pure shakenness as such.

Insofar as it gives any weight at all to other criteria, of whatever kind, a thinking is *ipso facto* 'metaphysical' in the Heideggerian sense. The thinking of Being – as the transcendence of metaphysics – is nothing other than a holding fast to the demands of pure shakenness alone. Quite apart from any further overlay of doctrinal orthodoxy.

Heidegger makes much play with the etymological origins of the Greek word for 'truth': *aletheia*, the primary sense of which is 'unconcealment'. The basic point here has to do with the radical otherness of 'unconcealment' from 'correctness'. Truth-as-correctness is a quality of propositions; truth-as-unconcealment is a quality of relationship. And the *aletheia* of postmetaphysical insight, as such, has essentially to do with the innermost relationship of one's whole existence (in German, *Dasein*, literally 'being-there') to the shaking-power of Being. Even the most perfectly correct formula, in the mouth of the wrong person or spoken in the wrong context, may in actual practice serve to 'conceal'. But true 'unconcealment' comes, precisely, from shakenness – the shaking away of that which conceals.

Everything, in short, depends upon the actual *appropriation* of the experience of shakenness. Heideggerian pre-theology is thus fundamentally an attempt at the most primordial account possible of what it means for shakenness to be 'owned'.

In its first stage, the pages of *Being and Time* (1927) feature a sustained play upon the terms '*eigen*' ('to own'), '*eigenst*' ('one's ownmost') and '*Eigentlichkeit*' ('authenticity') – all with reference to a shaken coming to terms with the sheer fact of one's mortality. But then, from his *Contributions to Philosophy* of 1936–8 onwards, he turns to focus more on the shaking-power of the given historical context. So he becomes the exponent of what he calls '*das Er-eignis*': 'the event', or 'event of appropriation'.[2] This concept of the *Ereignis* serves, in Heidegger's thinking, as his trans-confessional pre-theological equivalent to the confessional theological notion of an historic moment of revelation. In the first instance, it appears to be a general term for any experience of cultural shake-up whatsoever – insofar as this is experienced not just as a catastrophe, but also as a compelling stimulus to the radical re-evaluation of all values. Or in other words: any irruption of Being, wherever and whenever.

Prior to Heidegger one finds a comparable polemical opposition between truth-as-appropriation and truth-as-correctness, most notably, in the thinking of Kierkegaard. For Kierkegaard, on the other hand, the issue emerges first and foremost with regard to the theological term 'faith'. So Kierkegaard defines faith as 'an objective uncertainty held fast in an appropriation-process of the most passionate inwardness'.[3] Faith's claim to correctness dwindles here to an 'objective uncertainty'; nor does Kierkegaard have any wish at all to *defend* it, at that level, as enshrined in the propositional content of the creeds, or in any way to try and mitigate that 'objective uncertainty'. On the contrary, he revels in a wholesale abandonment of all conventional apologetic defences. If the objective aspect of faith is deemed 'absurd' – so far as he is concerned, well and good. For, considered purely in itself, it is of no real theological importance at all. Its theological truth-value lies solely in its God-given role as a means of providing some symbolic reference points for the 'appropriation-process' which is faith. And what counts is just the quality of that appropriation-process.

Kierkegaard's term for what true faith represents is 'truth as subjectivity'. And, translated into Patočka's terminology, this is precisely the truth of shakenness. It is from Kierkegaard that Heidegger originally derives his concept of '*Angst*'. Kierkegaard, one might say, sets out to develop a systematic analysis of the emotional dynamics of shakenness: beginning from the most inchoate forms of *Angst*, then tracing the process by which *Angst* is progressively elevated to the very highest pitch of articulate intensity, and thereby transformed. Herein lies the truth which he calls 'subjectivity': the inner truth of faith is just the truth of that intensification.[4] No doubt it will, in fact, always seem 'absurd' to the objectivist mentality – since it tends to render everything not easier, but ever more difficult, existentially. Yet this is very much the ultimate criterion for good theology, from a Kierkegaardian point of view: that it should have that effect, of confronting us, in the most pressing way, with everything most difficult in our reality.[5] (A criterion with which I entirely concur.)

It is clear that Kierkegaard is an important influence on Heidegger – indeed, the whole (strange!) structure of *Being and Time* is largely interpretable as an elaborate attempt to wrench the Kierkegaardian concept of *Angst* out of its original Christian-confessional context.

And yet it seems to me that there is good reason for such a project. For whilst there may be all sorts of reasons to *combine* a celebration of shakenness with an affirmation of Christian faith, Kierkegaard's dogmatic *identification* of the two surely just confuses the issue. Notwithstanding his decisively anti-metaphysical prioritization of truth as the appropriation of shakenness over truth as doctrinal correctness, from the Heideggerian point of view Kierkegaard still remains very much a metaphysical thinker, just because the shakenness he affirms is not yet shakenness as such. It is only that much narrower phenomenon: the shakenness of authentic Christian faith.

But what Heidegger for his part means to affirm, in his strictly pre-theological critique of metaphysics, is pure shakenness as such. At this level he allows no further qualifications, absolutely no distractions. Nor has anyone ever been more radical than he in excluding such distractions – *at this level*.

Das Ereignis, as a particular historic crisis, marking the moral bankruptcy of second modernity

When it comes to the *other* level, however, things are rather different.

Heidegger's counterposing of his discourse on Being to 'theology', as an altogether other domain of thought, rests on a definition of 'theology' in which it is assumed, even in its most shaken forms, to be always grounded in an apologetic confessionalism – and so to be, at least to that extent, metaphysical, as in Kierkegaard's case.[6] Yet he himself then speaks, with solidarity-building intent, of God (or rather – in postmodern neo-pagan fashion – of 'the God', and 'gods'). And why, after all, should not this be called another form of theology? For my part, I can see no reason other than a quite unnecessary deference to conventional academic departmentalism, in a world where all academic departments of theology remain strictly confessional.

So let us also speak of Heidegger as a 'theologian'. What I am calling his 'theology' essentially differs from his pre-theology in that it represents a much more direct response to the actual historical circumstances in which he found himself.

One might perhaps put it like this: at the pre-theological level Heidegger is concerned with the nature of the *Ereignis*, which is the highest truth, as a perennial possibility; always accessible, in one form or another, to every age, inasmuch as every age has its more or less significant experiences of cultural shake-up to be appropriated. But, at the same time, for him personally the *Ereignis* is also the appropriation of one very *particular* cultural shake-up. Namely, that which issued from the horrors of the First World War, along with the subsequent tribulations of the Bolshevik Revolution and its consequences.

Heidegger belonged to a generation of German intellectuals for whom the shock of these events had drastically, it seemed, invalidated all the hitherto predominant notions of 'progress', bound up with second modernity. For in its more liberal forms such progressivism now appeared quite powerless to help resolve the traumas deriving from all that bloodshed. Whilst in its militant Bolshevik form it was perceived to have turned most horribly destructive.

In his later thinking the resulting state of affairs is named '*das Ge-stell*': 'the framework' or 'the enframing'.[7] This is the decisive enframing context for his more constructive religious thought; or, in my terms, his theology.

The *Ge-stell* may thus be said to be a comprehensive term for everything that Heidegger felt he had been taught by the world-historical crises of his youth. As he puts it, it is a vision of the whole 'world of technology' – viewed in its aspect as a great force-field of potentially revelatory contradictions. Its moment of truth lies in its enframing of the *Ereignis* essentially as a revelation of the profound perils inherent in our present-day processes of technologization, in general. It is a term for the whole technology-driven background to our present-day culture, which we usually take for granted – as seen however by the thinker who no longer takes it for granted, but on the contrary is shaken into a sense of it as a great and troubling mystery, and so calls it fundamentally into question.

Again, this is in a sense just what Kierkegaard was doing, with paradigmatic radicalism, confessionally. The primary focus of Kierkegaard's culture-criticism was on the moral consequences of technological progress, especially in the communications-media; and his response was to call for a 'leap of faith', out of the banality of mass-circulation newspaper-reading herd-existence – and out of the sort of unappropriated, or merely 'objective', Christian belief which fails to challenge that banality. Heidegger, by contrast, identifies the *Ereignis* of the present with a philosophical 'leap', or 'step back' – not only beyond what Kierkegaard calls the level of 'objectivity' (faith rigidified into mere formulas) but also beyond the shaken confessionalism to which Kierkegaard still subscribes.[8] Yet, with his notion of the *Ge-stell*, he nevertheless seeks to transfer the Kierkegaardian fury against mass-culture into this new context.

Other German intellectuals of Heidegger's generation responded to the same experiences of cultural crisis by recoiling back, away from the apparently discredited progressivism of second modernity, to the older hopes of first modernity. I am thinking here especially of the circle around Karl Barth, who differed from Kierkegaard only in their concern to build a genuine solidarity-strategy on the basis of their critique. Heidegger aspires to be yet more radical. In his thinking there are accordingly two quite distinct fundamental impulses at work: on the one hand, his pre-theological bid to transcend 'metaphysics'; but on the other hand, also, a wholesale theological repudiation of modernity in all its forms.

In fact, it seems to me that the tragic flaw in his thinking is most instructively apparent at just that point where he starts to speak, in post-modern fashion, of 'the gods'. I am thinking partly of the section in his *Contributions to Philosophy* devoted to the concept of 'the last God'.[9] But perhaps the most thought-provoking texts of all from this point of view are his various lectures and lecture-series on the poetry of Hölderlin, dating from the period 1934–42, in which he is commenting on Hölderlin's 'gods'.[10]

These are quite richly evocative commentaries on some of the most poignantly shaken poetry ever written. And what they serve to evoke, more directly than any of his other writings, is the distinctive Heideggerian religious solidarity-strategy, or theology. But suffice it to say: whilst at the pre-theological level his thinking remains an altogether uncompromisingly strict affirmation of pure shakenness as such, at this secondary level the basic loyalty-principle at work is *not* the universal solidarity of the shaken. It is, rather, the solidarity of shaken German intellectuals – as German intellectuals.

Inasmuch as German-ness is not an identity definable by any doctrinal orthodoxy, it is not strictly speaking a 'metaphysical' phenomenon. And for Heidegger the solidarity of the shaken, in itself, was evidently still too abstract an ideal to be seriously entertained. By contrast to us today, he lived in a world largely devoid of concrete movements which might be said to embody it.

What he is advocating and exploring here is therefore a new, purified form of German nationalism, beyond the vulgarity of the prevailing Nazi version: a nationalism of pride in Germany, essentially, in its quality as a pre-eminent 'nation of thinkers and poets'. Hölderlin is important to him above all as a prophet of that ideal. (Whether such an interpretation actually does justice to Hölderlin is another matter....) The Hölderlinian gods are pagan deities. And Heidegger is clearly attracted to this paganism, in part, by its trans-confessional character: pagan tradition, of course, has no sacred scriptures to help define confessional limits.

Yet this is a species of trans-confessionalism in which confessional identities are merely supplanted by those of 'blood and soil'; by kinship loyalties and a shared dedication to the sacred places of one's homeland. And the experiment clearly fails. Heidegger's apocalyptic neo-paganism may have originated as a bid for maximum critical distance from the sheer mindlessness of the more ideologized versions of first and second modernity, but it ended up merely de-sensitizing him to the appalling potential destructiveness of Nazism – just because, it seems, of Nazism's essentially wobbly relationship to modernity.

It is true that in his Nietzsche lectures of the later 1930s he is already clearly pulling back from the political hopes he had entertained at the actual heady moment of the Nazi revolution in 1933. And then, in the dark days at the end of the war, he went further: qualifying the political expression of his Hölderlinian piety with a new – almost Buddhist – advocacy of what he calls 'Gelassenheit', 'releasement' from or 'hanging loose' to all worldly concerns.[11] In his posthumously published interview in *Der Spiegel*, he expresses his chastened sense of philosophy's necessary removal from the political domain with a splendidly flamboyant flourish:

> Philosophy will not be able to effect any immediate transformation in the present state of the world – neither philosophy nor any other merely human plotting and planning. Only a God can save us. The one possibility that remains to us is, in thinking and poetizing, to prepare a readiness for the appearance of the God. Or for the absence of the God, in our downfall – so that it is in facing towards the absent God that we go under.[12]

Yet one may well ask: was there no other lesson to be learnt from the great collective traumas into which he had been caught up, beyond such despair? What would it have taken to have actually prevented the rise of totalitarianism in twentieth century Europe? Surely not just the wider dissemination of *Gelassenheit*! As has indeed so often been complained – when all is said and done, the fact is Heidegger still appears to have been remarkably *un*-shaken by the revelation of the Holocaust. Essentially I think in consequence of his basic repudiation of the cosmopolitan-universalist sympathies constitutive of modernity, there is so much that his form of piety seems merely to blot out from consciousness, so many shaking memories that it is evidently incapable of fully appropriating.

The abiding value of Heidegger's thought surely lies in his systematically sublime pre-theological clearing out of a proper space for trans-confessional theology: that is, his critique of 'metaphysics'. And this remains the case, no matter how flawed his own actual follow-through. But it seems to me that, in the end, everything depends upon our going on to occupy the theological space he has prepared in another way, not his.

I do not think that he is entirely wrong in his interpretation of the *Gestell*. For, like him, I too would see both first and second modernity as processes which have largely now exhausted their creative potential. But what the Heideggerian experiment shows us, it seems to me, with the most painful clarity is just the ultimate futility of any generally anti-modern – and in theological terms therefore neo-pagan – alternative, such as he attempted.

And hence the significance of the idea of third modernity. The thinking of both first and second modernity is, in Heideggerian terms, intrinsically metaphysical. But what third modernity represents is nothing other than the dream of a new, *post*-metaphysical modernity.

Which then demands an equivalently new, post-metaphysical theology to interpret it ...

7 Post-metaphysical faith

Arguably one of the most promising anticipations of the general sort of theology required – albeit still largely couched in pre-political terms and so not yet related to the phenomena of new social movements – is to be found in the work of *Wilfred Cantwell Smith*. Not that Smith himself connects his thought to Heidegger's. And yet, so far as it goes, it nevertheless seems to me to fit the bill quite admirably.

Thus, Smith describes what he is doing as a form of 'world theology'. It is, essentially, a direct response to that world-wide confluence of religious traditions into a single, global conversation-process, which Karl Jaspers registered in terms of philosophical historiography with his notion of the Axial Period. As a young man Smith was a United Church of Canada missionary in what was then British India, working among the Muslims of Lahore. His governing preoccupation is with the preconditions for good inter-cultural religious conversation – in the first place between Christians and Muslims, and then more generally.

Conventional textbook discussions of Christian attitudes to 'inter-faith dialogue', as it tends to be called, usually differentiate between three basic possible approaches: 'exclusivism', 'inclusivism' and 'pluralism'. And Smith is widely taken to be one of the prime exponents of the 'pluralist' approach. 'Exclusivist' thinking (according to this scheme) is founded upon the metaphysical conviction that the ultimate truth of salvation is exclusively to be found within confessionally Christian tradition; and that Christian theology, for the purpose of defining the proper nature of Christian loyalty as such, is therefore exclusively charged with the exposition of that specific truth. From the exclusivist point of view, the ideal outcome of trans-confessional conversation – between Christians and the adherents of other, non-Christian religious traditions – would always involve the conversion of the non-Christians to Christianity, as the higher truth. Almost all traditional Christian theology, prior to the twentieth century, has as a matter of course been exclusivist in orientation. But – suppose one were to judge the conversation between different post-Axial traditions no longer in terms of any pre-ordained ideal outcome, but strictly in terms of its quality *as* conversation. What then? In this case, one surely would have to feel at any rate some misgivings about the intrinsic belligerence of that old traditional approach.

'Inclusivist' thinking differs in that it redefines salvation, so as to include the possibility of what Karl Rahner has famously called 'anonymous Christians'. In other words, it consistently tends to downplay the actual necessity – in order that one be 'saved' – for one explicitly to have recognized Jesus Christ as one's saviour. Jesus remains, for such thinking, metaphysically understood as the one and only true saviour; yet, it is argued, he somehow saves both those who recognize him and those who do not.

How, though? From a critical point of view, one may well wonder what inclusivism really expresses – beyond a rather vague benevolence. For, after all, an 'anonymous Christian' *as such* is not yet a proper conversation-partner for (overt) Christians. When I talk about religious matters with the adherents of other traditions I necessarily address them as the adherents of those other traditions, not as potential anonymous Christians. Perhaps in helping soften the aggressiveness of my missionary zeal the doctrine may help the conversation. Yet is that really all that a good conversation needs? Inclusivism is still not asking this question, with any systematic intent. In itself it simply seems to represent a desire that Christian faith should be made easier, because more modest; it is not yet a whole-hearted plunge into trans-confessional conversation.

Only 'pluralist' thinking really takes that plunge. It may be that the pluralist redefines 'salvation' once more: to admit the possibility that there are several paths to 'salvation', of which the Christian path is only one. Or else one reverts to the exclusivist notion that 'salvation' is the proper name for the valid promises of Christian faith; but then urges that the wisdom of 'salvation' is only one of several, complementary and mutually incommensurable forms of wisdom all ideally required by the highest truth. So that the ideal outcome of trans-confessional conversation, for the Christian, is simply that Christian insight be increasingly incorporated into non-Christian religious traditions – and *vice versa*.

Non-pluralist theology (whether exclusivist or inclusivist) may be deeply shaken, but the solidarity it affirms is still not the solidarity of the shaken as such; it is the solidarity of shaken Christians, as shaken Christians. A Christian theological affirmation of the pure solidarity of the shaken as such must I think be unequivocally pluralist. Of course not all new social movements are immediately confronted with problems of major religious difference amongst their adherents. And yet, in order that the solidarity of the shaken, in the strongest sense, should become the basis of its own theology this option for pluralism is still at any rate the *logical* first step. In itself, it remains a pre-political step. But that then is just what a doctrine of third modernity is intended to supply: the proper (anti-)political fulfilment of a pluralist approach.

'Esperanto pluralism'/'multilingualist pluralism'

By no means all pluralist thinking, however, is automatically post-metaphysical in the Heideggerian sense, as I have suggested Smith's is. In this respect I think the conventional tri-partite typology (exclusivism/inclusivism/ pluralism) needs some refining. By 'post-metaphysical', here, is meant a thinking entirely focused on the truth of the *Ereignis*. That is to say: the most thoughtful possible appropriation of shakenness, considered in itself, whatever the various cultural forms in which it may come to expression; quite without any other distracting interest in the supposed greater doctrinal correctness of one such set of cultural forms, as compared with the others, but solely concerned with how each one, in its own way, may best be opened up for the communication of shakenness. Yet there is also another species of pluralist theology which rests upon a distinct metaphysics of its own, namely one of radical *agnosticism*.

This other pluralism is not in fact primarily concerned with the inter-cultural communication of shakenness. Rather, its concern is with the simple promotion of peaceableness between traditions. Which, again, is certainly one of the preconditions for good conversation here – but by no means the only one. It is therefore alert to the deliverances of shakenness solely to the extent that those deliverances are compatible with a systematic devaluation of the given historical particularity of religious traditions, in view of the way in which conflict here derives from a rigid insistence on particularity. Preoccupied with the defusing of such conflict, this sort of thinking is in fact quite ready to risk desensitizing its adherents to the original and ongoing shake-up quality of the experiences giving rise to the particularity of each tradition.

It is, so to speak, a form of 'Esperanto pluralism': just as some utopians look to the development of a new, culturally neutral language, Esperanto, to be the vehicle of a future peace-making internationalism, so the theological Esperanto-ist, likewise, seeks to found peaceable trans-confessional conver-sation essentially on the basis of a metaphysically-conceived neutrality, altogether abstracted from actual history. The aim is to develop a new universal tradition, equally open to everyone. All the old divisions between traditions are progressively to be emptied of significance, and the highest form of religious truth is then supposed to lie, simply, in whatever is left.

The most distinguished Christian representative of this approach, in recent years, has been John Hick. It seems to me, however, that Hick's form of pluralism actually rests on a fundamental confusion. Thus: one of the key moves in Hick's argument is his conflation of two very different types of disjunction.[1] For brevity's sake, let us call them 'disjunction A' and 'disjunc-tion B'.

Disjunction A constitutes, in my terms, the very essence of the most radi-cally 'religious' insight. For it is the disjunction between the Transcendent as necessarily given in the propositional formulas of some particular tradition, and the Transcendent as that which nevertheless transcends all such given-ness. Hick himself gives numerous instances of this. Within Christendom, Meister Eckhart restricts the name 'God' to the divine datum of tradition – as contrasted with the tradition-transcendent 'Godhead'. Within Jewish tradition, the Kabbalists – and within the Islamic world, the Sufis – did like-wise, respectively referring to the Transcendent that transcends all givenness as *'En Soph'*, and as *'Al Haq'*. Certain strands of Hindu thinking, notably including that of Shankara, differentiate between 'saguna Brahman' and 'nirguna Brahman'; that is, Brahman 'with' and 'without attributes'. The first is Brahman mediated to us in the imaginative form of the creator-God Ishvara, the second is Brahman proper. There is a strand of Pure Land Buddhist thinking, for example, which defines the Transcendent given in tradition as *'upaya dharmakāya'*, dharmakaya-as-compassion; whereas the Transcendent that transcends all traditional givenness is *'dharmata dharmakāya'*, dharmakaya-as-suchness. The latter is – in propositional terms – purely inexpressible. So too, in the opening lines of the *Tao Te Ching* we read: 'The Tao that can be expressed is not the eternal Tao.' Indeed, one could cite many more such formulations, from each of the great post-Axial cultures. And the Heideggerian critique of metaphysics is essentially yet another variant of the same.

Disjunction B, on the other hand, is that made pre-eminently by Kantian philosophy: between the 'phenomenal' and the 'noumenal' levels of reality. It is, from a theological point of view, the outlawing of any serious talk of divine revelation in history – on the grounds that divine reality is 'noumenal', and therefore quite divorced from the 'phenomena' of history, as perceived in traditional terms.

This is a thoroughly anti-'metaphysical' move in Kantian terms; but clearly not at all in the very different Heideggerian sense of 'metaphysics'. Hick, however, effectively identifies A with B.

Note the jump which this involves. Disjunction A is the disjunction between two opposing *attitudes to religious language*: on the one hand, an attitude which treats it as if it were ideological, focusing on the propositions involved as though everything depended on their intrinsic correctness; on the other hand, a recognition of its truly religious character, as a testimony to Transcendence. Disjunction B, though, is the disjunction between two different *modes of experience*: on the one hand, concretely empirical experi-ence; on the other hand, the experience of 'Ideas' attained through pure abstract ratiocination.

For Kant the sacred is strictly 'unknowable', in the sense that to 'know' something is to have a concrete empirical experience of it. But one comes closest to an authentic apprehension of the sacred through a purely *abstract* consideration of the rational implications of ethical obligation.

There is no such celebration of abstract reflection in the various doctrines which affirm disjunction A. What they are celebrating is just the process by which truthful thoughts of every sort, abstract or concrete, come to be spiritually appropriated; the moment of insight, when the penny drops. The Kantian doctrine, in its theological application, serves essentially to de-emphasize the significance of whatever is culturally and historically distinctive about any particular religious perception of the world, inasmuch as this derives from the concrete imagery and narrative content of an authoritative tradition. That distinctiveness, it argues, can never constitute real 'knowledge', as is so often claimed. It is *only* – in the most demeaning, even damning sense – a perspective. (Hick adapts the doctrine by applying it to issues of trans-confessional conversation with which Kant himself was not concerned; nevertheless, there can be no denying that it does very natu-rally lend itself to such use.) Disjunction A, however, does not imply this at all. What is negated here is not so much the intrinsic significance of perspec-tival religious perceptions, in their concrete distinctiveness – as if the ideal were some sort of abstract Esperanto uniformity instead. But, rather, what the theoreticians of this disjunction are subverting is precisely any attempt to restrict the potentially infinite *multifariousness* of perspectival insight – by mis-identifying sacred truth with adherence to a particular set of 'correct' propositions.

Hick's identification of A with B produces a theology whose whole emphasis tends to be on the negation of exclusivist truth-claims, and nothing else. This is especially the case when, as a Christian theologian, he comes to tackle the dogma of the Incarnation.[2] In effect, he sets out to combat the historic ideologization of the dogma by entirely removing its excitement, pouring buckets of cold water on it. It is as though he has just one main thing to say: that the Incarnation, like the central teachings of other faith-traditions, is after all 'only' a metaphor.

In certain contexts, I certainly accept that that may well be worth saying. (An idol is a sacred metaphor which pretends to be something more, and so fails.) But can it ever be, so very much, the one and only thing to say? Is there not also a time for saying: yes – but, at the same time, this is no ordi-nary metaphor; and only to the extent that it is allowed to be extraordinary can its full shaking-power be unleashed?

And then there is the fundamental question which has always to be asked, with regard to any version of the Kantian doctrine: what can it actually mean to speak of an ultimate Reality which is absolutely 'unknowable'? Is not the paradox just a device to help theological liberals protect their liberal preconceptions, sheltered from direct exposure to the systematic study of historical phenomena? 'I have denied knowledge', Kant remarked, 'in order to make room for faith.' It is not just that he repudiates any metaphysical proof of the existence of God. In thus opposing faith to knowledge – of any sort – he also de-historicizes it. His 'faith' is his theological liberalism; and he thereby protects it from any too corrosive 'knowledge' of its own histor-ical relativity. (He tucks it modestly away, as it were, into a mental closet marked 'apprehension of the noumenal'. Everything else is historically rela-tivized, only not this 'faith'.) That is what Hegel meant when he accused

Kant of being in theological collusion with 'the sloth of Reason'.[3] Un-fortunately, though, Hick is just oblivious of the Hegelian critique.[4] The infinite restlessness of authentic thought is cut short not only by the dogmatic claims of a narrow-mindedly exclusivist religious orthodoxy – but equally by the dogmatic claims of Kantian agnosticism, which negates that orthodoxy with such undialectical absoluteness that no real conversation between the opposing positions can ever get going.

No. Good conversation surely requires two things, in tandem: a radical openness to the thought of other cultures *plus* a passionate affirmation of difference, both within and between cultures, as a positive good in itself. Universal agreement, after all, would be universal thoughtlessness. And what is most significantly true in any tradition is always what is most unique about its truth; its most specific contribution to humanity's collective quest for truth. Which is by no means necessarily that aspect of it which is most immediately consonant with a self-negating reference to the supposed 'unknowability' of ultimate Reality. To be sure, a passionate affirmation of difference will always risk evoking conflict. Well then, so be it. Good conversation arises out of the thoughtful sublation of conflict, not its mere suppression.

Smith is indeed very often bracketed with Hick, as if they simply represented two aspects of the same. But in fact he surely represents a completely different type of pluralism. He is by no means a theological Esperantoist. His thinking is quite independent of Hick's Kantianism. And, unlike Hick, he approaches the matter with all the instincts of an historian.

In sharp contrast to Hick's commitment to a philosophically-constructed neo-Kantian religious Esperanto, Smith's 'theology of comparative religion' is very much a form of religious *multilingualism*. It is, in his terms, a systematic process of translating 'faith'-insights from 'belief'-system to 'belief'-system, as from one language to another. Unlike Hick, he is not a metaphysician intent on establishing his own agnostic belief-system to rival the metaphysical systems of confessional thought. But he is simply a mediator, whose whole concern is just to try and help promote the very best possible inter-cultural communication – between the shaken.

'Dialogue'?

Note that Smith speaks of a 'theology of comparative religion'.[5] This is, I think, quite different from – and infinitely preferable to – the more usual designation, 'inter-faith dialogue'. In the first place, 'inter-faith' implies that it is legitimate to speak of a plurality of 'faiths' – a notion which Smith, in my view quite rightly, calls into question, inasmuch as it involves a highly dubious reification of faith; just as the notion of a plurality of 'religions', likewise, tends to reify religiousness. I will come back to this. But secondly, one may also wonder to what extent the specific notion of 'dialogue' is really appropriate as a designation for the type of conversation involved here.

Smith himself seeks 'something less occasional, less polarized' than this term suggests.[6] That is to say: not so much an 'inter-faith' frontier-negotiation process, as it were, between the peacemaking representatives of opposing ideological blocs; more a multilateral 'colloquy'.

So too, for instance, John Cobb urges a move 'beyond dialogue' in the merely diplomatic sense – towards a form of conversation in which all the participants are open to being changed fundamentally, in themselves, by the encounter.[7] Whilst John Milbank, again, urges an abandonment of the 'dialogue' model for inter-cultural conversation, and its replacement by, as he puts it, 'mutual suspicion'.[8] Such a formulation may well appear uncharitable. But, after all, the one thing that all post-Axial cultures, insofar as they are true to their Axial origins, most significantly *do* have in common is a basic suspicion of what I have called 'ideology'. That is their common truth, just as it is the source of all their intellectual rivalry. And what else is the providential benefit of there being a plurality of cultures – if not precisely the provision of this sort of stimulus?

The mediator's task

Much of the strength of Smith's work lies in its quality as a scrupulously fair-minded Christian registering, and mediation, of other cultures' suspicions of Christendom – which nevertheless eschews any, to my mind, over-defensive theological reductionism. It is a radically cosmopolitan enterprise.

And yet the primary target of his polemic is in fact the ideologization associated with that other great cosmopolitan enterprise, the self-promotion of secular academia.

Smith writes both as a Christian and as a secular academic. Using the term 'religious' in essentially the same sense that I have adopted, he sets out to defend the 'religious' elements in the heritage of academic secularity – the 'religiousness' belonging to its origins in Graeco-Roman philosophy, and in Renaissance humanism – against those who would ideologize that heritage.[9] More particularly, he is a fierce critic of any academic approach to the study of religion which proceeds simply from the standpoint of an external observer – as opposed to that of an engaged and open-minded participant in ongoing conversation with those whose religious culture is being studied. For such an approach ensures that nothing will be perceived, by the observer, other than what is consonant with an ideologization of the culture in question. Ideologized secular-academic objectivity only ever perceives expressions of ideology, everywhere it looks. That is its curse.

A theology of comparative religion, or world theology, reflects an attempt to understand the differences between religious cultures by, so to speak, imaginatively entering into alien modes of cultural consciousness. This is quite a different goal from trying to 'explain' the logic of other cultures to oneself and to one's own group (or indeed trying to 'explain' religion in general). And it must, Smith insists, have absolute moral precedence over that other goal.[10] Take for example Buddhist tradition. 'To understand Buddhists', he remarks,

> we must look not at something called Buddhism, but at the world; so far as possible, through Buddhist eyes. For this, we must among other matters learn to use the total system of Buddhist doctrine or world-view as Buddhists use it: as a pattern for ordering the data of observation – not as among the data to be observed. A conceptual framework ... has to be grasped as it has been: not part of what a person knows, but the vision by and within which he or she knows (knows, or guesses, or is aware of not knowing). It does not *mean* something; it confers meaning.[11]

This is the challenge for such theology – in a certain sense, it is precisely what constitutes it as the solidarity-building enterprise of 'theology' – even in relation to the, in another sense, quite un-'theological' doctrinal framework of Buddhist cultures. It is the challenge it faces in relation to all cultures, without exception.[12] Its task is systematically to mediate between them, at that level; to be an authentically religious thinking-through of religious difference.

One may well compare this to Kierkegaard's mid-nineteenth-century protest against the reduction of religious truth to something merely 'objective'; somehow discernible from outside. But Smith does not, as Kierkegaard does, simply seek to get beyond 'objectivity' by exalting 'subjectivity', as such. For, unlike Kierkegaard, he is equally anxious to get beyond the *collective* 'subjectivity' of his own given culture. He defines his ideal as the cultivation of a 'corporate critical self-consciousness'; which would, in that sense, transcend both objectivity and subjectivity.

'By "corporate self-consciousness" ', he writes, 'I intend knowledge that is in principle apt both for the subject himself or herself, and for all external observers; or, in the case of group activities, for both outside observers and participants.'[13] The theology which is to serve this goal thus becomes both a comprehensive translation-service, between religious cultures, and a polemical affirmation of its own translation-practice as the first priority for good religious thought today. Its distinctive 'truth' is the truthfulness of faithful but effective translation. Hence, from this point of view, 'no statement about Islamic faith is true that Muslims cannot accept'; at any rate, those particular Muslims which the statement intended. Yet – by the same token – 'no statement about Islamic faith is true that non-Muslims cannot accept', either.[14] That is to say, none that they cannot possibly accept just by virtue of their being and remaining non-Muslim. And so, too, with all other faith-traditions: in the end, only ideology resists this deeper-than-merely-linguistic mode of translation.

Or again, beyond objectivity and subjectivity, Smith advocates what he calls a form of 'personalism', honouring Martin Buber, for instance, as a pioneer.[15] He is deeply mistrustful of any preoccupation with academic 'methodology'. As he once put it: 'I feel that methodology is the massive red herring of modern scholarship, the most significant obstacle to intellectual progress, and the chief distraction from rational understanding of the world'(!).[16] Good conversation, after all, is far more a matter of flair than of method; and, in the 'humane sciences', that is surely what counts. 'I am haunted', he says,

> by the sense that method, technique, is a device for dominating. The relation between science and technology suggests that if we learn the right method, we can manipulate, control, exert our superiority. If there be any of that in the humanities, we are doomed as scholars. Our task is not to dominate, but to revere; to learn to revere.[17]

A methodology tends to represent a bid for power, within a particular academic 'discipline'. Smith deplores the academic organization of the humanities into self-enclosed disciplines, constituted by this sort of power-play, and the consequent fragmentation of university life into a multitude of more or less competing sects – whose members write only for one another, in their own jargon, or are chiefly interested in the specification of their own distinctive group-identity. He himself began his scholarly career as a Marxist, that is, as the member of a sect both academic and party-political.[18] In part, it seems, he is polemically repudiating his own past here. But the same is true of any strong commitment to a particular methodology: it will always tend to obstruct good conversation. And this is especially so where good conversation is in any case most difficult, because of being inter-cultural.

Once upon a time the leading ideologists of Western cultural imperialism were (the more crusading type of) Christian missionaries. Now however, he argues, that role has largely been usurped by secular academics, in their various methodologically-defined sects. These academics may be better *informed* than their missionary predecessors; but this does not, of itself, render them any better equipped as inter-cultural conversationalists. Methodologies differ from one another, essentially, in their approach to information-gathering. Good conversation, on the other hand, depends upon getting beyond the level of mere information-gathering. It is a mediation of the transcendent – and, whereas information is communicated to the intellect, the transcendent speaks to the whole person.

Indeed, the real shaking-power of Smith's theology, one might say, lies precisely in his attempt at the very strictest possible demarcation of language evoking the transcendent from information-language. In ordinary usage, the term 'religion' oscillates between these two sorts of context. And so, crucially, does the term 'faith'. He responds to such oscillation in the most drastic fashion.

A history of religion in the singular

Smith is in fact notorious for having, at one stage in his career, advocated the complete banishment of the term 'religion' from scholarly discourse. This is the basic argument of his book, *The Meaning and End of Religion*, first published in 1964.

Here, he distinguishes four basic common meanings for 'religion':[19]

1 It may be used as a straightforward synonym for personal 'piety'.
2 One may speak of Christianity, Judaism, Islam, Hinduism, Buddhism, Taoism, Confucianism and so forth as 'religions' in the plural, or each as 'a' religion; referring to the ideals these various cultural complexes are supposed to embody.
3 One may do the same, with reference to their actual, non-ideal practice.
4 One may talk (as for example I have been doing) of 'religion' in general, as a moral quality of whole cultures.

The trouble is that usages 2 and 3 render 'religion' the name of a certain type of 'thing'; in the sense of being an entity knowable essentially by way of factual information. Whereas in the other two usages – at least sometimes – it designates no mere thing, but on the contrary an inner movement of response to the transcendent. This ambivalence, Smith argues, tends to result in theologically disastrous confusion.

In the mid-1960s, he could see no valid use for the concept of 'religion' at all. But he was optimistic: within twenty-five years, he predicted, it was likely that it would have simply vanished 'from serious writing and careful speech'.[20] People would instead speak – in an altogether more discriminating manner – of 'piety', of 'cumulative traditions' and of 'faith'. They might perhaps persist in using the adjective 'religious'; but not, any longer, the noun.

Well, twenty-five years have come and gone, and it must be said that there is as yet very little sign of this actually happening. Smith himself has since reverted to speaking of 'religion', at any rate in the last of his four senses; not least readmitting the term into his programmatic formula, 'theology of comparative religion'. And yet he still does scrupulously continue to avoid any talk of this or that particular 'religion', or of 'religions' in the plural.

I myself think he is right to do so. For, as he points out, this latter way of speaking belongs very much to the dynamics of Western imperialism.[21] In fact, he finds the earliest example of the idea of '*the* Christian religion', set over and against other 'religions', in Grotius's book *De Veritate Religionis Christianae* (1627). In previous Christian theology, he suggests, the word had always meant piety – or the ritual expression of piety – in general; whether of Christians or non-Christians. Thus, in effect, it signified that which most momentously renders any human culture both human and cultured. (This remains the case in Calvin's thought, for instance: it is, Smith argues, a serious error of translation to insert a definite article into the title of Calvin's *Institutes of Christian Religion*.) But in the early seventeenth century the word which had hitherto meant that which all humane culture most deeply has in common was transformed, instead, into a designation for cultural division. The shift here is surely symptomatic of a heightened sense of inter-cultural conflict, in the pioneer age of Western expansion.[22]

And then, in the nineteenth century, this notion of 'the Christian religion' was further reinforced by Western scholarship's construction of a number of mirror-concepts: 'Buddhism', 'Hinduism', 'Confucianism', 'Taoism', 'Zoroastrianism', 'Shintoism'.[23] There are no originally Chinese terms with the exact meaning of 'Confucianism' or 'Taoism'; no indigenous Indian word for 'Hinduism'; no properly Buddhist concept of 'Buddhism', as one 'religion' among others.[24] But with these coinages Western scholarship sought to impose its own clear-cut Western-style order on the amorphous and multiply syncretistic phenomena of Eastern religion. Was this not indeed a crowning act of metaphysical creativity? Smith, on the other hand, breaks with it completely. He abandons (instead of trying to adapt) the terminology involved, essentially in order to signal the finality of the break.

To talk of 'religions' – as opposed to the single religious history of humanity as a whole, in which there are various 'strands', Christian, Jewish, Muslim, Hindu, Buddhist, Taoist, Confucian and so forth – is, it seems, to place a heavily ideological emphasis on the divisions between such cultural complexes, rather than their creative interaction; and on their elements of overall internal coherence, rather than their openness and pluriformity. It goes, historically, with what Smith calls the 'big-bang theory' of religious origins: an approach to the study of human spirituality consistently privileging those 'big-bang' moments of which it may be said that, here, some brand new 'religion' has been born – almost as though everything, in each case, entirely depended upon the intrinsic quality of that initial event alone.[25] He traces the sources of this attitude in Western scholarship back to the Reformation, with its polemical insistence on a return to the Bible. The same approach was reproduced, only somewhat more coolly, in Enlightenment theology, before (he suggests) going on to become a dominant prejudice of nineteenth-century religious historiography. In this context it serves as a labour-saving device, for simplifying matters. But it also has the effect of quite arbitrarily devaluing the later products of syncretism.

To the 'big-bang theory' Smith opposes what he calls a 'theory of continuous creation'. So, for example, he writes:

> Historians have tended at times not to notice the present tense in Christians' exultant cries at Christmas and at Easter, no matter what the century. 'Hodie natus est', they have exclaimed; and exuberantly sung, 'Jesus Christ is risen *today*'. Should one not speculate that they perhaps meant what they said? Some historians of religion have tended to opine that Christmas and Easter as celebrated in Europe and elsewhere are

symbolic representations of events that took place long ago, in the first century AD, in Palestine. Might they not rather interpret the observed facts the other way round? Should one not say that on each Easter morning, in this century and in that – and to a less intense degree, each Sunday morning; and in a suffusing way, constantly – something trans- forming and liberating and exalting, less or much, or simply but importantly sustaining, occurred in the lives of those Christians, of which the tales of first-century events served successive ages as the symbolic representation?[26]

The first Christian century, he insists, is not necessarily the most impor- tant from a theological point of view, just because it was when Christianity was at its cultural purest.[27]

'Faith'

Smith's doctrine of 'religion' may be said to represent the very purest form of post-metaphysical monotheism – and, then, in his doctrine of 'faith' he also goes on to develop an equally post-metaphysical soteriology. Clearly the situation is somewhat different here, in that as a Christian theologian he cannot just jettison the term 'faith', the way he advocates jettisoning the non-biblical term 'religion'. And yet in this case too there are major prob- lems of oscillation: between 'faith' as a placing of trust in the transcendent and 'faith', conventionally understood, as the giving of assent to a set of metaphysical 'beliefs'.

To be sure, Smith is by no means the first to draw that distinction. Nevertheless, he does develop it with quite singular radicalism. Thus, he constructs a theological history of the English words 'belief' and 'believe'. It is a story of decline and fall – corresponding, he argues, to a fundamental sickness of mainstream Western theological culture as a whole in the post- Enlightenment period, and above all from the nineteenth century onwards. The advance of this sickness is rendered especially clear in the English- speaking world, by virtue of its possessing the two closely related words 'faith' and 'belief', where other languages only have one. There has been a regrettable slippage in the meaning of both; but it was 'belief' which slipped first, and deepest, subsequently dragging 'faith' down by association. And the obvious remedy, in English – he urges – is therefore to draw the sharpest possible distinction between the two: abandoning 'belief' to its fallen meaning, whilst rescuing 'faith' by henceforth insisting on its absolute other- ness from 'belief', in that sense.

The link between the two words derives from the chance fact that, in English, 'faith' is a noun lacking a verbal cognate. In the Greek of the New Testamant, the noun '*pistis*' correlates to the verb '*pisteuô*'. It was natural for the translators of the King James version to render the noun as 'faith' and the verb as 'believe'. But, as Smith seeks to show at some length, the term 'believe' did not for them mean what it means for us.[28] Its prevailing connotations were quite different. For them, this was a word which still, in all its usages, retained a vivid flavour of its etymological origins: as being related to 'love', 'beloved'; the old English 'lief' ('dear'); the Latin *'libet'* ('it pleases'), *'libido'* ('pleasure'/'desire'); the German *'belieben'* ('to prize' or 'to hold dear').[29] As an equivalent to the Latin *'credo'*, it preserved all the original connotations of that word, too: literally, 'I set my heart'; hence, 'I pledge allegiance'.[30]

Now, however, everything has changed. As he puts it:

> The affirmation 'I believe in God' used to mean: 'Given the reality of God as a fact of the universe, I hereby pledge to Him my heart and soul. I committedly opt to live in loyalty to Him. I offer my life to be judged by Him, trusting His mercy'. To-day the statement may be taken by some as meaning: 'Given the uncertainty as to whether there be a God or not, as a fact of modern life, I announce that my opinion is "yes". I judge God to be existent'. Insofar as a moral commitment and one's life behaviour are involved, they could add: 'And I trust my judgement'. To say that so-and-so believes in God may mean: The Idea of God is part of the furniture of that man's mind.[31]

The former is the attitude of *pistis* in its New Testament sense. *'Pistis'* nowhere meant what, for the most part, 'belief' has subsequently come to mean. And 'I believe' has by the same token also become a completely inadequate translation for *'credo'*.[32] In contemporary English, he suggests, the creeds should no longer begin 'I believe' or 'We believe in God'. In view of what has happened here to the language, it would nowadays be far truer to the tradition for us to say, instead: 'I *commit myself*' or 'We *commit ourselves* to God'.

The balance of conventional usage has, he argues, shifted both with regard to the subject of the verb 'to believe', and with regard to its object, that which is said to be 'believed in'. With regard to the subject of the verb, in Shakespeare, for example, it appears by far the most often in the first person, to some extent in the second person, far less in the third person. Smith has actually counted the occurrences. In fact, it occurs about nine times more often in the first person than in the third.[33] Gradually, however, and above all in nineteenth- and twentieth-century academic literature, this has ceased to be the norm it once was. Thus 'belief' has become, far more, something one observes in others.

So too, in its earlier usage, even when it did refer to another person's point of view, it seldom if ever meant one with which the speaker disagreed; on those relatively rare occasions when one did say 'she believes' this was mostly equivalent to 'she acknowledges'. But then came the decline. And, rather than 'she acknowledges', it increasingly came to mean the more non-committal 'she is of the opinion'; or, indeed, the frankly disparaging 'she imagines'.[34] As a 'prize example' Smith cites the 1966 Random House Dictionary, where the entry for 'belief' begins with the definition 'an opinion or conviction' – as in 'the belief that the earth is flat'.

In the New Testament, by contrast, *'pisteuô'* is never 'I am of the opinion'; it is always 'I acknowledge'. Nor is the verb ever used to refer to anyone else's questionable opinions. Rather, it tends to connote a certain quality of response – far more religious than it is opinionatedly ideological – to the demands of difficult, but undeniable reality. In only a small minority of instances (one in eight, Smith reckons) does it refer to a proposition at all.[35] Often, it has no explicit object. And where it does have one, this is normally not a proposition – but the difficult reality of God, or Christ, as persons. Moreover, the use of 'believe' for *'pisteuô'* in the King James Authorized Version of the Bible also appears to correspond to the more general usage of the word in seventeenth-century English. In all the literature of that period, 'believing' seems mostly to have persons for its object. 'Belief' in a person, or persons, may well serve as the medium for an orientation to the transcendent, inasmuch as it is a laying of oneself open to being transformed by the encounter; 'belief' in propositions can, as such, only be an ideological stance. But, as the usage of the term evolved through the following period, it lapsed steadily from the one to the other.[36] Smith cites John Stuart Mill, for example, in the mid-nineteenth century: for (the immensely influential) Mill, it had become quite self-evident that 'the objects of all Belief and of all Inquiry express themselves in propositions'. He can envisage no criterion for the validity of 'belief' other than the correctness or incorrectness of its propositional expression. As he sees it, 'all truth and all error lie in propositions'.[37] This is a view which Smith calls 'not merely wrong, but tragically wrong', because of everything it so blithely leaves unaccounted for.[38] And yet – such was the evolution of Western intellectual culture that it seems sophisticated and serious-minded people like Mill had, by his day, effectively lost any sight of any real alternative. Therein lies the tragedy.

'Belief' was thus demoted from the sphere of authentic religion to that of ideology. Its usage became more and more restricted to the demarcation of competing metaphysical points of view. Yet, even so, it still retained its intimate relationship with 'faith'. And so it also tended to involve 'faith' in its downfall; with a gravely distorting impact first on Western 'philosophy of religion', and then on theology. By way of illustration here, Smith focuses in particular on A.J. Ayer's remark: 'Until we have an intelligible proposition before us, there is nothing for faith to get to work on.'[39] Once the meaning of 'faith' has been reduced in this fashion – from being a certain depth of interpersonal relationship to being a certain style in the construction of propositional belief-systems – it naturally tends to share the fate of 'religion'; so that, just as one already speaks of such-and-such 'a religion' or of 'religions' in the plural, it likewise becomes natural to speak of such-and-such 'a faith' and of the many 'faiths'. Or one starts to speak of 'the content of faith'. It tends to become a term for any culturally-limited, or arbitrarily-chosen attitude – essentially in its limitedness or arbitrariness. Until, finally, a cynic like Mark Twain's 'schoolboy' may even venture the succinct definition: 'Faith is believing what you know ain't so.'[40]

Nevertheless, of the two words, 'faith' still remains the less fallen; it is, after all, much better anchored in Christian theological tradition. Within that tradition, from St Paul onwards, faith is that which 'saves'. And, as a Christian theologian, Smith therefore takes up the traditional cry: salvation is indeed by faith *alone*.[41] He seeks to sever the link. We are saved by faith alone – and that means, *not by belief.*

It is, then, essentially on this basis that he aims to found that systematic process of inter-cultural conversation which he calls 'world theology'. For 'belief', in its fallen sense, is of course just what divides one tradition from another. But a capacity for articulating faith (as that which saves) is, he insists, at least latently present within every religious tradition as such.

In short: what he is advocating is a radically post-metaphysical notion of faith. The term 'faith', deriving its significance as it does primarily from Christian and Islamic tradition, carries with it strong connotations of modernist cosmopolitanism. It is therefore not surprising that Heidegger should have rejected it.[42] Yet here we have a trans-confessional theological account of faith which is just as closely and undistractedly focused on the intrinsic potential revelatoriness of what I am calling 'shakenness' as Heidegger's pre-theology ever is.

Thus by 'faith' Smith seems to mean precisely what Heidegger for his part calls the '*Ereignis*' – only, in its modernist mode. Or in other words: any properly modern and authentically religious response to the shocks of cultural shake-up, wherever and whenever they may occur; equally, whether it be within the religious traditions of first modernity, or within other religious traditions, originally pre-modern but now modernising.

This is, to be sure, a very untraditional doctrine of faith. In arguing along these lines Smith is not only rejecting the more recent, fallen usage of the term; he is also making quite a radical departure from earlier Christian tradition, which was always at least partly metaphysical in character. The point is, though, that in that earlier period the otherness of salvific faith from mere assent to propositional belief was for the most part just taken for granted. And so it remained blurred. Whereas, at least the pressures deriving from post-Enlightenment ideological confusions of the two have – it is to be hoped, once and for all – helped sharpen up the issue.[43]

Response to critics

Of course, there is a certain sense in which Smith's own doctrine might be said to be the expression of a particular sort of 'belief'. However, let us distinguish between two orders of belief: *first-order beliefs*, which, in themselves, are simply statements of personal commitment to some particular metaphysical account of the world; and *second-order beliefs*, which specify one's attitude to conversation with those who, in first-order terms, believe different things from oneself.

In that case, what Smith is articulating is a form of second-order belief. But one might, more precisely, further define his conception of 'faith' as a particular quality of shaken thoughtfulness and moral dedication attendant upon a person's appropriation of their first-order beliefs; such that – quite regardless of the actual propositional content of those first-order beliefs – the deeper the faith, the more genuinely inspirational that individual's testimony becomes, even to those from other traditions.

Critics have objected that the absoluteness of the distinction Smith draws is unsustainable. Granted that faith is indeed 'more than' the mere unappropriated holding of the (first-order) beliefs in which it is framed, this line of argument runs, it surely still does imply a certain (second-order) commitment to those beliefs: as being, at least to some extent exclusively, *the* truth. Hugo Meynell, for instance, puts it in robust, common-sense terms:

> Once the chips are down, all differences of expression due to culture and intellectual development taken into account, and all ambiguities removed, there cannot both be and not be a God; and the Qur'an bestowed through Muhammad both be and not be the final and culminating expression by him of his nature and will to humankind. However much the Muslim admits that he has positively to learn from the Christian or the Buddhist, he has, so long as he remains a Muslim at all, to insist that they are in error so long as they do not believe these crucial facts; which, of course, they cannot come to believe without thereby ceasing to be a Christian or a Buddhist.[44]

For Meynell, Smith's doctrine – insofar as he appears to deny this – is nothing but a sheer epistemological muddle.

But, first of all, let us be clear which level of belief we are talking about. At the level of first-order belief, the Muslim believer need not actually be saying anything more than '*In my culture* true shaking power is conceived as God, and the Qur'an bestowed through Muhammad is the final and culminating expression by him of his nature and will.' (For clarity's sake, I think we need to jettison Meynell's little question-begging phrase 'to humankind' here; if we are truly to engage with what Smith is saying, 'final and culminating' must, in the first instance, just mean 'final and culminating to *me*'.) The whole issue is, then, whether this first-order mode of belief *necessarily* has the sort of second-order implications which Meynell suggests it has. It may, in actual practice, usually be understood as having such implications – but must it, in principle?

That is what Smith is denying. And yes, in my view he is quite right to deny it. For – to use Meynell's own phrase – the simple fact is 'the chips' never *are* down. There can be no proper end to the process of taking 'differences in expression due to culture and intellectual development' into account. The 'ambiguities' Meynell speaks of can never be removed. What Meynell is defending is not the proper nature of religious language; it is merely metaphysics. But it seems to me that metaphysics is always, ultimately, a diminishment of religion. In just this sense: that religious language is precisely that form of speech in which one and the same proposition – the elementary proposition 'there is a God', for example – may very well be both true and false; inasmuch as what is really meant (in this case, by the word 'God') always so entirely depends upon *who* is speaking, *when* and *to whom*. Different people, using the identical theological phrases, may mean such utterly different things by them in practice. And the practice is what counts. I repeat: religious truth, and religious falsehood, inhere not in propositions, but in persons and conversations; they are qualities of life, and of encounter. What is muddled, it seems to me, is not so much Smith's post-metaphysical 'personalist' understanding of faith. The real muddle lies far more in the opposing, common-sense view, as it fails to recognize the infinite slipperiness of such language. Thus far at any rate, I see nothing wrong with Smith's resolute rejection of compromise.

Nor am I at all persuaded by any of the other major counter-arguments that have been proposed. William J. Wainwright, for example, has criticized Smith's basic formula for good religious conversation: 'no observer's statement about a group of persons is valid that cannot be appropriated by those persons'.[45]

Smith himself immediately goes on to add that, in this connection, he means statements about a group's faith, rather than about its traditions considered as historical data, the way they have objectively evolved. But, as Wainwright points out, he clearly implies the further qualification that group-members should be able to accept the observer's statements without in any way thereby abandoning their original group-loyalties. And if so, then – Wainwright objects – 'we would appear to be committed to the claim that any account of the most bizarre cult must be acceptable to its members'.

What this objection evidently overlooks, however, is the implicit presence of yet a third vital qualification to the formula: once more, the point is that Smith is only talking about faith as it is embodied in first-order belief. The principle cannot be meant to apply to views tying faith to particular restrictive forms of second-order belief; not even when such views are clearly held by most or all of the group-members in question. Certainly it applies to the faith of bizarre-seeming cults. But only in Smith's sense of the word 'faith', not the cultists' – insofar as the term 'cult' suggests some rigid sort of fundamentalism; since if a fundamentalist has faith, in the relevant sense, this is essentially *in spite of* his or her second-order views regarding the impossibility of salvation for others. We have to distinguish here between first-order bizarreness and second-order cultic bigotry, in the group's self-description. That which is bizarre demands imaginative openness – so the principle implies. Only the bigotry is intolerable. And yet, no bones about it – the bigotry truly *is* intolerable.[46]

From a rather different angle Smith has also been criticized – above all by John Cobb – for, it is said, illicitly and confusingly seeking to extend the usage of the Biblical/Qur'anic term 'faith' beyond its proper cultural limits. With his universalizing interpretation of 'faith', Smith himself, Cobb argues, is failing to respect other cultures' self-descriptions, as they should be respected. By using the term to designate the common denominator of all authentic religious culture as such, it is said, he has converted it into an extraordinarily abstract concept; which, from a Christian perspective, has been drained of most real meaning. At the same time, he appears to preclude any real openness to the insights of secular humanist traditions, such as Marxism – insofar as these explicitly repudiate the language of 'faith'. And, most damaging of all in view of his professed intentions, there is actually an intrinsic element of residual cultural 'imperialism' in such an approach, towards the non-fideist traditions of the East.

As Cobb puts it:

> The proposal fails, I am convinced, because Smith assumes without examination that we can affirm and realize our unity as religious persons only if we believe that at bottom we are already at one. This assumption is extremely widespread, and just for that reason it is worth challenging ... Recently the unity has been sought in mystical experience. This tends toward a Vedantist imperialism. Smith seeks it in faith, which tends towards a Christian imperialism.[47]

The pressing need, however, is to get beyond both those modes of 'imperialism' alike. True mutual understanding, in Cobb's view, can in the end only come from abandoning the futile quest for a common denominator: we just have to accept that different religious cultures are oriented towards radically different ultimate realities, each of which may nevertheless be valid in its way.

Cobb's critique derives from his own experience of Christian/Zen Buddhist conversation. As he points out, this is quite a different background to Smith's, inasmuch as Smith begins instead from an experience of Christian/Muslim conversation. Certainly, the term 'faith' lends itself very well to articulating what the Christian and Muslim traditions have in common. It is so close an equivalent to the Qur'anic term *îmân*. But in Zen Buddhist tradition there is no such equivalent.

Not all forms of Buddhist culture are equally alien to the Christian model; and where there are resemblances, as most notably in the case of the Pure Land tradition with its devotion to Amida, Cobb is not slow to latch onto them: the name 'Amida' may very well, he thinks, be taken as an effective Buddhist equivalent for 'Christ'.[48] Zen Buddhist doctrine, however, is different. It is altogether more intransigent in its testimony to Emptiness – as precluding *any* ultimate devotional attachments. 'Faith', in Christian parlance, refers to a certain turning of the individual will, towards conformity with the will of God. Zen Buddhist enlightenment, on the contrary, consists in an ultimate abandonment of all willing, in recognition of Emptiness. The difference could not be more basic. And yet, Cobb argues, Smith's doctrine is systematically incapable of doing justice to it.[49]

I can only respond by saying that I agree: no doubt, it would be – *if* Smith were indeed saying what Cobb thinks he is saying. However, it does not seem to me that he is. At least, not necessarily. Maybe his doctrine, as it stands, is ambiguous; but let us discriminate.

What Cobb is arguing against is the claim that there is a common something, namely 'faith', present under various forms in every religious tradition, yet essentially always the same; the expression of which, in each tradition, invariably constitutes that tradition's highest truth. Smith, though, does not *need* to be claiming quite that. All he is committed to saying is: every religious tradition contains within it some experiential analogue to that distinctive something, 'faith', the particular expression of which through the gospel constitutes Christianity's highest truth; such that – whilst the analogues in question may be more or less peripheral to the highest truth of other traditions – the fact that they are there nevertheless does give those other traditions the capacity, without absolute self-contradiction, to appropriate key elements of Christian insight for themselves.

At any rate, this reading would surely make much more sense than the one Cobb attacks. But, then, it also seems to render his whole counter-argument redundant.

Thus, there is in this case no necessary weakening of the Biblical/Qur'anic concept of faith, since the special definitiveness of Biblical/Qur'anic tradition in that regard is fully acknowledged. Nor is there any necessary closure to the insights of secular humanism. When it comes to a phenomenon such as Marxist tradition, the issue is actually somewhat comparable to that with Wainwright's 'bizarre cults'. Smith might well continue to speak appreciatively of the potential disclosures of (first-order) Marxist 'faith'. What he rejects is just the second-order element in mainstream Marxist self-description: the (in the worst sense) irretrievably ideological character of the Marxist appeal to 'science', as the putative authority by which other people's faith is to be supplanted.

And neither is there, after all, any veiled 'imperialism' involved. For the learning process is by no means dogmatically required to be only one-way. Other cultures may have much to learn from their encounter with the Biblical/Qur'anic traditions of faith; but they may also have much to teach those traditions. It is not only faith which needs to be strictly differentiated from the various metaphysical belief-systems within which it is lodged, in order that it may become a pervasive inspiration for good inter-cultural conversation. The same applies, with equal cogency, to the primary modes in which transcendence is articulated by non-fideist traditions as well. If Smith

privileges faith, it is over belief. Not, by any means, over such other liberating experiences as Zen Buddhist enlightenment. It is faith, not belief – he
is saying – which 'saves', in the Christian sense. Therefore non-Christian
traditions can also help 'save' us. But that is not to say that 'salvation', in
this sense, is the only possible form of spiritual liberation that counts.

What future for world theology?

Faith is the guiding spirit of any authentic Jewish, Christian or Muslim
confessional theology; and of any trans-confessional theology, insofar as it
remains open to the trans-confessional appropriation of originally Jewish,
Christian or Muslim insight.

In the thirteenth Christian century, when the university of Paris and its
sister institutions were developing, theology was widely regarded as the
Queen of the Sciences. Its status reflected the general consensus that faith is
the highest of intellectual virtues. (Or rather, to be more precise, a virtue
altogether higher than those that are merely 'intellectual'.)[50] Now, however,
in the secular universities of post-Christendom – and perhaps especially in
those of England – the theologian has become something of an anomaly.

As an intrinsically religious enterprise theology must, by its very nature,
make demands on its students quite unlike those made by any other
academic 'discipline'. Given that its truth is the truth of true community, as
conceived in faith, it necessarily presupposes a certain shared commitment
to active community-building; which in the context of a secular university,
open to all-comers with the requisite academic attainments, has come to
seem deeply problematic. And hence, in that context, the natural tendency is
for Departments of Theology to become places in which everything ancil-
lary to theology is taught – rather than theology, in the truest sense, itself.
Within the university, 'theology' – no longer the Queen of the Sciences – is
then reduced to being a mere misnomer for one particular specialist branch
of the history of ideas. It survives, in the true sense, for the most part only in
seminaries; and there, often only as a somewhat secondary adjunct to the
more practical aspects of ministerial training. Whilst at the same time a new
discipline of 'religious studies' arises, far better suited than theology to the
new academic environment, and partly aiming to displace it.[51]

I am inclined to think that theology *is*, in principle, the true Queen of the
Sciences, within Biblical/Qur'anic culture; and that it is called to be a perpet-
ually awkward, critical participant in the secular university. But it is the
Queen of the Sciences, and authentic in its awkwardness, only insofar as it
successfully escapes ideologization, that is, being penned back into the business of defending a particular first-order belief-system in an aggressive
competition with others for power. A thinking which merely criticizes one
set of ideologies in the name of another, supposedly godlier one is just bad
theology. Phenomenology of religion, the staple practice of 'religious
studies' – with its systematic attempted withdrawal from the very possibility

of ideology – is indeed a greatly preferable approach. It is the essence of good theology to be a faith-driven positive critique of *all* ideology – very much including those forms to which its own community is mostly tempted.

That is why *Karl Barth*, for instance, was such a great theologian.

Thus, Barth's greatness lies perhaps above all in his decisive subordination of apologetics to dogmatics: in the sense that 'apologetics' is the defence of belief, and 'dogmatics' the deployment of belief, both for self-critique and critique of the world. Apologetics may come either in conservative or liberal versions. The liberals clearly tend to be the more sophisticated, with their systematic narrowing-down of the front to be defended; and that is why Barth is mainly concerned to combat them. But in both cases alike theology has become a mode of defensive self-assertion: an upholding of the truth-claims of one's own belief-system, against the sceptics.

Hence, it has fallen away from its chief vocation precisely to encourage a community's abandonment of its ideological defences – against the moral claims made upon it by the truth of faith. Barth's whole thinking, from his 1918 commentary on *Romans* onwards, is eloquently focused on this basic contrast. So he criticizes liberal apologetic theology for having become altogether too sucked into the world of the secular university. The trouble is, these theologians are preoccupied with justifying themselves to their colleagues in other academic disciplines; they have largely forgotten theology's prior task, to provide training for preachers, so that the word of God may be proclaimed in all its proper shaking-power.[52]

And yet, of course, his critique remains locked within the constraints of a strict confessionalism, setting drastic limits to the possibilities of inter-cultural conversation. What is worse, he sees that confessionalism as a necessary precondition for the critique. His is certainly a profoundly shaken form of theology – herein lies its truth. But its founding loyalty is not to the universal solidarity of the shaken; for, like Kierkegaard, he still exclusively identifies true shakenness with Christian faith.

Barth by no means denies that Christians may have much to learn from the wisdom of non-Christian traditions; nor does he have any difficulty in speaking of the possible 'salvation' of non-Christians. Nevertheless, he draws the line at the idea of non-biblical 'revelation'. And he speaks of 'faith' only as an explicit relationship to the God of Abraham, or the three persons of the Christian Trinity. 'Jesus Christ', he writes,

> is *the* light of life. To underline the 'the' is to say that He is the one and only light of life. Positively, this means that He is the light of life in all its fullness, in perfect adequacy; and negatively, it means that there is no other light or life outside or alongside His, outside or alongside the light which He is.[53]

Any other view, as he sees it, is merely an evasive attempt to do away with the necessary 'offence' of Christian faith, to have done with its proper challenge.[54] In other words: the only kind of pluralist theology he envisages is one that belongs to liberal apologetics – or perhaps the sort of sheer theological sell-out to worldly ideology typified for him by the Nazi 'German Christians'.[55] It is also, he insists, in flat contradiction to the consistent testimony of Scripture.[56]

But this is surely a disastrous oversimplification. No doubt there is a potential liberal-apologetic motivation for theological pluralism: to enhance the credibility of Christian belief by softening its truth-claims over and against its rivals. Such thinking, however, may equally spring from very different roots. What I have been arguing for here is not, in the first instance, a device for rendering Christian belief easier to defend. It is, rather, a matter of carrying one step further the self-same de-ideologizing process in which Barth himself is engaged; not retreating from the true offence of the gospel – which, I would argue, is its offence to the *libido dominandi* – but, on the contrary, seeking to preserve the purity of that offence from any confusing overlay (or misleading appearance) of Christian cultural chauvinism.

And neither is the biblical evidence quite as unequivocal as Barth suggests. Granted, the Hebrew prophets are consistently hostile to the sacred cults of their pagan neighbours; as are the evangelists and Apostles of the New Testament. But the paganism in question here is essentially pre-Axial; magical rather than 'religious', in the strict sense I prefer.[57] The Bible records the emergence of one particular species of religious tradition, in its dialectical inter-relationship with the pre-existing world of magic. It does not speak directly of any very serious encounter between two or more different species of *religion*. The only such encounter of which certain slight traces are to be found, in the Wisdom literature and in the New Testament, was with the traditions of Greek philosophy – and there was nothing about the actual form which that encounter took, in those texts, to inhibit its future and highly positive development in the theology of the patristic period, and subsequently. Christian theology, in short, cannot find any decisive precedents in the Bible to guide it, one way or the other, in its response to other religious traditions. All we are left to rely on is our own first-hand, faith-informed experience of them.

And how then can one persist in the sort of fixed *a priori* attitude proposed by Barth? In direct contradiction to his deeper anti-ideological intentions, his stance at this key point scarcely seems to transcend conservative church-ideology. Thus, it seems to me that the issue becomes: how best to preserve the Barthian spirit of intransigence with regard to liberal apologetics, whilst nonetheless liberating it from that residually ideological Christian-exclusivist wrapping.

English universities today have Departments of Theology; of Religious Studies; of Theology and Religious Studies. There is a fissure here between, on the one hand, theology as an essentially confessional enterprise and, on the other hand, religious studies as a trans-confessional antithesis to theology. In an ideal world I think that this fissure would be *aufgehoben*, into a new unity.

Instead, we would simply have Departments of World Theology, in Smith's sense – trans-confessionally theological, theologically trans-confessional. Some would be engaged in mediating between the trans-confessional and the confessional, with a distinctive emphasis on the heritage of one specific confessional tradition. Others would be more philosophical in orientation. A third category would place a greater emphasis on the phenomenological propaedeutics. And yet all would be explicitly conceived as complementary contributions to that one larger enterprise of critical faith.

8 Expressivism and individuality in new social movements

What I am looking for is an appropriately post-metaphysical modernizing framework of theology, to think through the religious significance of the general new social movement ethos. Smith's work, discussed in the preceding chapter, provides one very notable model of theology which may indeed be described as being both post-metaphysical and (at least implicitly) modernizing.

But this still remains a largely pre-political version. And if we are to develop a similar approach in more political – or anti-political – terms, it is clear that we will need to draw on a whole range of other sources as well.

There is, you will have observed, a basic ambivalence about my account of 'new social movements'. Thus, I have in the first place defined the concept in ideal terms, as referring to a species of community with a unique new openness to the solidarity of the shaken. But at the same time it is a borrowed phrase, already referring to a particular array of empirical phenomena. My project is to develop a theological interpretation of the ideal, in conjunction with a certain set of practical proposals concerning religious liturgy. On the other hand, from the point of view of actually existing new social movements in the empirical sense, this suggestion may well seem somewhat high-faluting, and quite remote from their immediate practical concerns as activist enterprises. For their business is, of course, campaigning; each in their own distinct area, with their own often quite narrowly-defined agenda.

The ambivalence of the concept is nevertheless vital to the project. For it is my essential aim here to try and show two things:

- the potential linkage of the ideal to this type of empirical phenomena, above all others; and
- the potential long-term usefulness to new social movements, in the empirical sense, of contemplative reflection on the solidarity of the shaken, as a unifying ideal above all others.

What is involved is a thinking which, as it were, places itself right in between the two aspects of the concept – its ideal aspect and its empirical one – in order systematically to try and pull them together.

How can that be done? In the end, I am arguing, everything comes down to how persuasively one is able to situate the immediate empirical facts in a larger historiographical context, determined by the ideal. Thus, if I were only concerned to analyse the actual self-understanding of new social movements in the empirical sense, I would not need to consider any stories other than those directly bound up with their own various processes of development. Nor would I need to tell any story at all if I were only concerned with the solidarity of the shaken as a transcendent ideal. (Except perhaps, incidentally, by way of illustration.) But, as it is, my concern is with the theological issue of how in general this transcendent ideal has historically come to be embodied, in organizational form. And then I want to place the diverse empirical phenomena of new social movements within that larger story.

It is indeed the distinctive dynamic of religious modernity, in general, to identify its very highest ideals with the quite down-to-earth world-transformative efforts of specific moral-campaigning organizations, and yet to insist that those ideals should at the same time be allowed to retain an infinitely elusive allure. At each stage of modernity one finds a similar restless back-and-forth between the two demands. So Christian first modernity counterposes the 'kingdom of God' or 'heavenly city' to its partial Messianic embodiment in the actual church, which is also its betrayal. And second modernity secularizes this, with an ideal of secular Reason both embodied within, yet also forever calling to account the various agencies of its progressive vanguard. The theology of third modernity, as a thinking-through of the potential of new social movements, grows out of these earlier projects by virtue of its intimate analogousness to them in this respect. Its truth-potential, as I see it, lies not only in its ultimate transcendence of them, but also in its direct continuity from the best that is already in them; its dialectical carrying forward of their concerns to another level of questioning. But – in what sense, exactly?

So far we have considered the advantages of new social movements: their strict self-distancing from party-politics and the seductions of the state; their trans-confessionalism. Now, however, let us start to focus on what they might also more positively continue to draw from older modern traditions, for their collective self-understanding.

One-sided enlightenment

In its essence the new social movement ethos is one of perpetual dissent; for one of these movements to achieve its aims would be for it to disappear. But any dissident movement straight away has to justify itself against the primal objections of those who are inclined to see it as mere arrogant presumption.

The defenders of established custom and the apologists for arbitrary power are quick to ask, by what *right* do you go against us? Who, or what, gives you the necessary *authority*?

There are, it seems to me, two basic different types of possible response here.

The *first* consists in a simple appeal to one's innate rights as a rational individual: to trust one's personal experience, to think for oneself, to experiment freely. In its pure form this initial response is too individualistic to be especially religious – in the sense of not really needing the sort of community-support which religious ritual supplies. But, where it still does make theological authority-claims, these tend to take shape as an appeal to the God of deist metaphysics.

In 1793 Immanuel Kant published his classic version of such theology (or, perhaps better, 'anti-theology') under the title *Religion Within the Limits of Reason Alone*.[1] And, as Kant understands it, 'within the limits of Reason alone' there can be no authoritative tradition founded in a history of divine revelation.

The God of Kantian 'religion' is a God who has renounced any hold over individual consciences other than that which is implied by a general affirmation of Reason, decisively abstracted from the concrete processes of history. 'Reason' in this context is so narrowly delimited as in effect to eliminate all the usual resources for actual religious community-building. Liberty of conscience is envisaged simply as a matter of breaking free from the past.

Kant still advocates a certain form of grand narrative – as emerges in his essay entitled 'Idea for a Universal History with a Cosmopolitan Purpose' (1784).[2] This grand narrative, though, belongs in a quite separate compartment of his thinking from his (anti-)theology 'within the limits of Reason alone'. The theme he envisages for his 'universal history' is grandiose enough by any standard: nothing less than 'the hidden plan of nature to bring about an internally – and *for this purpose* also externally – perfect political constitution as the only possible state within which all natural capacities of mankind can be developed completely'.[3] Or: humanity's gradual progress down the centuries towards the sort of cosmopolitan international order capable of guaranteeing 'perpetual peace' – first explicitly envisioned and advocated in the mid-eighteenth century, by the Abbé St Pierre and Rousseau. And yet note what follows from his repudiation of the concept of divine revelation. The study of history, he argues, may be useful to the extent that it helps *encourage* those who are striving for this ideal, with the morale-boosting sense that history is on their side. But that is all. However useful the historian's findings may be as an encouragement, the ideal itself is one whose ultimate validity remains strictly independent of them. Kant does not *identify* the 'enlightenment' he looks for, in any sense, with a heightened historical self-consciousness; he merely looks to history for a source of incidental emotional sustenance to the otherwise enlightened.

'Enlightenment' is famously defined by Kant, precisely, in terms of an absolute insistence on one's positive vocation to think for oneself:

> Enlightenment is man's release from his self-incurred tutelage. Tutelage is man's inability to make use of his understanding without direction from another. Self-incurred is this tutelage when its cause lies not in a lack of reason but in lack of resolution and courage to use it without direction from another. *Sapere aude!* 'Have courage to use your own reason!' – that is the motto of enlightenment![4]

His proposed grand narrative would be nothing other than a systematic account of humanity's collective coming of age, in the attainment of 'enlightenment' so defined. For he sees the 'enlightened' individualism of 'having courage to use one's own reason' as the one and only agency ultimately required in order that humanity should progress towards his cosmopolitan ideal.

In general, the grand narrative of the Enlightenment oscillates between, on the one hand, a radically individualistic form of the solidarity of the shaken and, on the other hand, that very different phenomenon, the solidarity of an up-and-coming educationally defined élite – opposing Reason to tradition as a means of undermining the traditional authority of older élites.

Kant is the Enlightenment's most refined (anti-)theologian; but, inasmuch as all he provides by way of actual narrative is a brief programmatic statement of intent, the tension here remains latent in his thinking. However, consider for example the slippery slope that leads from what is perhaps the greatest single work of Enlightenment grand narrative, the Marquis de Condorcet's *Sketch for a Historical Picture of the Progress of the Human Mind*,[5] to the later thinking of Condorcet's admirers, Saint-Simon and Comte. A major figure among the leaders of the French Revolution, Condorcet in fact wrote the *Sketch* during the winter of 1793–4 whilst in hiding, after the downfall of the Girondin faction with which he was identified. And he represents the revolutionary spirit at its most liberal-democratic. Yet the story he tells already has a clear ideological thrust to it: pointing, as it does, to the emergence of a new 'enlightened' élite, to supplant the Christian clergy in their role as the shapers of the public conscience. Saint-Simon and Comte simply discard the liberal-democratic packaging. The ideal they envisage is for the new élite to take over the administration of the world's affairs, in a 'scientific' fashion that would put an end to democratic political choice once and for all.[6]

The new social movements of today generally represent a spirit of universal egalitarianism which is in the starkest possible contrast to Saint-Simonianism or Comtean 'positivism'. This is not to deny that they too are, in part, inheritors of the original free-spiritedness of the Enlightenment, in the ethical domain. For, after all, the whole thrust of their work is to promote greater public recognition of the individual's rights: not only the right to question the established order, in private – but also openly to express that questioning, and to pioneer alternative life-styles. (What we have here is, if you like, the 'Amnesty International aspect' of third modernity as a whole.)

And yet that is only half the story. For these movements are, at the same time, potentially heirs to another, completely different sort of tradition as well.

'Expressivist' critique

Just as the Enlightenment originated as a vindication of dissent on the basis of the individual's innate rights, so this *other* tradition derives from the other basic possible mode of critical response to the would-be censors of free thought.

Thus the necessary self-assurance of the censors may be said to depend upon two main factors. First, a certain element of sheer contempt for those they seek to keep under control, as individuals – which is what the polemic of the Enlightenment, with its affirmation of individuals' rights, confronts. But then, also, a powerful – albeit unreflective – instinctual conviction that *nature is on their side*. In other words: that the established order, whose defenders they are, is the natural option; the one truly serious possibility in the given circumstances; the only real, available alternative to chaos.

To which the obvious response is, precisely, *that they should look again at history*. For how could anyone who had genuinely taken to heart the actual historic diversity of human cultural traditions still continue to think that way?

If the study of history teaches nothing else, at least it surely ought to leave one with some deeper, heartfelt sense of the ultimate contingency – not to say downright oddity! – of one's own culture. (Especially when such study is combined with non-touristic foreign travel and immersion in other worlds.) So many various types of social arrangement have in the past proved viable, the more deeply a true appreciation of this has penetrated one's soul, the less easy it becomes just to dismiss the fresh imaginings of moral dissidents, as regards the future, out of hand. Furthermore, it becomes clearer that nature is not on anyone's side – in the sense that would put an end to questioning. Or rather, it becomes clearer that nature is always on the side of those most ready to respect and learn from the experience of others shaped by different backgrounds.

The theoreticians of the Enlightenment tend not to argue in this spirit. On the contrary, their usual inclination is to try and show that nature is on *their* side. Hence no doubt, in part, the special vulnerability of Enlightenment thought to ideologization. But already in Kant's own day a distinct counter-current had begun to emerge, critical of the Enlightenment on very much these grounds.

The chief original exponent of this critique was J.G. Herder. Herder (1744–1803) was, like Kant, an East Prussian. As a student he had attended Kant's lectures at the University of Königsberg (nowadays the Russian enclave of Kaliningrad, on the Baltic). Only, whereas Kant never once left his native province, Herder travelled. His first major work – although unpublished in his lifetime – was a travel journal.[7] And his thinking is the thinking of a traveller.

Although the term is anachronistic, there is a sense in which Herder is an eighteenth-century postmodernist. His ironically entitled 'Yet Another Philosophy of History for the Enlightenment of Mankind' (1774) is in fact a polemical attack on Enlightenment grand narrative in all its various forms.[8] The particular writers he focuses on in this attack are the Swiss historian Isaak Iselin, the Scots William Robertson and David Hume, and Voltaire; but the argument is equally applicable to the later work of Kant himself, or of Condorcet and his successors. Herder is indeed consistently critical of Kant, across the board.[9]

He is by no means hostile to the Enlightenment's appreciation of individual free-spiritedness, even though that is not his own main theme. What he rejects, in his repudiation of Enlightenment grand narrative, is simply the ideological confusion of that ideal with the special sophistication of an educational élite. The 'enlightened' élite may pride themselves on the broad intellectual horizons their education has given them; and therefore on being more 'cosmopolitan' than their neighbours, more universally humanist in their sympathies. But then –

> Who has not found that an unlimited extension of his feelings serves only to weaken and destroy them? ... The savage who loves himself, his wife and child, with quiet joy, and in his modest way works for the good of his tribe, as for his own life, is, in my opinion, a truer being than that shadow of a man, the refined citizen of the world, who, enraptured with the love of all his fellow-shadows, loves but a chimera. The savage in his poor hut has room for every stranger ... the inundated heart of the idle cosmopolite, on the other hand, offers shelter to nobody.[10]

What is needed, he argues, is a form of historiography which responds to true generosity, *wherever it is found*, with real generosity of its own. Kant values the study of history only for the extrinsic encouragement it may possibly offer to the shaken; Herder advocates the cultivation of sense of history for the sake of history's own intrinsic shaking power – when approached with proper generosity.

Nor does Herder dogmatically deny the possibility of progress. But he is preoccupied with the danger of a mere dogma of progress, which – even while its advocates dream in the abstract of 'perpetual peace' – all too easily permits the members of the 'enlightened' cultural élite to ignore the cry of those who are victimized by the violence of self-styled 'enlightened' regimes.

He is the great champion of endangered or suppressed folk-culture, in all its forms; a pioneer in urging the collection and treasuring of folk song, for instance; whose long-term influence is perhaps most spectacularly to be seen in his role as an inspirer, even though he was a German, of the nineteenth-century Slav national revival – and in particular the restoration of the Czech language, after centuries of German-speaking rule in the Czech lands, to be the vehicle of its own rich literary culture.[11]

Herder was fascinated by comparative linguistics, and comparative anthropology. And he further invested such studies with fundamental ethical significance. Charles Taylor speaks aptly here of his ethical 'expressivism': for him, ethics is defined by each people's, or each community's corporate vocation to seek out its own unique form of cultural self-expression – in the light of its distinctive historical heritage.[12] That is what the 'enlightened' historians he attacks have failed to recognize. Partly this perception stems from the wild enthusiasm for the world of Greek antiquity, as one of unsurpassed creative achievement, which had swept over the German intelligentsia of Herder's day, and which he also fully shared.[13] He was driven to recognize the valid co-existence of incompatible cultural ideals by the need to reconcile this enthusiasm for pagan Greece, philosophically, with his Christian faith. (He was himself a Lutheran pastor – from a Pietist background.) However, then he universalized the principle. No culture, he urged, should just be dismissed; not even that of the then generally despised Middle Ages. He deplores any sort of cultural imperialism – as in the case of ancient Rome and its (chiefly francophone) heirs – but otherwise affirms every well-rooted and creative cultural tradition without exception.

The new social movement ethos is heir both to the primary, not yet ideologized insights of the Enlightenment and also to this expressivist counter-current to the Enlightenment, represented by Herder. For these movements tend to resist the potential repressiveness of the state not only by appealing to the rights of the individual, but also, very much, in the name of cultural pluralism; a pluralism to which, moreover, they themselves – as community-constructive enterprises in their own right – contribute directly.

Hegel

I think that the theologian of third modernity must attempt to draw the two aspects of this double heritage together, as closely as possible. But, back in the heyday of second modernity, the philosopher/theologian who, in fact, went furthest in attempting such a drawing-together was G.W.F. Hegel (1770–1831). And so now let us turn our attention to the Hegelian doctrine as a possible model.

Right from the beginning, Hegel's thought actually emerges as a balancing act between what might loosely be termed Kantian and Herderian impulses. Among his earliest manuscripts, collected and published after his death, there is a document – written during his time as a student in

Tübingen – in which he sets out what he regards as the three most fundamental requirements of a healthy form of 'folk religion':

  I.   Its doctrine must be grounded on universal reason.
  II. Fancy, heart and sensibility must not thereby go empty away.
  III. It must be so constituted that all the needs of life and the public
       affairs of the state are tied in with it.[14]

   The first of these points is evidently intended as a straightforward affirmation of the Kantian impulse. Hegel at this early stage was an unreserved
admirer of Kant, and by 'universal reason' here he means the guiding spirit
of Kantian enlightenment, in all its radical individualism. In his later writings, he adopts other terms for the same. There, he speaks of it as '*the
principle of subjectivity*': a recognition of, as he puts it, 'the infinite value of
the individual as such'; the internalizing of which constitutes true 'freedom
of self-consciousness'; or 'the Idea of freedom'.
   The second and third points, on the other hand, are far more Herderian
in spirit.[15] Together, they articulate an expressivist ideal, which in his later
works he calls '*Sittlichkeit*'. The standard translation for this in English is
'ethical life'. More precisely, one might perhaps say 'corporate ethical self-
expression' – but for brevity's sake, in what follows, let us stick with the
German original.
   Hegel's chief paradigm, both in his early essays and in his later work, for
a truly vibrant religious *Sittlichkeit* – rich in its mobilization of 'fancy, heart
and sensibility', and ideally expressive of every aspect of a people's experience, without any distortion deriving from sectarian or denominational
intolerance – is always ancient Greece. At the time when he wrote the fragment I have quoted he was in fact ostensibly training to become a Lutheran
pastor. Yet his thinking sprang from a fierce rejection of church-
Christianity: like his friend Hölderlin, he idealized Greek antiquity all the
more because of its sheer otherness from what he saw as the lamentable
imaginative decadence of Christendom. Subsequently, however, his attitude
changes. And his mature thought, in fact, essentially arises out of a
profound re-evaluation of church tradition. Not that he ever was ordained;
but he nevertheless goes on to become arguably the most thoroughgoing
advocate there has ever been of reconciliation between second and first
modernity.
   Thus, in his mature thought Hegel still continues to be very much an heir
to the Enlightenment in the elementary sense of affirming the secularity of
the secular state, as prime guarantor of 'the principle of subjectivity' over
and against the intellectual repressiveness of narrow-minded church dogma-
tism. But he also goes decisively beyond the Enlightenment, at any rate in its
Kantian mode. For, at the same time, it becomes his major theological
preoccupation to try and show the countervailing latent truth of the
Christian gospel itself, as an expressivist medium. So he sets out to demon-

strate its potential capacity – once properly reinterpreted – to achieve just what he had earlier looked for from perfected 'folk religion': namely, with a minimum of compromise, to incorporate the pure claims of 'universal reason' into the most vivid and all-embracing form of *Sittlichkeit*.

With a view to reconciling the conflicting grand narratives of embattled first and second modernity he is compelled to attempt a new, more comprehensive grand narrative of his own. Like the Kantian mode of grand narrative, the Hegelian one also culminates in the emergent new intellectual openness of secular liberalism.[16] But, unlike Kant's, it is also framed as a direct extension of the older grand narrative of Christian orthodoxy; the Christian gospel-story is still there, unreduced, at the heart of it. As we have seen, Kant envisages what one might term a grand narrative of simple encouragement for the enlightened. Hegel by contrast envisages a grand narrative of divine revelation, nothing less. Only, as he remains determined to break free from the restricted perspective of traditional first modernity, this is no longer revelation exclusively in biblical and church history. It is now understood as extending throughout world-history *as a whole*.

What leads him back to Christianity is the expressivist impulse he shares with Herder. And yet Hegel is a much more complex theologian than Herder ever was. Herder has a traditional sense of divine providence at work in world-history as whole, but no grand narrative to analyse its actual workings on that scale. He simply attacks the grand narrative of the Enlightenment, in its more ideological forms. The real power of Hegelian theology, by contrast, lies in his attempt to develop the very grandest sort of grand narrative antithesis to grand narrative ideology.

I have spoken of the solidarity of the shaken. This is not Hegel's terminology, nor does he have any very direct equivalent to the concept. Nevertheless, *the ideal itself* is very much there in his thinking.

His whole commitment to grand narrative indicates his fundamental concern with issues of solidarity-building – since that is what grand narratives are for. And he articulates his equally fundamental recognition of the demands of shakenness by means of the concept of *Geist*. The grand narrative he constructs is above all the history of *Geist*, that is, 'spirit' or 'mind': the spirit/mind of God, infusing the spirits/minds of mortals, both communally and as individuals. But *Geist* is precisely a dynamics of infinite shaken negativity; above all by virtue of the endless pull and counter-pull it represents between 'the principle of subjectivity' on the one hand and the principle of *Sittlichkeit* on the other.

Revelation in world-history as a whole

In essence, Hegelian grand narrative may be said to be the history of *Geist*'s progress to a final clarity of grand-narrative autobiography. (Which is virtually the same as to say: the history of the gradual emergence of the possibility of the solidarity of the shaken, as a more or less articulate ideal.)

For this to be possible requires a certain sort of religious culture, informing and informed by a certain sort of political culture, a certain sort of aesthetic culture, and a certain sort of philosophical culture. And so, always with the same goal ultimately in view, Hegel embarks on his various encyclopaedic lecture-series, tracing the course of world-history in each of these aspects: the history of religion, the history of politics, the history of art and the history of philosophy.

Inasmuch as he is a reconciler of first and second modernity, his general argument serves in particular to vindicate both the Christian faith and the secular state. His *Lectures on the Philosophy of Religion* (delivered in four different versions between 1821 and 1831)[17] culminate in an account of Christianity as the proper form of 'consummate religion'. And, of all the varieties of Christian church-life, the one he most approves of is Lutheranism. He sees Lutheranism as the most natural background for a thinking such as his – largely because of its intrinsic impulse to secularization. Luther himself may not have been much of a friend to philosophy. But Hegel wants to translate the core Lutheran doctrine of the priesthood of all believers into philosophical terms, so as to draw out its critical implications, and to show how these transcend the immediate context of the original unphilosophical Reformation polemic. It is a matter of liberating the gospel – once and for all – from its distortion into the ideology of a clerical hierarchy, set over and against the secular state as a rival establishment, on the same plane. The immediate carrier-community for Hegelian grand narrative is a Lutheran secularizing élite, refined by a rigorous philosophical education.

However, let us emphasize the strict *provisionality* of these specific politico-theological conclusions.

This is crucial for a proper understanding of the Hegelian project and its continuing urgent relevance today. There are, so to speak, two distinct levels on which the truth-claims of Hegelian grand narrative are to be judged. At one level, we have to ask: to what extent has Hegel got his hermeneutical priorities right? Is he pursuing the right questions, in the right sort of way? As he envisages it, the ultimate defining goal of *Geist*, informing all its struggles, is just the very purest possible *Sittlichkeit* of 'self-conscious freedom'; that is, the most cohesively *sittlich* expression of 'the principle of subjectivity'. Is this, we first of all have to ask, truly the most promising of hermeneutical approaches to world-history as a whole?

But then we need to keep that primary level of enquiry quite distinct from the secondary level, where we also ask: given the criteria he has established, to what extent are Hegel's actual historiographical judgements valid? His assertion of the superiority of Christian faith over all other forms of religion belongs to this secondary level; as does his commitment to the cause of the secular state. Yet all his claims on this level are essentially provisional. They are, as he freely acknowledges, just the way he sees things, from his own inevitably limited historical perspective. The only claims he makes that are *not* provisional, in this sense, are those that belong to the primary level:

having to do with the first principles of his hermeneutics. Thus, he does not originally set out to construct a vision of world-history that will prove the excellence of Christianity or the necessity of secularization; that would indeed be nothing more than an exercise in ideology. But, rather, he sets out with a primary guiding concern for (as I would say) the solidarity of the shaken. And then he ponders the question of why it has evidently only now in his day, for the first time, become possible for someone like himself to frame the issues in the way he does? Is it not, perhaps, something to do with his background as a Christian (and more specifically Lutheran) thinker, in a newly secularized society?

He thinks so. And no doubt it is. Yet the provisionality remains. All too often Hegel has been caricatured, and attacked, as if he were a mere apologist for the given values of his own cultural milieu. Among later Christian theologians, that is the classic error of Kierkegaard for instance; it has also been a commonplace of Marxist critique. But this is entirely to confuse the two levels. And it just shuts off the real challenge of his thought.

That challenge, I think, lies first and foremost in his primary-level elaboration of the concept-clusters associated with the core ideas of '*Sittlichkeit*' and 'subjectivity'. For which the key text is his (unfortunately) most difficult work, the *Phenomenology of Spirit*.[18] The *Phenomenology* in general may be said to be a systematic study of what it means to live in the truth, in the sense of a maximally open-minded capacity to learn the lessons of experience. It is a phenomenology of 'spirit' – *Geist* – inasmuch as *Geist* is, in the first instance, the universal mind-opening process. The argument accordingly takes shape as a survey of mentalities (these are the 'phenomena' in question) from the very simplest to the most complex, at each stage probing the particular limitations they impose on that process. Always, at whatever stage is being discussed, the underlying question is the same: what needs adjusting, in order that new experiences may henceforth bring new insights? What are the blockages which need removing? But this question is asked at every different level possible. It is asked, first, at the level of the infant's initial coming to terms with the world of objects; then, at the level of elementary relationships between one individual and another; then, at the level of each individual's self-understanding, in relation to the pressures of society in general; and finally at the level of comparisons drawn between various more particular types of cultural formation.

For our present purposes, the most immediately relevant section of the *Phenomenology* is in fact Chapter 6, which is simply entitled '*Geist*'. This is where Hegel is setting the scene for his consideration of the actual history of religion – the topic of the following chapter. Here he elaborates the fundamental problem which he sees religion, above all, as being called on to resolve.

The essence of the problem can be formulated quite simply. In order for an entire culture to be maximally open to learning the moral lessons of experience, it must be maximally affirmative of the solidarity of the shaken.

For that is just what shakenness is: an especial moral sensitivity to the shock of the new.

Such sensitivity demands, in the first instance, a deep-rooted free-spiritedness. In Hegelian terms: a basic reconciliation of 'the principle of subjectivity' with the principle of *Sittlichkeit*. But the difficulty is, these two principles appear to be almost inevitably inimical to one another. 'The principle of subjectivity' is the self-assertion of individuals against the un-thinkingness of their communities. *Sittlichkeit* is the moral incorporation of individuals into the historic self-expressiveness of a community. It is not only oppressive power-structures which 'the principle of subjectivity' endangers; it may also be perceived as endangering the genuine good of social coherence, the mutual trust of those bonded together by a common *Sittlichkeit*. And in fact most forms of *Sittlichkeit* will indeed be endangered by it: every sort of ethos grounded in an unreflective reverence for customary values. Only a *Sittlichkeit* explicitly established on the basis of a consensual affirmation of 'the principle of subjectivity', itself, will be immune from that principle's devouring negativity. Yet this is to establish *Sittlichkeit* precisely on the basis of an energy which, by its very nature, tends to dissolve *Sittlichkeit*. Nothing could be more difficult! So that if – as Hegel suggests – that is the ultimate goal towards which *Geist* is world-historically working, it is perhaps little wonder that the process has involved the labour of millennia.

A genuine *Sittlichkeit* of 'self-conscious freedom' would be the most diffi-cult mode of *Sittlichkeit* because it would be that which was capable of containing the maximum of potentially disintegrative truth, without disinte-grating. And, the better to set up the question of what this might entail, Chapter 6 of the *Phenomenology* is therefore a progressive analysis of cultural disintegration. It begins with a brief look at the simpler forms of *Sittlichkeit*, and their potential internal tensions: as illustrated for example by the representation of the culture of an antique city-state in Greek tragic drama. Then it traces the evolution that has at length, in the eighteenth century, rendered possible the emergence of the new cosmopolitan-individualist doctrines of the Enlightenment – and the contrasting individualism of its Romantic aftermath – by which traditional bonds of *Sittlichkeit* are, at the actual time of Hegel's writing, being placed under such unprecedented pressure. In other words, in this chapter Hegel returns again to some of the earliest sources of his thinking: the dialectical interplay between the three criteria for an ideal 'folk religion', as set out in the Tübingen fragment. And he weaves that dialectical interplay into a story.

The débâcle of the French Revolution, played out in the meantime, also figures largely here. Thus, the Enlightenment appears as a necessary moment in the educative self-unfolding of *Geist*; but at the same time, by virtue of its undermining of traditional *sittlich* restraints, as being heavy with the latent violence of the French Revolutionary Terror. Against this background, the present-day vocation of religion emerges as a healing of what has been broken in the process – without in any way losing what has been learnt by the opening up of a new freedom to question, along the way. But, again, the question is: how?

In response, Hegel first considers what he has now come to see as the inner self-contradictions of the Kantian theological answer, with its attempt entirely to replace the *Sittlichkeit* grounded in traditional doctrines of divine revelation, and traditional public worship, by private faith in a minimal set of ahistorical 'postulates': the existence of a Creator; human moral freedom and ultimate responsibility; and divine judgement, in the context of eternal life. And nothing more. Granted, a religiousness grounded in such theology is immediately liberated from all the old repressiveness of authoritarian Christendom. But Hegel's basic objection is that it just cannot do the actual motivational job it has been allotted, as the supposed spiritual mainstay of a future liberal civilization. Kantian ethical theory is a meditation on the purity of pure moral duty – formally, in abstraction from any sort of *Sittlichkeit*. Hegel terms this abstract form of moral thinking '*Moralität*'. Then, however, the reductionism of Kant's theology drives a substantive wedge between *Moralität* and *Sittlichkeit* in general. And the result is a theory, of radical individual autonomy, which is forever doomed to be only a theory. On the one hand, Kant's recourse to his 'postulates' derives from a recognition that the demands of *Moralität* must somehow be made attractive: bound up with a love of God, a pride in responsibility, a hope of eternal reward. Yet, on the other hand – as Hegel sees it – the fact is, cerebral *Moralität* can only really be rendered properly attractive by being incorporated into the whole rich emotional life of a thriving historically self-conscious *Sittlichkeit*. The 'postulates' on their own do not solve the problem, he argues. They merely highlight it, in various ways.[19] To this extent, he is entirely at one with Herder.

But then, having tested the blind alley of Kantian theology, we are invited to explore a more general, not yet theologically articulated affirmation of radical moral autonomy – in terms of a simple invocation of 'conscience'. Such an invocation represents *Moralität* no longer rigidified, as in Kantian theology, into a form which necessarily inhibits its incorporation into religious *Sittlichkeit*, yet nevertheless continuing to present a pressing demand for the anti-authoritarian loosening up of *Sittlichkeit*. And what follows is in fact a dialectical celebration of conscientious 'action': true religion, Hegel in effect suggests, is religion which cultivates a cheerful readiness to *forgive* the self-assertion of the one who 'acts' – just so long as that individual is reciprocally ready to confess his or her own frailty, and not claim any special exemption from public judgement. Thus, it is in this movement of forgiveness – as the 'judging consciousness' is reconciled with the 'confessing consciousness' – that 'absolute *Geist*' first appears on the scene; which is Hegel's term for the proper content of religion.[20]

An unfortunate mistake sometimes made by commentators, however, is to suppose that essentially the type of action meant is what one sees in the career of someone like Napoleon.[21] It is nothing of the sort! True, the argument of the chapter up to now has been allusively illustrated by a series of examples which have all fallen into proper chronological sequence; and the last major event referred to was the French Revolution. It is also true that Hegel was an admirer of certain aspects of Napoleonic policy, at any rate in the matter of law reform. And, with reference to the mean-spirited figure of the not-yet-forgiving 'judging consciousness' he does admittedly cite the Napoleonic dictum that 'no man is a hero to his valet'. (He succumbs to the temptation because he wants to append his own little witticism: 'not, however, because the hero is not a hero, but because the valet – is a valet.')[22] However, this interpretation surely distorts the whole logic of the context. For what is at issue is just the purest kind of *conscientious* action – and can Napoleon really be taken as a model of that? It is not so much the 'great leader' who has to appeal to conscience. It is, rather, the *dissident*.

The argument therefore opens with a critique of dissent which remains in-'active': that is, apolitical, or political only in the most wilfully naïve fashion. For of course the conservative upholders of prevailing *sittlich* norms find it much easier to forgive dissent which mildly confines itself to ineffectuality; but the test that counts is not just our readiness to respect the dissident 'beautiful soul', in that sense.[23] Rather, it is Antigone, the heroine of Sophocles' tragedy, who reappears at this point. The chapter comes full circle. It was with her tragic act of civil disobedience that it began: her public upholding of the ethos of family-loyalty against the ethos of state-sponsored patriotism, encapsulated in her insistence that her rebel brother, killed in battle, should receive the honour of a proper burial even though King Creon had expressly forbidden it.[24] This story is alluded to by Hegel at the beginning of the chapter to illustrate the most immediate weakness of the simpler modes of *Sittlichkeit*: namely, such cultures' lack of any overriding criteria by which to resolve that sort of moral conflict – deriving from the strict differentiation of given social roles.

In the two figures of the 'confessing' and 'judging' consciousnesses both Antigone and Creon return. Only, they are transformed now, from being the protagonists of two opposing types of role-determined world-view, into modern conscientious individuals; both therefore equally independent of their given roles – and hence at last capable of reconciliation, insofar as they are able to transcend the natural prejudices associated with those roles.[25]

This is by no means to say that Hegel is an uncritical defender of every appeal to freedom of 'conscience'. Far from it. Indeed, it has to be admitted that at first sight the discussion of 'conscience' in his later work, the *Philosophy of Right*, looks almost like a lapse back to the standpoint of the not yet reconciled 'judging consciousness' criticized in the *Phenomenology*: there, all Hegel's energy goes into denouncing the 'hypocrisy' of the appeal to conscience one finds in the more self-indulgently antinomian expressions of Romantic moral sentiment.[26] But that is because he is writing in the *Philosophy of Right* only with a view to the requirements of the state; not, as in the *Phenomenology*, of religion. The perspective of the *Phenomenology* is more comprehensive. Taken together, the two works present us with the paradoxical ideal of an hegemonic religious culture which positively welcomes rational (that is, non-sectarian) dissent – against the norms which however it also upholds, as the necessary consensual underpinning of the state.

The false rhetoric of 'conscience' Hegel is attacking in the *Philosophy of Right* is one which merely serves to justify a wholesale disrespect for *sittlich* tradition; without even the lingering sense of unease still suggested by Kantian theology. It is a glorification of personal opinion, arbitrarily protected from any challenge by the relative devaluation of all more public moral criteria. In its most honest form, it becomes an ironical subjectivism which has finally lost the capacity to be serious about anything; a complete abandonment of the sort of public-spiritedness on which the moral health of the state depends. In terms of the argument in the *Phenomenology*, it is a dissident 'consciousness' which refuses the path to reconciliation through 'confession'; an attitude of sheer confrontation, that is to say, towards the other, 'judging consciousness' which upholds traditional values. It will not 'confess': it will not acknowledge its inevitable one-sidedness.

And yet, at the same time, the whole theme of the Hegelian grand narrative is the gradual emergence of the possibility of an ethical culture capable of maintaining its coherence even whilst paying the greatest possible respect to properly thoughtful conscientious dissent, as such. It comprises whatever history there is that might serve to articulate the authority proper to the true 'idea of human freedom', so defined; or to establish truly effective bonds of solidarity – drawing upon every resource of cultural tradition which might be available – in the defence of that 'Idea'.[27]

Christology, in this context

Now, the fact is, the cultural tradition of Christendom is especially rich in such potential resources. Already in the context of first modernity, the pure 'principle of subjectivity' acquires *sittlich*-religious form, inasmuch as it is quite directly symbolized by the figure of Christ. The crucified individual dissident is revealed as God incarnate. And that revelation becomes the absolute foundation of the *Sittlichkeit* of the church – is not this just what is wanted?

Herein, for Hegel, lies the essential truth of the Christian gospel. But the only trouble is, there are two basic alternative ways of interpreting the gospel-story. These two ways correspond to two different modes of reflection: in Hegel's own terminology, *Vorstellen* ('picture-thinking') and *Denken* (thinking proper or 'conceptual' thinking).[28]

Vorstellen is the natural element of story-telling. Stories may evoke universal ideas, but in the first instance they have to do with particular events, involving particular individuals. At the level of *Vorstellen* the dogma of the Incarnation is thus an affirmation about the particular individual, Jesus of Nazareth, simply in his unique particularity. That particularity is what counts: everything depends on acknowledging the fundamental difference of Jesus from all other human individuals.

Denken, by contrast, is what comes to its fullest articulacy in philosophy; and in the philosophical interpretation of stories. It deals directly with the universality of universal truth.[29] So that when it comes to the dogma of the Incarnation it therefore focuses on the sense in which the life of this particular individual represents a universal truth – about *individuality* in general. Interpreted in Hegelian philosophical terms, the uniqueness of Christ is effectively identified with the uniqueness of that special world-historical moment in which – for the first time – it had become possible for the infinite value of every human individual, as a child of God or vessel of *Geist*, to be symbolically represented in such a fashion. Hegel still wants to affirm the notion of God having become 'incarnate' here, in a strong sense. But the possibility of salvation is no longer supposed to consist in the sheer difference of the Saviour from all others; rather, it consists in a relationship of symbolic identity-in-difference.

For a theology still confined within the limitations of *Vorstellen*, Christ the unique exception represents humanity *en masse*, as its (to all intents and purposes) mythic advocate. An emancipated theology moves beyond that, to see Christ the historic individual as representative of each and every one of us, precisely in our true individuality. Hegel was the first to suggest that the opposition between these two approaches is really *the* crucial issue for Christian theology. And I think he is right.

In other words, he insists on seeing the Incarnation as nothing other than a great symbolic affirmation of shakenness: the shakenness of the individual, ideally out of all the prejudices of his or her social conditioning. According to this understanding, God's verdict on Christ, the verdict of the resurrection – in its symbolic overturning of Pilate's verdict, the verdict of the cross – is precisely a universal verdict, symbolically expressed, in favour of thoughtful conscientious dissent; a dramatic incitement to free-spiritedness, vindicating the necessary self-confidence, wherever appropriate, to be a dissident.

Hegel himself speaks of it as a vindication of 'happiness'. Or rather, in the *Phenomenology* he presents it as the symbolic antithesis to what he calls the 'unhappy consciousness'.[30] The notorious difficulty of the *Phenomenology*, generally, derives in large measure from its combining a very compressed, impressionistically interlocking discussion of world-views with all sorts of more or less veiled illustrative allusion; and the original passage on the 'unhappy consciousness' is, in fact, one of the most difficult of all. The actual phenomenon in question is meant to be a universal feature, in varying degrees, of all human self-awareness – yet the allusions are all to Christian history. This is because it is in the dialectic of Christian history that the universal underlying problematics are most vividly brought to the surface.

The 'unhappy consciousness' is simply mental servitude; a state of mind tending to preclude authentic dissent, because it already precludes the shaken questioning out of which dissent of any sort proceeds. Hegel describes it as a clash within the self, between two sub-selves or 'self-consciousnesses': the 'unchangeable' and the 'changeable'. The 'unchangeable' sub-self is unchangeable by virtue of its fixed attachment to prejudice. The 'changeable' sub-self is that which is potentially shakeable, and hence potentially dissident. But the 'unhappy consciousness' is the internal censorship and suppression of the 'changeable' by the 'unchangeable'; in which the 'unchangeable' has usurped the role of moral super-ego – 'the *essential* Being', as Hegel puts it, morally speaking – and the 'changeable' has been forced into the perceived role of amoral id. The self of the 'unhappy consciousness' is at the same time both of these two sub-selves:

> Here, then, we have a struggle against an enemy, to vanquish whom is really to suffer defeat, where victory in one consciousness is really lost in its opposite.[31]

Both sides are equally distorted: the 'unchangeable' because of its unchangeableness, the 'changeable' because of its relegation to demoralized and un-self-confident 'inessentiality'.

This elemental struggle is a universal phenomenon. But it is most vividly dramatized when the 'unchangeable' sub-self projects itself in metaphysical terms – representing its 'lordly' will as the will of a censorious 'Lord God', conceived in its own image. In principle, the Incarnation – as Hegel understands it – signifies the absolute reversal of that whole symbolic projection-strategy. Here, a worldly tale of conscientious dissent against worldly tyranny, Jesus' challenge to Roman imperialism, has been sublated into – a metaphysical uprising, of universal significance. The false 'Lord God' of the theologically-minded modes of the 'unhappy consciousness' is deposed. The true Lord God – the authentic truth of *Geist* – is revealed as a self-emptying God, taking the form of a slave (Philippians 2: 7). Pure unchanging spirit becomes mortal flesh: the metaphysical projection of the 'unchangeable' enters into a symbol of self-affirming 'changeableness'. And the two sides are thereby symbolically at-oned.

That symbolic reversal, though, is initially communicated only in the form of *Vorstellen*. And so its universal truth is all too easily obscured, by the particularizing dynamics of the medium. In actual practice, the 'unhappy consciousness' is therefore able to reassert itself once again within Christendom. Its original reversal, at the level of fundamental symbolism, is itself reversed at the level of the church's historic appropriation – or, rather, misappropriation – of the primal gospel symbolism. The old Lord God of the 'unhappy consciousness' rules again. It now appears that he just so happens to have a Son. Instead of a universal divine vindication of shaken human individuality as such, we are presented at the level of *Vorstellen* with the exaltation of one particular individual, precisely in his particularity as the founder of the church; in effect, occluding the universalist symbolism. So the gospel is reduced to church-ideology, a pioneering example of what we nowadays call a 'cult of personality'.

It is, then, the fundamental calling of what Hegel calls 'speculative' Christian theology to reverse, once again, that practical reversal of the original symbolic reversal of the theology of the 'unhappy consciousness'; the reversal which is the authentic truth of the gospel.

'Speculative' is Hegel's technical term for any compacted set of insights positively demanding to be elaborated in the form of philosophic grand narrative. And, in his version, the gospel of the Incarnation provides the 'speculative mid-point' of world-history. However, the 'unhappy consciousness' is not only a problem of religious symbolism. It is also, just as much, a political problem. Its full overcoming demands two things: not only a more rational interpretation of traditional religious dogma, in itself, but also a certain corresponding process of political liberation. And, as Hegel sees it, it is only with the gradual emergence of the secular liberal state that we are, in fact, at long last finally enabled to comprehend the real truth for which the Incarnation stands. What renders possible a doctrine such as his, explicitly dedicated to the quest for a true *Sittlichkeit* of 'self-conscious freedom' – and therefore to a corresponding Christology – is the actual progress that has been made in that direction, politically.

Thus, as he puts it in the *Philosophy of Right*:

> The principle of modern states has prodigious strength and depth because it allows the principle of subjectivity to progress to its culmination in the extreme of self-subsistent personal particularity, and yet at the same time brings it back to the substantive unity and so maintains this unity in the principle of subjectivity itself.[32]

The 'substantive unity' in question here is the *Sittlichkeit* of liberal second modernity, the consensus behind its programme of secularization. Hegel's grand narrative culminates in the emergence of that *Sittlichkeit*, just because of the way he sees it carrying forward the original gospel struggle for 'freedom'; thereby, so to speak, liberating the gospel from the more reactionary churches and their ideology.

In short, the notorious Hegelian glorification of the state is really a theological celebration of secularization for the way it removes, at any rate, the grosser political motives for the distortion of the gospel.[33] The theological constructions of the 'unhappy consciousness', designed to inhibit dissent within the religious community, naturally serve the purposes of the *libido dominandi*. The more a church institution has political power-interests of its own, set over and against the state, the more reason its leaders have to stick to this theology. What Hegel seeks to affirm in Lutheranism is just its basic organizational and devotional discouragement of such power-interests.[34] His was, let us remember, still a world in which all the most immediate threats to the freedom of serious thought came from, or were associated with, hardline church-ideology (Jacobinism having faded from the scene). And he is an advocate of secular second modernity in just as consistently anti-ideological a spirit as Kant. Like Kant, what he affirms is simply the general long-term tendency of the age to open up the practical scope for individual moral autonomy. The only difference is that he advocates the new modernity in a more complex fashion – insisting on its potential reconcilability with the original liberative impulse of first modernity, which Kant does not see.

The same principles reapplied today

In my view, the Hegelian vision of history is fundamentally true. However, actual history has of course moved on. And I also think there is a sense in which Emil Fackenheim (writing in the late 1960s) is right: 'Such are the crises which have befallen the Christian West in the last half century that it may safely be said that, were he alive today, so realistic a philosopher as Hegel would not be a Hegelian.'[35]

It seems to me that, today, Hegel would in fact be an enthusiastic advocate of third modernity.

Again, we come back to the distinction between the two strata of his thought. To the primary level, of (I think) enduring validity, there belongs his basic affirmation of philosophic faith: that 'reason rules the world, and that world history is therefore a rational process'.[36] What does this mean?

If we are to understand it, we must immediately note that he is using the word 'reason' here in a very particular sense. In the *Phenomenology* he arrives at the concept of 'reason' directly by way of his analysis of the dialectic of the 'unhappy consciousness'. The chapter entitled 'Reason' follows straight after that analysis, and the juxtaposition is crucial. It is with our first glimpse of the possibility of an ultimate overcoming of the 'unhappy consciousness', at the very end of his account of it, that 'reason' originally appears on the scene. In other words, 'reason' functions in this context as a term precisely for any sort of thinking insofar as it is premised on that overcoming.[37]

Elsewhere, in the *Philosophy of Right* and the *Encyclopaedia Logic*, Hegel abbreviates his statement of faith to the elementary formula, that 'What is rational is actual and what is actual is rational'.[38] This is sometimes misinterpreted – almost as if Hegel were a real-life version of Voltaire's Doctor Pangloss, saying all is for the best in the best of all possible worlds, so we need not let any of the great disasters of human history bother us. (Indeed, already in the *Encyclopaedia Logic* he is having to defend himself against that sort of crude misreading.) But, rather, what he is in fact arguing is that, if we wish truly to understand the proper nature of 'reason' – that is, the full implications of an overcoming of the 'unhappy consciousness' – then we need to tell stories about it. Above all, we need to retell the key historical stories which tell us who we are – as stories illustrative of the issue. For only so can we begin to comprehend what liberation from the 'unhappy consciousness' means, in all its concrete 'actuality'. The 'actuality' of reason – the one true 'actuality', in the technical Hegelian sense of that term – is whatever, in all the multifarious phenomena of our history, best helps serve this purpose. Abstract thinking, abstracted from history, will not do: we can only understand what reason is by exploring its history, its actuality. And, conversely, we only get to the deepest actuality of history when we approach it with an interest in the self-unfolding of reason. Thus, Hegel constructs his grand narrative essentially as a contribution to the overcoming of the 'unhappy consciousness'. It is framed as a universal history of freedom, at the level where 'freedom' is primarily defined as the antithesis to such 'unhappiness'.[39]

Francis Fukuyama has quite recently, in a spirited manner, sought to resuscitate Hegelian grand narrative from a contemporary perspective.[40] But he does so entirely at what I would regard as the *secondary* level; that is, in terms of Hegel's identification of 'freedom' with the politics of anti-ideological second modernity. There is a sense in which the conclusion of every grand narrative appears as an account of the 'end' of history: every such narrative is the story of how its own distinctive perspective on history as a whole has at length become possible; in that sense, it culminates in itself. But, Fukuyama argues, the very same end of history which Hegel already glimpsed in his day is nowadays progressively being confirmed – by the current spread of 'liberal democracy' around the globe. Hegel himself did not yet speak of 'liberal democracy', nor did he fully anticipate all its eventual requirements; he still rejected the idea of universal suffrage, for instance. But his basic vision of world history is nevertheless hereby confirmed. For 'liberal democracy' – so the argument runs – is just the most successful attempt to give political embodiment to the Idea of 'freedom', as Hegel conceived it; and this is what most fundamentally gives it legitimacy. No other system is so effective in giving political expression to the essential moral equality of all individuals; which, for Hegel, must be the true goal of the state.

Well, maybe so. Only, the trouble is, Fukuyama's analysis altogether ignores those other, theologically more significant aspects of the Hegelian doctrine of 'freedom' in the *Phenomenology*: the dialectic of the 'unhappy consciousness', with its Christological connotations, and the dialectic of conscience and forgiveness.[41] And so, in my view, he fails to see the full implicit radicalism of the concept.

As we have seen, the Hegelian ideal is a moral culture, or *Sittlichkeit*, maximally open to the potential contribution of conscientious dissent, grounded in the overcoming of the 'unhappy consciousness'. To be sure, it cannot be denied that having a general framework of liberal democracy does help. But the primary need must be for the flourishing of appropriate solidarity-networks. Which in our world surely means, first and foremost, the potential carriers of third modernity: the new social movements – a set of groups campaigning for a far more radical transformation in prevailing *mores* than the mere attainment, or reinforcement, of conventional liberal democracy in itself.

Each new stage of modernity begins as a great impulse towards the liberation of conscientious dissent. But let us immediately distinguish between, on the one hand, a commitment to this, that or the other particular dissident cause and, on the other hand, the affirmation of properly conscientious dissent *per se*. In Hegelian terms, the overcoming of the 'unhappy consciousness' implies an affirmation of properly conscientious dissent *per se*: for its intrinsic service to truth as a quality of conversation. What he is looking for, it would appear, is an ethical culture which fully appreciates the perennial need for such dissent – whatever its form – as a means of keeping the processes of public conversation dialectically alive, at the deepest level; combating the sheer spiritual deadliness of an unquestioned consensus.

To argue along these lines, however, is to suggest the need for *continual* dissent. Or, at least, a continual unqualified readiness to dissent. What needs valuing is that readiness *in itself*. If, on the other hand, what one is upholding is just this, that or the other particular dissident cause, then one will continue to uphold it, just the same, when it comes into political power and becomes an ideology of government; as Christian first modernity originally did in the days of Constantine, and as all the various schools of second modernity also aspire to do, with different degrees of actual success. But the very aspiration to this sort of power, even long before it is achieved, already serves to compromise the conversation-enhancing qualities inherent in properly conscientious dissent *per se*. Movements possessed by such ambitions will always be prone to exploit the herd-behaviour prompted by the 'unhappy consciousness', rather than simply to oppose it. For it may well serve their tactical interests to do so.

With new social movements, this is no longer the case. They begin as solidarity-networks for the shaken, and that is what they also remain. As moral consciousness-raising movements, pure and simple, they attempt to affect political decision-making only indirectly, by working on public opinion and so transforming the political decision-makers' context. And so they, by contrast, have every interest in promoting the transcendence of the 'unhappy consciousness'. Hegel had no experience of this sort of movement. He lived at a time when the only apparent choice was between first modernity and second modernity. But the underlying *criteria* he develops, for assessing cultural phenomena in general, would surely lead him to affirm what is now emerging, with these movements, in just the same qualified terms as in his day he affirmed the new secularity of the secular state.

And, moreover, I think that he would also therefore be compelled to revise the narrow Christian confessionalism which went with his secularism. He lived in a world where a strictly confessional Christian faith was the only real alternative option to 'enlightened' irreligion. Today, however, the emergent trans-confessionalism of the new social movement ethos represents something quite different from either of those.

For Hegel, Christianity stands alone as 'consummate religion': the theme of Part Three of his *Lectures on the Philosophy of Religion*. All the other religious traditions of humanity, surveyed in Part Two, are presented by him merely as more or less inadequate anticipations of the higher truth of Christianity, as philosophically interpreted. That philosophical interpretation is designed to show the latent 'absolute' truth of the Christian gospel as the potential framework for a *Sittlichkeit* of pure reason, a coherent ethical culture of the most radical free-spiritedness.

But my question is: why should this ideal be confined to only one sort of confessional form?

In fact, there are I think three distinct issues here, intertwined:

(a) the validity of Hegel's philosophical critique of traditional Christian theology, inasmuch as that theology still remains at the level of *Vorstellen*, with all the resultant ambiguity;
(b) the accuracy of his historiographical analysis of the actual long-term emancipatory role of Christian faith, already prior to its philosophical transfiguration in his thinking; and
(c) the logical cogency of his Christian-confessional apologetics, in relation to other religious cultures.

For my part, I am completely convinced by his critique of theological *Vorstellen*. But his assessment of Christianity's actual historical record seems to me rather more debatable. And as for his apologetics – I think one can only say that they are a response to circumstances quite different from those of today.

Thus, let us take each point in turn. In the first place, good Christology, surely, is a set of arguments tending to demonstrate the underlying logical *coherence* of the gospel-story; a demonstration of the logical necessity, to that coherence, of each of the story's central elements. But herein lies the intrinsic weakness of *Vorstellen*-theology.

Often it presents the Incarnation as a sheer arbitrary datum, without any attempt to explain why it should be by that particular means that atonement is achieved. Or else it resorts to the sort of argument classically developed by St Anselm, back in the late eleventh century: a demonstration of the theoretical necessity of the Incarnation in quite ahistorical terms – as if it were something that could have happened at any time or in any circumstances whatever. As Anselm conceives of it, Christ's substitutionary act of satisfaction for the guilt of human sin is essentially an event of mythic quality. The identity of this Christ with Jesus of Nazareth is, still, just an arbitrary datum. Hegel, however, shows the 'necessity' of the Incarnation as the actual historic event it was, against the background of Roman imperialism and its decadent religious culture: in the sense that only such an event could ideally symbolize the at-onement of what the 'unhappy consciousness' puts asunder; and only in such a context was the liberated faith it founds, for the first time, historically possible. It required Jewish tradition, a religious void in the pagan world, waiting to be filled, and an oppressive regime to dramatize the whole issue of dissent. Indeed, Hegel's argument implicitly does even more work than he spells out. For, inasmuch as the at-onement in question is a vindication of conscientious dissent, this also shows why it was necessary for Christian faith to be focused precisely on the figure of a *crucified* saviour. The Hegelian interpretation hooks straight into the primal pre-Christian symbolism of the cross – as a deterrent measure of the Roman authorities, against dissent in general. And it helps show the necessity of the resurrection: as a direct reversal of the deterrent message intended by the crucifiers; a symbolic restoring to life of the dissident they had put to death.

Hegel is uniquely radical in his focus on the universal subversiveness of the gospel symbolism, in relation to any sort of thought-control – even the most ostensibly Christian and devout thought-control. That, as I see it, is the real strength of his Christology. But then he goes further. It is not just that the gospel is open to a liberating interpretation. What is more, he suggests, the whole history of the Christian West follows a consistent trajectory towards spiritual and political liberation, which his thinking simply helps carry one stage further.

As he famously puts it in the Introduction to the *Philosophy of History*, the ancient Greeks were the first to develop 'the consciousness of freedom'.[42] Earlier civilizations tended to know only 'that one is free', namely the ruler. But this was not true freedom, since freedom demands a community of the free; it was mere caprice. The Greeks, however, still knew only 'that *some* are free': that is, free in their true selves, or gifted with the vocation to political freedom. For they retained the institution of slavery. The essential historic achievement of Christendom, down the centuries – he argues – has by contrast been a developing awareness of the truth that freedom is for *all*, and that slavery is therefore intolerable. Only a civilization founded on Christian faith, he implies, could have achieved this. Granted, slavery in itself is not yet condemned in the Christian scriptures; it is accepted as part of the natural order. And in Hegel's own day, of course, it continued to be a thriving institution in Christian America. Nevertheless, there had by then emerged a powerful campaign against it, which was church-based. (1807, the year he published the *Phenomenology*, was also the year in which the British government finally banned the trans-Atlantic slave trade.) And deep down, he thinks, this really represented the intrinsic tendency of Christian faith all along. Such a momentous transformation in human self-understanding required centuries to mature. But consider: first slavery had disappeared in the original heartlands of Christendom, and now, at long last, Christianity was inspiring moves for slavery's abolition also in the colonies.

How valid, though, is this suggestion as an historiographical hypothesis? It is undoubtedly a very striking fact that slavery for the most part disappeared from early mediaeval Western Europe. And it is true that Christian preachers not only taught people to regard slaves as human beings rather than mere animals, by admitting them to the sacraments, but also always advocated the manumission, or release, of slaves as a meritorious act of piety. Yet suffice it to say that current scholarship has become increasingly sceptical as to the real significance of this as a causal factor for the change – as distinct from other, more purely economic factors.[43] The system of serfdom, which developed in the period following slavery's disappearance, was not much less demeaning. When serfdom, in its turn, disappeared, the major reasons once again seem to have been economic ones. And even though the anti-slavery movement of the eighteenth and early nineteenth centuries was largely church-based, there is really no evidence to show that *only* a Christian culture could have produced such a movement.

Nor – by the same token – does it by any means follow from a philosophic argument like Hegel's, showing how well suited the Christian gospel is for translating the highest form of existential truth into religious terms, that *only* a Christian culture can do that job; or that Christianity alone can therefore fulfil the role of 'consummate religion'. Here again I repeat what I said above about Kierkegaard's equivalent confessional-exclusivist assumptions: the claim is surely excessive.

Hegel's term for the highest existential truth is 'absolute knowing'. This is the title, and topic, of the concluding chapter of the *Phenomenology*. To apply my terminology, one might say that 'absolute knowing' signifies a radical solidarity of the shaken, rendered fully articulate. It is an absolute shakenness, in the first place, out of any fixed subjective sense of one's own identity; and second, out of any fixed objective metaphysical world-view. And it is the acknowledgement that such shakenness is *itself* the true essence of the divine. As a study of *Geist*, the *Phenomenology* as a whole is a systematic study of the dynamics of shakenness at every level of human spiritual life, in the broadest sense; at this highest level, these dynamics are finally recognized as the multi-layered experience of human participation in the divine – or the self-revelation of the divine in the human.[44] But to speak of shakenness as the essence of the divine presence is at once to affirm it as the basis for true solidarity, demanding positive religious articulation. 'Absolute knowing', then, is the final philosophic clarification of the truth of religion, in the sense of an absolute transcendence of *Vorstellen*. And 'consummate religion' is definable as the ideal practice corresponding to that clarification.

Hegel, still living in the religious culture of traditional Christendom, thinks of this exclusively in terms of his philosophic clarification of the Christian gospel. But why, after all, should it only be the Christian gospel which is open to such transfiguration? What counts is the formal shift from

Vorstellen to *Denken*. Yet this shift in form may surely be accomplished with regard to all sorts of different substantive traditions – just so long as they are open to the deliverances of shakenness. And it therefore seems to me that, in principle, 'absolute knowing' ought to be seen as a state of wisdom potentially attainable within the framework of *any* authentically 'religious' culture, in the strict sense of that term. That is to say: within any post-Axial culture – insofar as it is purged of ideology. So that *every* form of religion, as such, has at least some capacity to become what Hegel calls 'consummate'.

True, Hegel himself was only able to arrive at his insights by way of a meditation on his own Christian heritage. And, more generally, no doubt the development of Christian faith has had a quite crucial role to play in the global self-unfolding of divine truth, for just the reason he suggests: namely, inasmuch as the gospel represents such a perfect symbolic refutation of the 'unhappy consciousness'.

Yet that still need not mean that '*absolute knowing*' is only attainable to the actual practitioners of Christian faith. Other religious traditions have other truth-bearing qualities, more or less necessary in other ways. And why should anyone worry which of them is most necessary? For the partisan of the solidarity of the shaken, there is surely an intrinsic value to their very plurality – as diverse systems of *sittlich* practice, each with their own distinctive perspective to contribute to the larger conversation-process on which such solidarity depends. 'Absolute knowing' is not the prize in a competition, it is simply a commitment to that conversation-process at its best.

The new context of third modernity, it seems to me, positively demands a correspondingly new theological pluralism; in order that – just as Hegel sought to reconcile second modernity with the truth of first modernity – third modernity may also, in its turn, be reconciled with the truths of its two predecessors.

9 Against 'recoil-theology'

Do the failures of second modernity really compel us to go backwards?

The original grand narratives of second modernity, those of the Enlightenment, owed their grand-narrative character to their role as a counter-blast to the – decayed and corrupted – grand narratives of first modernity. So they exalted the ideal secular state as a guardian against the sort of tyranny which justifies itself on the basis of an appeal to Christ, as Christ is envisaged by established church-institutions; or on the basis of a particular interpretation of Islam. Then, though, there also developed another variant. Namely, socialist grand narrative: where salvation is still looked for from the secular state, as an instrument in the hands of the enlightened; but where the earlier solidarity-project of resistance to confessional bigotry has been supplemented by other solidarity-projects – now concerned, rather, with resistance to the natural inertia of capitalism.

The nightmares of twentieth-century totalitarianism have tended to undermine both these variants, equally. For a while it was possible, even for those who genuinely deplored the extravagant cruelty of the totalitarian regimes, to regard this as just a passing aberration; and still to place serious hopes in the redistributive promises of socialism in its hardline Marxist–Leninist mode. But what Francis Fukuyama announces as 'the end of history' was of course the moment at which that hope, for most of its adherents, finally expired.

Fukuyama himself looks towards the possibility of a new, post-socialist form of grand narrative for second modernity, in celebration of 'liberal democracy'. However, there is something rather artificial-seeming about this. For 'liberal democracy' in Fukuyama's sense scarcely seems to have much *need* for grand-narrative underpinning. Whether it has such underpinning or not, it will surely thrive in any case – just because of the way it goes, so naturally, with the sheer flow of global-capitalist economic rationality.

Certainly, in many countries there still are political problems deriving from confessional bigotry which might seem to revindicate the original secularizing dynamics of second modernity. And yet – consider the Stalinist Soviet Union or Nazi Germany. Were not these also secular states? Indeed, they were the most militant sort of secular states: seeking to confine the practice of religion quite strictly to private life alone. The earlier pioneers of second modernity, in the Enlightenment period, could not see beyond the dangers inherent in the ideological corruption of church-religion. Therefore they were tempted to regard secularization, simply in itself, as a virtual panacea for all social ills. But, already, the French Revolutionary Terror warned of another species of danger; and the twentieth century has repeatedly underlined that warning, in the most horrific fashion. As a result, there is just no longer the necessary impulse of ardent hope to sustain the old grand narratives of second modernity in all their original grandeur.

Amongst the most fundamental questions for any contemporary political theology must be: How were those totalitarian horrors possible? What was it about the cultures out of which they developed that most significantly contributed to them? And what would it take, in principle, to render a culture properly immune to the risk of their repetition? But to ask these questions with any real persistence is surely to step right outside the traditional confines of second modernity. In a sense, what confront us here are the foundational questions of third modernity: inasmuch as the thinking of third modernity is essentially a celebration of solidarity-initiatives from below, of the sort which constitute the basic building-blocks of a critical civil society. And such initiatives are precisely the purest possible antithesis to totalitarianism in any form – the very thing that totalitarian regimes most fundamentally seek to eradicate.

Many of the most interesting theologians of the twentieth century, however, have responded to second modernity's misfortunes somewhat differently. The moral of the story, they have suggested, is clear enough. What is really needed now is a chastened *recoil* back to what second modernity began by rejecting: *the prior traditions of first modernity*.

For the Christian theologian of third modernity, the loyalty of church-members to their church is primarily to be affirmed as a unique potential contribution to the larger solidarity of the shaken. (More or less along the lines suggested by Bonhoeffer's formula: 'the church is the church only when it exists for others'; that is, when it corporately participates in Christ's own absolute being-for-others.)[1] Recoil-theology differs, in that it affirms church-loyalty rather for its own sake – urging that it be kept strictly separate, not only from the secular political-society loyalties of second modernity, but from *all* other loyalties without exception.

This is the main thrust of the whole Barthian tradition, for example; which served the Confessing Church in Germany so well, in its struggle with Nazism. Other more recent recoil-theologians of note include Lesslie Newbigin, as a missiologist; Stanley Hauerwas, as an ethical theorist in the North American context; Hans Frei and George Lindbeck, as theological epistemologists – to name just a few.

And there are also numerous others. The particular two I want to focus on especially in this chapter, though, are Oliver O'Donovan and John Milbank.

'Recoil-theology' (i): the issue of political authority

O'Donovan's book *The Desire of the Nations* represents recoil-theology in its purest form, and at its politically sharpest.[2] Thus, it is in essence a vindication of old-fashioned Christian authoritarianism. Not, obviously, 'authoritarianism' in the sense of a sheer rigid clinging to unquestioned prejudice – as suggested by the psycho-sociological notion of 'the authoritarian personality'.[3] But, rather, in the very different sense of a political thinking for which the absolutely central issue is: what is it that rulers need to be and do, in order that they may in fact acquire for themselves a proper authority? That is to say, an authority properly subordinated to the authority of God.

Of course, all Christian theology as such is grounded on the authority of God, as mediated by the authority of Scripture; and all Christian political theory involves, amongst other things, at least some consideration of how that authority relates to the authority of rulers. But not all professedly Christian theology, any longer, makes this specific issue – about the status of rulers – *central*. It used to be central to most traditional political theology, in the context of first modernity; however, it tends to be much less so today. And O'Donovan is a recoil-theologian, above all, in the sense that he thinks it ought to be made central again.

To be sure, he is by no means advocating an indiscriminately wholesale return to every single dominant tendency of old-style political theology. He calls himself a 'liberal': he entirely rejects the illiberal coerciveness which so often disfigured the politics of pre-Enlightenment Christendom. But what he advocates is a critical recoil to the heritage of *'early modern* liberalism'. As he himself immediately concedes, this is something of an artificial historiographical construct. The actual heroes of his story are Wyclif, Vitoria and Grotius: a pre-Reformation English reformer of the fourteenth century, a sixteenth-century Spanish Catholic and a seventeenth-century Dutch Protestant; very diverse figures, who would no doubt have been quite startled to find themselves grouped together as 'liberals'! But never mind. What is meant is just the general authority-orientedness of pre-Enlightenment political theology as a whole; minus the violence.[4]

O'Donovan is a theological advocate of 'early modern liberalism', against 'late modern liberalism'. The historical caesura between the two comes with the Enlightenment. And the crucial difference lies in their contrasting fundamental predispositions towards political authority, as such.

Thus, by way of critical extrapolation from O'Donovan's own argument, let us distinguish in this context between the following two fundamentally contrasting ideal-types of political theology. On the one hand, there is what might be termed 'authority-prioritizing' political theology. This, as I understand it, is what he favours: effectively, a conversation among theologians arising in the first instance out of their experience (or perhaps their dreams) of addressing political rulers; for guidance or reproof. In such theology the goodness of the good community is quite naturally, therefore, defined by reference to the wisdom and effectiveness of its rulers, under God; as consisting in the political articulation of Christian charity, or at any rate some approximation to it, by ruling institutions and individuals which command a maximum of uncoerced respect. The existing authorities are criticized insofar as they fail to be properly and sufficiently authoritative, in the most godly sense. Politics is understood, first and foremost, as the art of authoritatively mediating the transcendent authority of God.

But on the other hand there is what I would call 'solidarity-prioritizing' political theology. Here, by contrast, the stimulus is not so much the actual or imagined experience of addressing political rulers; it is rather the experience of addressing politically-, or anti-politically-concerned members of the general public, with reference to their own spontaneous solidarity-initiatives. Essentially at issue between the two approaches is the question of which category of addressees does one trust more to actually hear – and not mishear – what is being said? Solidarity-prioritizing theology certainly does not deny the possibility of authentic political authority. Yet it is nevertheless premissed on a basic suspicion of all rulers, even the most devoutly religious and orthodox. The theologian is no longer so concerned with how valid authority is to be made more *effective* – naturally a primary concern if one is intent on conversing with rulers, in terms which rulers can immediately relate to. But instead, true ruling authority is defined first and foremost in terms of its restraint: the scope it still leaves for the free exercise of individual autonomy. Whereas authority-prioritizing theology, in other words, tends to invoke the authority of God in a *directly* political way, a solidarity-prioritizing approach therefore invokes it in a politically much more *indirect* (or anti-political) way: as mediated first, pre-politically, through the conscience of the autonomous individual – and then through solidarity-building initiatives from below. The ideal community of faith is, in effect, conceived here as a confessional expression of the solidarity of the shaken; the political truth-quality of Christian charity is defined, above all, by its building-up of thoughtful free-spiritedness.

It is not that an authority-prioritizing theology is by any means necessarily more conservative, in political terms, than a solidarity-prioritizing one; it does not merely affirm authority for authority's sake. The difference is simply one of theological methodology. Of course, a solidarity-prioritizing theology may well have things to say about the authority of those rulers who come to symbolize the inspiration of the solidarity it celebrates. And an authority-prioritizing theology will also serve to express the solidarity of those who seek to defend the authority it celebrates, against all threats. There is no absolute opposition between the two. Yet they nevertheless remain two approaches with quite different starting points; and, hence, often widely divergent emphases.

This contrast I have drawn between the two ideal-types is mine. It is not O'Donovan's. But the specifically theological shift he deplores, from 'early modern liberalism' to 'late modern liberalism', may I think be equally well described as a move away from the authority-prioritizing approach towards the solidarity-prioritizing one.[5]

Hegel is the great pioneer here – with his direct response to the Enlightenment, as represented by Kant. Later on in the nineteenth century, the rise of Christian Socialism provided another major creative impulse. More recently, it has been the 'liberation theology' movement, originating in Latin America, which has taken the lead. For the whole thrust of that movement has been to promote a form of solidarity from below: the solidarity of the theologically articulate classes with the poor, in their struggles for justice.

O'Donovan concentrates especially on the liberation theologians. He calls them 'the Southern school'. And he sharply counterposes his own thought to theirs.

In the first place, he approves of the seriousness with which the Southern school has sought to develop a position grounded in the exegesis of particular scriptural concepts: 'though its stock of these sometimes appears rather small, they are undoubtedly foundational to its enterprise'.[6] But he complains that the social-scientific concepts brought to bear on this exegesis are too narrow. They are too narrowly focused on one single set of problems: namely, those directly bound up with the economic exploitation of the poor by the rich. In the thinking of the Southern school, the whole political thrust of the gospel is reduced to its vindication of God's 'preferential option for the poor' – as a basis for solidarity. O'Donovan is not at all denying that this is indeed a vital aspect of the gospel. But he nevertheless argues that to focus on this one aspect of the matter *alone* is, to a considerable degree, to cut oneself off from the actual riches of the older patristic, mediaeval and 'early modern' traditions of political theology.

In short, the Southern school 'has lacked a concept of authority' properly to back up its concern for solidarity with the poor.[7] O'Donovan's complaint is not that these theologians have a false concept of authority. But rather, as he sees it, there is a whole range of authority-related issues they fail to address:

> Can democracy avoid corruption by mass communications? Can individual liberty be protected from technological manipulation? Can civil rights be safeguarded without surrendering democratic control to arbitrarily appointed courts? Or stable market-conditions without surrendering control to arbitrarily appointed bankers? Can punishment be humane and still satisfy the social conscience? Can international justice be protected by threats of nuclear devastation? Can ethnic, cultural and linguistic communities assert their identities without oppressing individual freedoms? Can a democracy contain the urge to excessive consumption of natural resources? Can the handicapped, the elderly and the unborn be protected against the exercise of liberty demanded by

the strong, the articulate and the middle-aged? Should the nation-state yield place to large, market-defined governmental conglomerates?[8]

Political theology of the sort pioneered by the Southern school, O'Donovan argues, tends just to ignore such issues – which can only properly be addressed by way of a systematic return to the problematics of authority.

To some extent, he thinks the one-sidedness of the Southern school is a natural consequence of the actual socio-political context in which the theologians of the South find themselves. Yet, unfortunately, there has been little adequate counterbalance supplied from the North, where the sorts of issues listed above are more immediately pressing. On the contrary, in recent years the leading Northern political theologians – people such as Jürgen Moltmann, Johann-Baptist Metz and Dorothee Sölle – have largely been concerned to appropriate, for the North, the lessons to be learnt from the South. Over and against these thinkers, O'Donovan urges that Northern political theology now has quite another special vocation of its own: at long last, to break with the prejudices of 'late modernity', in which the Southern school is still embroiled; to re-prioritize the problematics of authority; and then 'to say to theologians of the Southern school that, just as poverty was their issue first, but also ours, so authority is our issue first, but also theirs'.[9] He seeks to move beyond the instinctive suspicion of all governmental authority as such, which the theologians of the Southern school tend to have in common with their Northern allies, so as to reconnect with the older – as he sees it, unjustly forgotten – traditions of pre-Enlightenment political theology. And in *The Desire of the Nations*, as a whole, he is exploring what this might imply.

Recoil-theology (ii): desire unbounded

John Milbank is a rather different sort of recoil-theologian – a recoil-theologian who is also something more. Thus he differs from O'Donovan in a number of respects.

To begin with, although both are Anglicans, O'Donovan is an evangelical but Milbank is Anglo-Catholic. At the same time, Milbank is much more of a philosophical theologian and much less of a dogmatic theologian than O'Donovan. Unlike O'Donovan, he calls his theology 'postmodernist' – which at any rate indicates a certain sense that there might be valid new insights available to us today, which decisively transcend what O'Donovan calls the 'early modern'. (O'Donovan, for his part, has no time at all for 'postmodernism'.) And, again unlike O'Donovan, Milbank is clearly committed to some form of Christian Socialism; a movement entirely belonging to what O'Donovan would call 'late modernity'.

Nevertheless – in terms of my argument – he is still very much a critic of second modernity, in the name of the lost wisdom of first modernity. And it is this recoil-theology aspect of his thought that I want to focus on here.

Milbank is a thinker of protean energy, throwing out a bewildering multiplicity of swift and sweeping arguments, often highly erudite. But at the heart of his thinking – at any rate as I understand it – there stands one key thought of particular suggestiveness and power. He is preoccupied with what renders the Christian gospel unique. And in effect his central theme is the way in which the gospel represents an unfettering of *infinite desire*.

'All desire is good', he writes, 'so long as it is a restless desire (a more-desiring desire) which is moved by infinite lack, the pull of the 'goal'. Such desire is non-violent for it could only be content with the unrestricted openness, non-possessiveness and self-offering of resurrected bodies.'[10]

By contrast, the sort of desire that may lead to violence is urgent but *finite*: that is to say, the desire of the addict. (I am restating the point here in my own way, but I think that this is the implicit contrast.) Thus – whether one be addicted to drugs, or to the pursuit of wealth, or to sexual promiscuity, or to glamour and fame, or to the excitement of danger, or to manipulative power, or to vengeance, in each case it is the same. One's desires are confined to getting the next fix, by whatever means available.

But the thing is, there are two ways of not being addicted, and only one of them is the way of faith. The other way is through the diminishing of desire, the cultivation of contentment, the leading of a quiet, settled, innocent life – with no great intensity of thought, therefore. The way of faith is the exact opposite to that.

For faith is the expression of infinite desire. Namely, the desire for God. What comes to expression in authentic faith is the desire whose goal is symbolized, in Christian terms, by the image of the resurrected body; the whole self in communion with God. It is the desire to be Christlike, nothing less. In principle, it is precisely the desire for that which is most difficult, demanding the greatest intensity of real thought for its achievement; the impulse to the deepest thoughtfulness. By virtue of this difficulty, this demandingness, it is the truth of desire. Or – truth *as* desire. This is, one might say, what most *truly* saves us from our proneness to addictions (that proneness being understood as the very essence of 'original sin'). It saves us, inasmuch as it connotes an intensity of restlessness utterly transcending the limited horizons of addiction, and decisively outbidding it.

The whole logic of the gospel is one of infinite intensification, with regard to desire. To begin with, the twin doctrines of creation and providence appear as the retrospective vindication of that infinitude, inasmuch as they amount to a symbolic proclamation that everything truly desirable is ultimately possible. And then, looking forward, the same attitude classically issues in the Augustinian notion of the 'heavenly city'. That is to say: the vision of an (anti-)political ideal, radically non-violent, entirely purged of every last trace of coercive domination; infinitely remote from the ways of the actual earthly cities of the present day, and yet urgently present to faith as an object of desire; the more urgently present, the deeper the faith. Herein, Milbank suggests, lies the unique genius of Christianity. Everything, in short, depends upon our insisting on its *absolute* otherness from any advocacy of wisdom-in-contentment. Or, crucially, from any sort of so-called 'realism' – setting fixed limits on what is to be hoped for, in faith.

Milbank develops his polemic on several fronts. Partly, it is framed as an argument against paganism; both antique paganism and, more especially, the postmodern paganism of our contemporary 'Nietzscheans'. In this rather broadly conceived category he includes both Lyotard and Heidegger; along with Deleuze, Derrida, Foucault and their various followers.[11] These thinkers are all, indeed, vivid advocates of infinite desire in the specific context of the *pre-political* moral self-creation of free-spirited individuals. Yet when it comes to politics – and hence to the claims of the Christian gospel as politically, or anti-politically, mediated through the church – they appear to draw back. Their wisdom is, in Milbank's terms, 'nihilist' inasmuch as it connotes a basic political rejection not only of the church, for its historic failings, but also of the 'heavenly city' as a transcendent ideal in itself. There is no infinite desire in their politics. Instead, we find them more or less cheerfully *resigned* to the supposed inevitability of discord and violence in human relationships. As Milbank puts it, in opposition to the Christian 'ontology of peace' their thinking effectively presupposes an 'ontology of violence'. In other words, whereas Christian spirituality systematically points beyond the immediate actualities of conflict – both back towards the original peaceableness of creation, and forwards to its looked-for restoration by redemptive grace – these 'Nietzscheans' simply assume that the natural order, as such, is irredeemably conflictual.

But this is after all, he insists, a quite arbitrary option. Nietzsche himself disguises that arbitrariness by wrapping it up in a rhetoric of 'honesty'; Milbank sets out to unmask Nietzschean 'honesty' for the arbitrariness it really is. Thus: the difference between Christian faith, at its most authentic, and Nietzschean neo-paganism is not that Christianity is necessarily dishonest about violence. It is not that it, in any way, necessarily de-sensitizes its adherents to the actual realities of violence – on the contrary, the fact that its worship is focused on the violent image of the cross surely signifies a fundamental commitment, at least in principle, to ever-deeper sensitivity in that regard. But the real difference is just that true Christianity insists on a cultivation of infinite desire *in every domain of life*. Unlike Nietzscheanism, it does so in the political domain just as much as in the pre-political. And so it refuses to be paganly fatalistic about violence. In fact, it represents the absolute antithesis to any such fatalism.

Similarly, another of Milbank's arguments is directed against the sort of ethical purism primarily represented by Emmanuel Levinas – with whom he further associates Patočka, Derrida once more, and Marion, for instance.[12] Whilst the Nietzscheans look away from Christianity to ancient Greece, Levinas's thinking emerges out of the twentieth-century experience of

European Judaism. And then others have gone on to find a fundamental affinity between the Levinasian argument and the innermost original ethical core of the Christian gospel. As with the Nietzscheans, so also here we have an affirmation of infinite desire. But in this case the trouble is it is affirmed only in one form: namely, insofar as it is *self-sacrificial.*

What Levinas affirms above all is the infinitude of infinite self-sacrificial desire. And he places the accent just as much on the aspect of self-sacrifice as on the infinitude. Hence, moral goodness is here defined as a purely *disinterested* generosity; it is primarily supposed to be apparent where it is most clearly independent of any hope or expectation of reciprocity. Theologically, therefore, it is taken to be at its purest where it is radically dissociated from any mythic imagery of post-mortem rewards. There is at least this much advantage in secularization, it would appear.

From the Milbankian point of view, however, this is altogether too narrow an approach. He criticizes it as a sort of moralized masochism, half in love with suffering and death, as the price the ethical individual is prepared to pay – the more the better, ethically. To be sure, the self-giving that springs from faith does not demand any prior calculation of returns, or any contractual guarantees. Yet that is still not necessarily to say that it is always at its truest only where it is most self-sacrificial, or that its goodness is primarily to be measured in those terms. Christ's death on the cross is by no means a symbol of pure self-sacrifice in the Levinasian sense. Rather, Christ died for love of the community he had gathered round him; a love which was passionately reciprocated. He died because the only alternative would have been to betray that community. And, in gospel terms, every such experience of vibrant community is to be regarded as a foretaste of the heavenly marriage banquet, which is the true image of the highest good. Infinite desire may appear in many different forms, all sorts of different mixtures of (inevitable) self-sacrifice and erotic self-fulfilment. But just as, against the Nietzscheans, the Milbankian argument is effectively an advocacy of infinite desire in every context, so against the Levinasians it is an advocacy of infinite desire in every form alike.

Again, at another level, Milbank seeks to defend the claims of infinite desire against the pretensions of the 'sociology of religion' – this indeed is what seems to make his blood boil most of all.[13] For what is sociology? It is the study of 'society', essentially as conceived in strict abstraction from any perspective determined by infinite desire; a reflection on cultural phenomena, systematically turning away from any advocacy of infinite desire towards 'scientific', observational neutrality. (At this point his argument runs parallel to Smith's, discussed above.) But one cannot truly comprehend infinite desire by detached observation, from the outside. It can only be comprehended, in its actual infinitude, by those who themselves participate in it. To know it is, quite simply, to feel its pull; whereas, by contrast, all that can be identified by looking in and surveying the scene from outside is the reactive interplay of various different groups' corporate self-interest. Another possible name for infinite desire is 'the sublime' – and Milbank defines the sociology of religion accordingly as a reductionist 'policing of the sublime'. For, insofar as sociology in general seeks to privilege its own specific notion of 'society' over all other accounts of human living-together, it therefore becomes, in his terms, the mortal enemy of true political theology. Granted, it still allows space for the authentic expression of infinite desire in the context of purely private religious experience – such matters being beyond what it claims as its special sphere of competence. But its whole tendency is nevertheless just to devalue any more political expression of such desire, which it precludes itself from understanding, and consequently tends to misrepresent as a mere ideological mystification of corporate egoism. In response to this sort of sociological suspicion, Milbank advances his own 'meta-suspicion': namely, that the sociology of religion itself is nothing but an elaborate pseudo-scientific device for the self-protection of ideologized self-interest against gospel-truth.

Each of these various modes of thought has tended to influence recent Christian theology. Milbank's basic project is to purge it of these influences. But then, in the process of so doing, he also becomes a recoil-theologian.

Thus, he seeks to go 'beyond secular reason'; 'secularism', of any sort, is a major bugbear to him. He defines his position as a form of neo-Augustinianism. It is also (with some qualifications) explicitly anti-Hegelian.[14] Just as much as O'Donovan, he is from the outset fundamentally mistrustful of any project like Hegel's, insofar as it aims at the general reconciliation of first modernity with second modernity.

And the underlying logic of this mistrust, on his part, is I think quite straightforward. It follows from the essential nature of second modernity, as a set of projects all immediately bound up with attempts to gain control over the levers of power within political society. Thus, as soon as one identifies one's hopes with such a cause, one is inevitably caught up in, at least to some extent, the complex tactical considerations and moral compromises of worldly *Realpolitik*. The ultimate goals of an enlightened worldly *Realpolitik* may well be altogether valid in themselves, so far as they go; however, the question is to what extent it can ever be right, precisely, to *identify* true Christian hope with them. Christian hope can be quite compatible with all manner of actual engagement in secular politics. But compatibility is one thing, identification is quite another. And if the real truth of Christian hope, in its distinctive essence, derives from the sheer infinitude of the desire it expresses, then it surely needs to be quite strictly differentiated from any more limited species of ambition – even the noblest.

On these grounds, Milbank – like O'Donovan – is also a particular critic of Latin American liberation theology.[15] The liberation theologians have of course been widely criticized by politically more conservative theologians for their readiness, in large measure, just to adopt and baptize the secular ideology of their Marxist allies. And Milbank also deplores the compromises which he sees this as involving. Only, he is by no means criticizing liberation theology from a more conservative point of view, in political terms.

On the contrary, what he deplores in Marxism is precisely its fatalistic resignation to the immediate demands of 'revolutionary' *Realpolitik*, in a capitalist context, as opposed to the altogether more uncompromising – and hence, in the long run, more truly realistic – political testimony to infinite desire which he finds paradigmatically present, for example, in the original, pre-Marxist forms of Christian Socialism. Thus, he advocates a return to something like the gospel-based politics of Pierre Buchez and his circle, the protagonists of 'the very first unambiguously "socialist" theory', in mid-nineteenth-century France.[16] For here we encounter a species of socialism belonging far more to civil society than to political society; a socialism conceived not so much as a stream within second modernity, but rather as a recoil against it, in its liberal capitalist mode – back towards the old 'gothic' spirit of the mediaeval guilds and confraternities. Milbank's own recoil-theology represents a recoil of the identical sort: in effect, an attempt to recapture that same spirit, adapted and radicalized, to meet the challenges of an industrialized economy. Thus, he is the exponent of a theologically framed socialism which looks for justice not from any further extension of secular state power but, instead, from a restoration of the older sort of 'complex space' which the centralizing dynamics of the secular state have all too often tended to erase.[17] And so his thinking bears witness to the Augustinian ideal of the 'heavenly city', still unco-opted by the *Realpolitik* of any secular political party. The basic failure of liberation theology, from the Milbankian perspective, is simply that it allows itself, with so little resistance, to be co-opted that way.

Response

Up to a point, I agree with the Milbankian argument – as I understand it. I think that there is, indeed, every reason to identify religious truth with the infinitude of infinite desire; and to insist that we should therefore seek to read the gospel first and foremost in that light. Basically, I would see this as another way of restating the central Hegelian insight, that the innermost truth of the gospel lies in its symbolic overcoming of the 'unhappy consciousness'; for what else is the 'unhappy consciousness' if not the most elementary stifling of infinite desire?

And, moreover, I also think that Milbank is at least partly right in his critique of Hegel, inasmuch as Hegel's systematic reconciliation of the gospel with secular liberalism surely does involve a certain watering down of the core gospel-truth he himself had so persuasively identified.

But – just as in the case of Hegel – I am much less convinced by Milbank's attempt to tie his rethinking of Christian truth to an exclusive confessionalism. Insofar as he is saying that the innermost truth of the gospel lies in its capacity to articulate the claims of infinite desire, and that this is therefore the proper basis for Christian self-criticism, yes I agree. However, it also seems to me that the same may be said of every other properly religious tradition, as such; each after its own distinctive fashion. But Milbank appears to deny this. It is a matter of principle for him that he thinks only, ever, from within the given world-view of the Christian-confessional story; and with the aim of demonstrating the ultimate superiority of that world-view to any other.[18] I have the same objection here as I have to Hegel's exclusive identification of 'consummate religion' with Christianity: surely the deeper truthfulness always lies in a confessional orientation towards self-criticism – and not towards self-congratulatory competitiveness.

Unlike Hegel's, Milbank's exclusive confessionalism is part and parcel of his general repudiation of second modernity. I am inclined to think that he represents the very strongest possible line of argument in favour of such a recoil. And yet the strength of that argument depends entirely upon his turning a blind eye to the very different possibilities of third modernity.

Thus, let us take another look at the historical dialectic of infinite desire and governmental *Realpolitik*. From this particular point of view, there is actually a certain sense in which the life-cycle of second modernity rather resembles that of first modernity before it. Both began alike with a great surge of infinite desire, a great cultural shake-up. And both alike were then faced with the problem of how to reconcile the intransigent idealism of their origins with the legitimate demands of *Realpolitik* – as an inescapable fact of life for responsible rulers. Of course, this problem took some time to impose itself on the Christian theologians of first modernity, only appearing in its full seriousness after the conversion of Constantine; whereas for the protagonists of the Enlightenment it was a problem from the beginning. But both these forms of modernity have in fact had the greatest difficulty in sustaining a proper tension between the two poles. Second modernity originates as a reaction against the perceived failure of Christian first modernity here: its falling apart into the excessive ambitions of great church-establishments on the one hand, cynically given over to the most corrupt and oppressive forms of *Realpolitik*; and, on the other hand, the alternative excess of a rigidly other-worldly sectarianism, which just refuses to acknowledge the actual realities to which responsible *Realpolitik* must respond. Recoil-theology, then, originates as a reaction against the perceived failure of secular second modernity in tackling the selfsame task – as the original liberating vision of the Enlightenment has been more or less swallowed up into the *Realpolitik* of twentieth-century political parties, with their mindless propaganda machines.

And yes, the recoil-theologians are clearly quite right to insist that there must be other ways for Christian tradition to transcend the historic collapse of first modernity, as represented by old-fashioned Christendom, besides the way of simple accommodation with second modernity. Only, one has to ask: where are there any actual church-communities in existence truly equal to the task of carrying the burden of hope these thinkers would impose on them? It is not obvious.

Consider, though, how the new social movements of potential third modernity come at this problem. Insofar as these movements are committed to remaining part of civil society, not political society, they seem to me to be – at least in principle – uniquely well equipped to succeed where the carrier-communities of both preceding stages have foundered. For, whilst their role as ethical lobby-agencies brings them continually into conversation with the world of *Realpolitik*, their strategic commitment to perpetual outsider-status nevertheless always serves to protect them against its grosser temptations.

It is surely in the solidarity of the shaken that political desire is most truly infinitized – and what is there in the pure consciousness-raising activity of civil-society movements to dull the appetites of such desire? To put it in Milbankian terms: are not the new social movements precisely creating a new sort of 'complex space', for the resurgence of the 'gothic' spirit? They are doing it, necessarily, in trans-confessional terms. And yet Milbank, alas – with his absolute commitment to an exclusive confessionalism – turns a theological blind eye to their creative potential. That is the trouble.

And so does O'Donovan. But then O'Donovan also goes further: he is altogether more closely enclosed within what I would see as the constraints of recoil-theology than Milbank ever is – by virtue of his deliberately antique attitude to the whole inter-relationship of nature and history.

This emerges most directly from the polemic to be found in his book *Resurrection and Moral Order* against what he calls 'historicism'. O'Donovan himself defines what he is attacking here as follows:

> The heart of historicism can be expressed in the thesis that all teleology is historical teleology. The concept of an 'end', it is held, is essentially a concept of development in time. Nothing can have a 'point', unless it is a historical point; there is no point in the regularities of nature as such. What we took to be natural orderings-to-serve and orderings-to-flourish within the regularities of nature are in fact something quite different: they are orderings-to-transformation, and so break out altogether from nature's order. The natural exists only to be superseded.[19]

As he makes clear, he is thinking especially of the theological influence of Hegel in this connection – and, more recently, of Marxism; or the evolutionary cosmology of Teilhard de Chardin. But the great anti-historicist movement in twentieth-century theology has been that of Barthianism, and he is to that extent entirely on the side of the Barthians. In effect, O'Donovan seems to regard 'historicism' as being, at bottom, a merely arbitrary prejudice in favour of whatever is world-historically new, just on the basis of its being new and therefore presentable as moral 'progress'.

And yet – is that really fair, with regard to any of the actual thinkers he cites? In the case of Hegel, at least, surely not. Hegel's commitment to a grand narrative of ever-unfolding ethical insight has nothing whatever to do with arbitrary prejudice. Hegel does not affirm anything just because it is new; but he is nevertheless resolute in always holding open the possibility of radical new insight, inasmuch as such openness is essential to a properly rational attitude to historical experience in general. And then he records the emergence of new insight wherever he finds it. His historicism simply consists in the deliberate cultivation of historical consciousness as a means of relativizing, and so calling into question, customary norms – in order that, instead of being unthinkingly taken for granted, they may henceforth become the subject matter of the most free-spirited rational debate.

From an historicist's point of view, on the other hand, O'Donovan's de-historicizing ethical invocation of 'the regularities of nature' appears to be nothing but the expression of a (one is tempted to say, truly very arbitrary) prejudice in favour of a certain set of attitudes mysteriously exempted from historical relativization by the 'authoritative' say-so of the theologian – as a representative of orthodox church-tradition. O'Donovan appears to be an anti-historicist on the anachronistic grounds that strict, philosophically self-conscious historicism is nowhere to be found in Christian Scripture. Which surely begs the question.

By appealing to 'the regularities of nature' as a basis for ethical judgement, he seeks to sidestep historical relativization – almost as if he were thereby stepping right outside the limitations of his own specific historical context to apprehend 'nature' direct. But this cannot be done. In reality, the moral attitudes he wants to privilege as being 'natural' are those he finds by looking, in traditional orthodox fashion, at the underlying assumptions of Scripture. Thus, in particular, the authority-prioritizing approach to political theology seems to him to be the 'natural' and proper way because it is so clearly the prevailing approach both in Scripture and in early church-tradition. Whereas, by the same token, he considers 'late modernity' – because of its historicism and its relative loss of interest in the problematics of authority – to be far less 'natural'.

O'Donovan criticizes whatever he considers to be contrary to 'nature'. Historicism, by contrast, criticizes whatever it sees as depending upon a fundamental blindness to the actual state of affairs, in historical terms – whether this blindness be due to simple narrow-mindedness or, perhaps, to the positive dishonesty of ideologists seeking to cover over their traces. And so, when it comes to the shift O'Donovan describes – from 'early modern' to 'late modern' political theology – the historicist's immediate concern is not so much to ask whether this is in accord with some predetermined standard of what is 'natural', but, rather, to consider the actual historic reasons *why* it has happened, and to what extent it genuinely registers a thought-provoking development in the historical context.

As a matter of fact, there surely are some very good historic reasons for the shift. The old world of Christendom was one in which rulers expressly sought to derive authority from their professed allegiance to biblical principles; likewise the world of pre-exilic Israel, *mutatis mutandis*. Of course, this gave a special significance to the problematics of authority – as prophets and theologians set out to call those rulers to account. The pre-Constantinian church, like post-exilic Israel, was faced with rulers making authority-claims which were expressly contradictory to biblical principle, in that they appealed to other gods. In such a context, political theology could only be focused on the resulting authority-conflicts. Yet in 'late-modern' societies like contemporary Britain neither of these situations any longer obtains. Here the triumph of liberal second modernity has changed everything, it seems, for ever. Where once political power was legitimated in religious terms, by appeal to divine providence, now it is legitimated by elections instead; no longer from above, but from below. The role that churches once played in the generating and licensing of political authority has been taken over by political parties, which are for the most part confessionally neutral. When it comes to questions of religious authority, the whole tendency of the system is thus to render these politically peripheral. Nostalgic theologians may deplore this state of affairs as much as they like; the truth is, they cannot change it.

And then, at the same time, we are also faced with a whole set of urgent new solidarity-problems – in relation to which theological decisions *do* have a direct impact. Above all: the unprecedented challenges of third modernity. To what extent, and on what exact basis, are Christians positively called *as Christians* to engage in practical solidarity-building with non-Christians, as co-participants in new social movements?

So unprecedented are the new opportunities now emerging that Scripture and tradition provide only rather oblique guidance on how to respond. Yet respond we must, one way or another.

No doubt a complete political theology must deal with both sorts of issues: both those to do with the horizontal networking of solidarity-relationships and those to do with the vertical authority-structures of government. But it is a question of priorities: is political theology *primarily* to address itself to the political authorities, seeking to guide them in the performance of their duties – even when they are no longer listening to theologians, and in any case have so seldom shown any great aptitude, even in the heyday of Christendom, for actually appropriating a prophetic message? Or is it more important to address ordinary citizens, in their potential vocation as creative participants in civil society? O'Donovan appears to assume that, when it comes to considering the affairs of the secular world, it is theology's 'natural' vocation always to prioritize the concerns of political, not civil, society. As in the Bible, so therefore for evermore. Surely, though, the priorities may change. One thing, and one thing alone, I would argue is unchanging: precisely, the need to try and do justice – on the basis of tradition – to whatever is most thought-provokingly *not yet thought through* in the evolving historical environment.

And yet O'Donovan's sense of priorities unfortunately seems to rule out any very sympathetic engagement with the new, not yet thought through, possibilities of third modernity, *a priori*. He remains preoccupied with the older issues involved in the struggle between first and second modernity: how to reconcile the political authority-claims of an exclusive Christian confessionalism with the actuality of a secular state. And, moreover, he thinks that this still remains the properly central preoccupation for all contemporary Christian political theology, as such. With the result that his thinking effectively serves to occlude the newer problematic: by what principles loyal Christians should be guided when it comes to their participation in the trans-confessional solidarity-building work of new social movements. The issue of trans-confessional solidarity does not actually figure in his thinking at all. Such solidarity depends upon a shared respect for the deliverances of authentic moral autonomy, overriding all differences deriving from allegiance to different confessional authorities; but an authority-prioritizing political theology automatically tends to reinforce the blockages to this.[20]

'Not in the immanence of social movements is hope to be found', O'Donovan declares, 'but in the revelation of divine justice at Calvary.'[21] Yet how else are we to grasp the true significance of a saviour revealed in the form of a crucified dissident, if not by a maximum of open-minded exposure to the contemporary experience of (as he puts it) 'social movement turbulence'? If the story of Good Friday is to be anything more, in practice, than an item of self-serving church-ideology, it must surely be retold in precisely that context. I cannot accept O'Donovan's dichotomy.

I would certainly agree that the priorities of 'Northern' political theology must tend to differ from those of the Southern school. But not because it is the special vocation of us 'Northerners' to lead the way back towards a more authority-prioritizing approach.

Rather, the most striking contrast between the theological contexts of 'North' and 'South' seems to me to lie in the very different opportunities each typically provides for the new solidarity-projects which constitute third modernity. Thus, the theology of the Southern school is essentially an attempt to rethink the potential significance of the gospel as 'good news to the poor' – beyond the mere offering of heavenly consolation. But this rethinking emerges out of a situation where Christian faith, in general, is already well rooted within the culture of the poor themselves. And the political agenda of these theologians may quite easily therefore be presented as a straightforward extension of the mainstream church's pastoral concern for its own members.

In large areas of the Northern world, on the other hand, things are very different. Let us take one particular concrete case to illustrate the point. Over recent years, I personally have had a good deal to do with Leeds Industrial Mission (LIM), a little ecumenical enterprise, in the city of Leeds, with a theological outlook quite closely akin in fact to that of the Southern school. Beginning in the late 1980s, LIM developed a particular concern for the plight of industrial homeworkers, as one of the very poorest groups in the local labour market. Not only are such workers, on the whole, extremely low-paid; but inasmuch as they remain separated from one another, each in her own home, they also have virtually no scope for spontaneous self-organization. Nor are trade unions able to operate at all in this environment. During the 1980s there appears to have been a major increase in the number of homeworkers in Britain. They were doing a great variety of jobs: anything from tailoring and garment manufacture to packing charity Christmas cards, soldering circuit boards, or assembling budgerigar cages, and the like. But their poverty was compounded by a complete lack of effective legal protection. And they had no public voice.

Working in conjunction with the Yorkshire and Humberside Low Pay Unit, LIM set out to try and help remedy this. The West Yorkshire Homeworking Group was very much a new social movement type of project, entirely independent of any political party. It was dedicated partly to community-work: producing a free newsletter; setting up a telephone information service; helping provide appropriate equipment for health and safety purposes; organizing holiday coach-trips for homeworkers' families; and offering all sorts of pastoral support. Partly, it was a political campaigning agency: directly confronting the more unscrupulous local employers; drawing the attention of the large transnational corporations, whose subcontractors these were, to what was going on; publicizing the situation through newspaper articles and television documentaries; lobbying Parliament and the European Commission; and networking with analogous or sympathetic agencies overseas. It achieved some notable local successes. And in the end it was also instrumental in the establishment both of a national Homeworking Group and of a formal international network of such groups – which in 1996 persuaded the International Labour Organization, for the first time, to agree a theoretically binding convention on homeworkers' rights.

But not many homeworkers are church-members. The decaying inner-city neighbourhoods and dismal housing estates in which they live are, for the most part, an environment in which church-congregations struggle to survive. Moreover, LIM's partnership with the Low Pay Unit meant working in conjunction with a completely secular agency; indeed, the work involved a whole series of alliances with people who would normally be quite mistrustful of the church. And, besides – homeworking in contemporary Britain is a thoroughly multicultural phenomenon. There are a great many white women involved, but also many from the Asian immigrant communities: Muslims, Sikhs and Hindus. The Homeworking Group aimed to work in solidarity with all homeworkers, and therefore recruited to its staff, amongst others, community-workers drawn from these non-Christian religious communities.

LIM is a church-based group, inspired by a certain vision of the gospel. It became involved in the Homeworking project on the basis of the Bonhoefferian principle that 'the church is the church only when it exists for others' – above all, those amongst its neighbours who are most disadvantaged, whoever they may be. Yet, at the same time, it is a group which also seeks to be fully *owned* by the institutional churches of the city, on whom it has always depended, not least for its funding. These churches, however, are institutions under increasing financial pressure. And their natural response to that pressure is, more and more, to want to turn back inwards, concentrating all their resources on the self-serving pastoral monoculture of ordinary congregational life. For the theological advocates of enterprises like that of LIM, this gives rise to a fundamental problem – not faced, to anything like the same extent, by the theologians of the Southern school. How is such an enterprise to be justified, as a church venture, in view of its solidarity-building character, way out beyond the confines of conventional church loyalty?

LIM's work is just one small-scale example of Christian discipleship mediated through commitment to a new social movement mode of organization. That is to say, in the terms of my argument, a small, but pioneering contribution to third modernity. Yet there are also innumerable others one might cite, as belonging in the same general category. All, or virtually all new social movements have specifically Christian sub-groups active within them.

Together, these make up the global community which the World Council of Churches for instance has sought to draw into its 'conciliar process' for 'justice, peace and the integrity of creation'. Again and again, however, the same elementary theological issues arise. They have arisen very sharply, at times, within the particular forum of the World Council of Churches. But, more generally, they arise wherever loyal Christians are also active participants in new social movements. The essential trans-confessionalism of this whole species of enterprise, to my mind, surely needs defending. It needs defending against both the scepticism of those who adhere to more timidly institutionalized understandings of the gospel, and against the outright hostility of resurgent fundamentalism.

The real trouble with recoil-theology in any form, I think, is simply that it systematically downplays the urgency of that need.

10 The healing of Christendom's original trauma

Against a theology without absolutes

Over and against recoil-theology, my most immediate practical proposal for a possible religious contribution to realizing the still latent potential of third modernity is a fundamental reform of the church's liturgical calendar. This would involve extensive experimentation with new types of civil-religious observance. In theoretical terms, my basic aim is therefore systematically to try and establish the proper theological criteria for such experimentation.

And so – what is liturgy for? I would say that its primary job is to enshrine fragile moral insight within durable customs. To this end, it is first and foremost a medium for the corporate appropriation of corporately significant memory.

But, I would also argue, memories are corporately significant in the true religious sense – they have the quality of 'revelation' – essentially by virtue of combining two key characteristics. In the first place, the memories in question are those that most decisively serve to shape who I am, as a member of the various overlapping moral communities I belong to. They are not immediately my own memories. But they are the corporate memories through the owning of which I become incorporated, at a spiritual level, into community-life. And, secondly, revelatory memories are memories that compel me to think – by confronting me with the experience of other individuals who have been intensely made to think. Herein lies their 'spiritual' quality: they are memories of cultural shake-up.

Texts acquire authoritative significance for liturgical purposes, it seems to me, by virtue of their power to transmit such memories. This need not mean that they are in every aspect morally right. To take an extreme example: I do not want to affirm the teaching of Deuteronomy 20: 10–18, which commands the regular practice of genocidal massacre, in the course of holy wars. And yet the book of Deuteronomy clearly does have great significance in the sense suggested above – directly springing as it does from such a very acute experience of cultural shake-up, the whole process issuing in the great reforms of King Josiah. It has, for instance, from this point of view, far more significance than the book of Proverbs, which is altogether more distanced from any cultural shake-up, even though there is a good deal less to disagree with in Proverbs. That is to say, there is potentially altogether more to be gained from liturgical reflection on Deuteronomy, however critical that reflection may have to be. It is much more important to include books like Deuteronomy and Leviticus in our lectionary than Proverbs.[1]

Good religious liturgy is not just a matter of celebrating what we (currently) hold to be good and right. That would simply be an ideological observance. But, rather, it is a community's honest exposure to the shaking-power inherent in significant memories of shakenness. An ideal liturgical culture would surely be one in which people were maximally exposed to *every* such memory which was relevant to their condition, to the precise extent of its relevance.

Therefore my question is: why, as an actual matter of fact, does this not happen with us?

Why is mainstream Christian culture so very narrowly selective about the memories it chooses to focus on? Why is the church, at this level, so *self-obsessed*, for ever focusing only on the stories of its own founding, its own institutional history and pre-history? What is it about church history, in other words, that gives recoil-theology such a powerful appeal?

I am urging that we church-members should also pay due attention to all those other great shake-up memories which serve to define our various non-ecclesiastical, or civil identities: the whole legacy of twentieth-century totalitarianism, for example, and of the resistance to it; the legacy of European imperialism, and the trans-Atlantic slave trade; the legacy of the various struggles for democratic liberty, in the context of the Industrial Revolution and its aftermath; and so forth. The more I think about it, the stranger it seems to me that so little of the church's official liturgical time is in fact allotted to remembering these other stories – allowing them to interact with, and to illuminate the central gospel-story.

The more I think about it, the more I want to ask: *why*? What is it that has tended to produce such a remarkably inflexible sort of liturgical mind-set?

Church history: the persistence of the original trauma

At the roots of church history there is, I think, a major paradox. The most fundamentally necessary practical precondition for the original possibility of the reception of gospel-insight is also, more or less inevitably, the source of the most radical distortion of that insight.

By this I mean the early church's experience of persecution. Only a persecuted community – only a community recruiting, in the teeth of persecution, people whose exuberant sense of thereby being spiritually liberated from worldly oppression made them ready, if need be, to endure all manner of affliction for the sake of their new faith – could have arrived at such a revolutionary insight as that which is captured in the image of a crucified God. A crucified God! This was such a wild departure from every previous notion of the divine, no other sort of community could ever have seen the point.

But *they* knew just what it meant to encounter God in the figure of a perse-cuted dissident – for the simple reason that they too had become persecuted dissidents, as a result of the encounter. The defiant truth of that insight directly fitted their own first-hand experience. It was confirmed, over and over again, in the indomitable resilience of their own community – which, if anything, actually grew by being persecuted.

Here – in this image of a conscientiously dissident free spirit condemned and crucified by the state, but symbolically vindicated by the divine act of resurrection – we have, potentially, the most vivid possible religious affirma-tion of conscientiously dissident free-spiritedness in general; and hence of the solidarity of the shaken, in its most embattled form.

And yet this is the problem: in order for a community to survive persecu-tion, it must *shape itself to do so*; and all the more so if it is a new community, bonded not by the fixed givenness of an ethnic identity but by freshly acquired and easily renounceable ideas. This, though, can only be done at a certain price. After all, a persecuted community, certainly one which lacks clear ethnic coherence, can scarcely afford to encourage much free-spiritedness in its own *internal* debates. For this will tend to be divisive – and the first requirement of survival is strict unity.

The early church survived by virtue of its unity. Or, rather, those elements of it survived which best managed to hold together – thanks to a strategic cultivation of moral and intellectual conformity. The free-spirited anti-patriarchal impulses of the original group around Jesus, still visible in the Gospels, necessarily had to be moderated to make it easier to attain consensus. An undisputed canon of Scripture had to be established, as well as creeds, as a disciplinary constraint on free-spirited intellectuality. 'Heretics' had to be readily identified and cast out, so dogma had to be more and more tightly defined. (Irenaeus, bishop of Lyons in the 180s – that great polemicist against 'heresy' – still allows for some areas of 'legitimate disagreement' among Christians; but the inexorable tendency was progres-sively to close those areas down.) There was a need for the most regimented structure of leadership possible, a unified hierarchy on the basis of apostolic succession. The role that bishops came to play, as lifelong religious monarchs, was completely unprecedented in either pagan or Jewish tradi-tion; nor was there any direct New Testament authorization for it. Yet the pressure of circumstances nevertheless demanded it – just as that same pres-sure also demanded an extravagant, not to say fanatical, glorification of Christian martyrdom. The impassioned confessionalism of mainstream Christian theology largely originates from the martyrs' confession of their faith before their pagan accusers. Church unity was emotionally grounded in loyalty to their memory, and anything that might endanger it was stamped as treachery. All of these developments may be seen to belong together, each one constituting a key element in the church's mental armour.

They are, I think, essentially post-Pauline developments. Paul's letters, at any rate the ones indisputably attributable to the Apostle himself, still reflect the apocalyptic spirit of a community which was convinced that the end of time was imminent; and which to that extent, therefore, remained quite indifferent to the logic of long-term survival. But in the later writings of the New Testament the adaptation process is already well underway. And here we also find the beginnings of the Catholic struggle against Gnosticism.[2] The Gnostics are interesting in this context, inasmuch as they were, precisely, principled upholders of a radical free-spiritedness in the internal life of the Christian community: being, in general, far more critical than the Catholics were of traditional patriarchy; rejecting the Catholic demand for a fixed canon and publicly authoritative creeds; repudiating the Catholic clerical hierarchy; and, it would seem, often evincing considerable suspicion of the Catholic martyr-cult.[3] But then Gnosticism succumbed to the persecutors – no doubt very largely as a result of these characteristics. It is clear that the Gnostics' demand for intra-ecclesial free-spiritedness was premature. Looking at their fate, one sees just how necessary the Catholic response really was.

Nevertheless, as regards the historic articulation of gospel-truth in its highest form – as, in Hegelian terms, a symbolic overcoming of 'unhappy consciousness' – it seems to me there could scarcely have been a more disastrous sort of beginning for church tradition than this!

True enough, the persecution was only occasional and sporadic – considered from the point of view of the persecutors, it was much too little, and mostly too late to be at all effective as a means of repression. Still, that did not prevent it from having the most momentously deep-seated consequences for the whole self-understanding of the church. Christianity, I think, is a religious tradition which resembles an abused child; one so deeply damaged by his early experiences of abuse that when he comes of age he simply repeats the mistreatment he has grown used to regarding as normal, and so becomes an abuser himself. Nor – I would further venture to suggest – have we Christians *fully* recovered, even now.

The trouble is that, when it eventually came to power, the machine for surviving persecution – with its ingrained commitment to a regimented moral and intellectual conformity, and its extraordinarily coherent hierarchy – so easily became a most effective machine for persecuting. The very qualities which had originally equipped the church to survive also now equipped it to persecute.

This did not happen all at once. Indeed, for some hundreds of years the catastrophe lay mostly latent. It took the dramatic growth of early mediaeval towns, in Western and Central Europe, beginning around the end of the eleventh century, to trigger it. In the period from 1100 to 1250 many towns grew five- or sixfold. This growth generated a series of moral panics: for here were great crowds assembling, of uprooted people, often economically insecure – with, it seemed, no effective authority-structures in place to keep them quiet. And the response of those in power was of the same general type that one also sees for example in twentieth-century fascism. Sensing the inchoate simmering rage of the mob, it would seem, and anxious not to become its target themselves, they wanted scapegoats against which to divert it.

Over the following centuries there followed wave after wave of persecution.[4] The targets varied, and included Jews, heretics, homosexuals, 'lepers',[5] usurers, prostitutes and 'witches'. And there were, of course, many secondary factors at work as well, so that each mode of persecution had its own distinctive history. The persecution of the Jews began as a series of popular eruptions: the first being the Rhineland massacres of 1096, in the context of the First Crusade; and then the pattern grew steadily more and more recurrent. The persecution of heretics was initially a response to the rise of new dissident movements through the eleventh century; but it was the Albigensian Crusade, beginning in 1208, which really marks the shift to large-scale and sustained repression. The transition from a culture largely tolerant of homosexuality to one of widespread popular homophobia appears to have started around the end of the twelfth century; it then escalated gradually, until by around the mid-fourteenth century such homophobia had more or less become the universal orthodoxy of Western Christendom, enshrined in law. The great 'witch'-scare came last, gradually building up over the period from the late fourteenth century to the mid-fifteenth. Each of these waves had its own more immediate causes. Yet they may surely also all be seen as so many variants of the same basic dynamic – all symptoms of one and the same deep-rooted disease.

No doubt the underlying social pressures that gave rise to this dynamic would have caused some trouble in any culture. And clearly Christian tradition cannot be held entirely responsible: there was nothing in that tradition to authorize the persecution of 'lepers', for instance; and it was often the secular authorities who took the persecuting initiative, rather than ecclesiastics themselves.[6] Nevertheless, it can scarcely be an adequate theological response just to want to make excuses. One has, at any rate, to ask: why was there so little actual recorded resistance – within the community of the devoutly orthodox – to the church's being co-opted for such oppressive purposes?

Nowadays, thank God, these horrors mostly seem rather ancient history. And so we tend to forget the great debt we owe to the pioneers of second modernity, whose great achievement was to put an end to them. But what exactly did second modernity accomplish in this regard? The development of the secular state served to put an end to the more extreme forms of persecutory behaviour on the part of the mainstream, more institutionalized church-institutions. And this, in itself, certainly did represent a huge advance in civilization.

Yet for a trauma to be fully healed surely requires that it be recognized as such, in all its long-term destructiveness; and for the memory to be worked through in those terms. In the church's case that has clearly still not happened, anywhere. The old nightmares continue to haunt the Christian psyche – resurfacing especially in revivalist movements. Precisely where the gospel is proclaimed at its liveliest, and where Christian preaching is most effectively populist, the old syndrome reappears, now in the form of 'fundamentalism'. Fundamentalists claim to be going back to the 'fundamentals', the uncorrupted origins of the Christian tradition; but what they are in fact reviving – with their insistence on rigid moral and intellectual conformity, and their visceral hostility towards 'the world' – is surely just the ancient neurosis deriving from the church's original trauma.

To be sure, the memory of the early church must be allowed to have immense religious significance: its emergence represented such a tremendous cultural shake-up. But, as I understand it, true Christian liturgy would be an attempt at bringing Christian imagery prayerfully to bear on the shake-up quality of cultural shake-ups *in general*. This is what we are at present failing properly to do. The exclusivism of traditional orthodoxy which sets the shake-up experience of Christian origins radically apart from all other shake-up experiences, as belonging to an altogether different order of revelation, makes perfect sense in situations where the church is being persecuted and needs to reassert its claims against the persecutor. There, indeed, it has a perfectly defensible rationale. But it makes much less sense where that has ceased to be the case. No other post-Axial tradition involves quite so difficult an interior struggle with the impulse to ideology as Christianity does – because of its traumatic origins.

In order that Christian tradition be loosened up, as I would advocate, to become more directly responsive to the great cultural shake-ups of the present, there would surely also have to be a complete reframing of the church's commemoration of its own past: a much more searching acknowledgement than is usual today, of that history's radical ambivalence. Only so, it seems to me, can the gospel-truth finally be liberated from the historic limitations essentially constitutive of Christian first modernity.

'Erring'

On the other hand, I am by no means denying that it is also possible to go too far in uprooting Christian thought from its past. Thus I certainly do not want to go quite as far as a thinker such as Mark C. Taylor, for example.

Thomas Altizer, in the Foreword he wrote to Taylor's book *Deconstructing Theology*, describes Taylor as

> the first American post-ecclesiastical systematic or philosophic theologian, the first theologian free of the scars or perhaps even the memory of Church theology, and the first theologian to address himself to the purely theoretical or cognitive problems of theology.[7]

And it is true, Taylor does seem to represent a form of Christian thought in which the scars left over from the original traumas of church history have after all finally healed.

He is, like Wilfred Cantwell Smith – only more flamboyantly so – a radically post-metaphysical Christian thinker, signalling his complete indifference to the metaphysical claims of traditional theism by referring to his work as a form of 'a/theology'. But where he seems to me to go wrong is by then proceeding (like Heidegger, only Christianized) to try and combine strict post-metaphysics with strict postmodernity.

In Taylor's 'postmodern a/theology' we actually have the very purest possible antithesis, within the general ambit of contemporary Christian thought, to any sort of 'recoil-theology', but especially O'Donovan's. For what he rejects about modernity are precisely its intrinsic authority-claims. And he rejects these simply because the whole thrust of his thinking is, as it were, to try and hollow out traditional authority-claims of every sort. All religion necessarily involves some sort of authority-claim, in dialectical relationship to its expression of worshipful desire. Taylor's 'a/theology', however, is nothing but a supposedly therapeutic minimizing of the former and a countervailing systematic maximizing of the latter.

In his book *Erring* he presents this approach in fourfold fashion.[8] To begin with, it takes shape as a gospel-proclamation of 'the death of God'. The God who has 'died', it seems, is just the old authority-God: the God of the Law and the prophets, the God whose authority irradiated, and was supposed to confer a special representative authority on the church. But, secondly, the 'death' of this God is by no means – he argues – to be interpreted as opening the way to the establishment of some rival 'humanist' authority, as an alternative definer of our true 'selves'. For 'the death of God', properly understood, further signifies 'the disappearance of the self': that is to say, the decisive abolition of any notion of objectively-definable individual vocation – for would-be authorities to latch onto and exploit.

At the same time, moreover, 'the disappearance of the self' clearly implies 'the end of history'. Here is the specifically postmodernist moment in the argument. For, in the absence of 'selves' with their vocations to be defined, no role remains for any sort of authoritative grand narrative to set the context for that defining. And with 'the end of history', finally, we come to 'the closure of the book': there is no role left for the grand narrative-shaping, community-forming authoritative sacred text, or authoritative commentary on the sacred text. But, instead, we are left with the infinite play of 'writing' – writing which henceforth, at its most thoughtful, will continually proclaim that it is 'just' writing, nothing more. The true a/theological writer, as envisaged by Taylor, necessarily remains out on the margins of church-life; for ever playing with words and ideas, endlessly subversive of institutionalized piety; clowning around; cheerfully 'erring'.

It seems to me, however, that *this* form of healing for the traumas of Christendom comes at altogether too great a price.

For (O'Donovan's purely antithetical stance is surely justified at least to this extent) religion without serious authority-claims is religion no longer having any distinctive contribution to make, whatsoever, to the political world. As I would use the term, this so-called a/theology has no real 'theology' in it at all.

Indeed, the cost of Taylor's strategy becomes perhaps most vividly apparent when one looks at it in its formative relationship to the thought of the two earlier Christian thinkers who remain most important to him: namely, Hegel and Kierkegaard.

Taylor values both Hegel and Kierkegaard as thinkers who, each in their opposing ways, stand decisively outside the mainstream of conventional church theology and call it into question. They may appear to be incompatible opposites; yet his early writing is very largely dedicated to the task of mediating between them, in a reconciliatory spirit.[9] And in his later writing too – in which the supervening influence of Derrida, and hence of Heidegger, becomes more and more apparent – he nevertheless continues to refer in unfailingly positive terms to both. In the end, it is just these two loyalties which constitute his continuing link to the Christian tradition.

Taylorian a/theology is presented as being, in some sense, a radicalization of Hegelianism. Hegel figures in this scheme of things as the culminating thinker of 'the epoch of selfhood', which is more or less inaugurated by Augustine. The 'epoch of selfhood', it seems, is on the one hand a movement of thought in which knowledge of God is largely identified with each individual's own self-knowledge, as being subject to a distinctive individualized vocation – the two forms of knowledge mutually mirroring and mediating each other; whilst, on the other hand – as it culminates in Hegel rather than Kierkegaard – it is also, increasingly, an epoch of progressivist politics, in which progress is precisely identified with an expansion in each individual's freedom of self-expression (what Hegel calls 'the principle of subjectivity'). Taylor, however, is intent on articulating, as he sees it, a yet more radical mode of individualized free-spiritedness. And he therefore turns away from Hegelian progressivism with its persistent authority-claims – authority-claims which, in his view, still continue unacceptably to constrict the free play of the spirit. He takes up the Hegelian formula for true free-spiritedness, as liberation from 'unhappy consciousness', and reinterprets that liberation as entailing a wholesale release from History; that is, from any would-be authoritative rhetoric of progress. Every authority-claim becomes, for him, a symptom of 'unhappy consciousness' – even Hegel's own.

But does this shift really represent an authentic radicalization of Hegelian free-spiritedness – or just a rather cavalier renunciation of philosophy's proper political responsibilities?

Hegel for his part certainly has no ambition to neutralize, or even in the slightest degree to moderate the traditional authority-claims of Christian faith. Rather, he seeks to mobilize them – through his philosophic reinterpretation of the dogma of the Incarnation – in an essentially new way: as a direct contribution to the political project of second modernity. The basic difference is surely just that, unlike Taylor, he is serious about politics.

Granted, Hegel is far too much of a political realist to see the philosopher's role as a straightforwardly legislative one, in the way that Plato dreamed of. In a still benighted world, he acknowledges that the philosophers of the future may well have to resign themselves to acting as 'an isolated order of priests', who cannot 'mix with the world, but must leave to the world the task of settling how it might find its way out of its present state of disruption'.[10] But that is certainly not to say that they should rejoice in such a restricted role; nor that they are therefore to abstain from any attempt to expand it, by the judicious invocation of religious authority to back up their cause. On the contrary, he notoriously speaks of the truth of true philosophy as '*absolute* knowing'. It is 'absolute' in the sense that it is authoritative: seeking to pick up as much of the traditional authority of Christian revelation as is compatible with his strict secularism. This claim to 'absoluteness' is essentially expressive of his political seriousness. The wisdom of valid philosophy, Hegel is saying, is not just of significance for its immediate practitioners; philosophy is not just an academic game, to be played for its own sake alone. Insofar as it is valid, it is of 'absolute' significance. That is: it demands real transformation, not just in the lives of those who have caught the bug, but in the whole culture of both church and state.

Hegel has actually already anticipated the possibility of something like the Taylorian standpoint – for it may well be regarded as a prime instance of what in *The Phenomenology of Spirit* he criticizes as the world-view of 'the beautiful soul'. Purely reliant on the inner voice of conscience to the complete exclusion of any notion of objective authority, in political terms 'the beautiful soul', as he puts it, 'vanishes like a shapeless vapour that dissolves into thin air'.[11] And Taylorian a/theology does much the same. Paradoxically enough, moreover, in view of Taylor's attempt to turn the critique of 'unhappy consciousness' against Hegel himself, Hegel actually describes this standpoint of 'the beautiful soul' as being, itself, a somewhat rarefied variant of 'unhappy consciousness'. This is because, as *he* understands it, the true overcoming of 'unhappy consciousness' comes only in the attainment of a proven capacity for actual free-spirited political action.

Nor, though, is Taylorian *a*political anti-authoritarianism really at all compatible with the furiously prophetic, albeit unorganized, *anti*-politics of Kierkegaard. For whereas Kierkegaard is equally opposed to Hegelian progressivism, what he by contrast sets over and against 'absolute knowing' is 'absolute paradox': in other words, a no less 'absolutist' countervailing authority-claim of his own. No less than Hegel, Kierkegaard seeks to exalt the authority of the gospel – in order to deploy that authority in direct antithesis to the Hegelian celebration of second modernity. Hegel backs up his authority-claim by the construction of a monumental pedagogic system; Kierkegaard backs his up by means of savage caricature, chiefly of Hegel. The two styles could scarcely be more different. But in each case the underlying claims are nevertheless equally inflammatory.

Taylor's whole project, however, is designed, so far as is possible, to lower the temperature. This is how he is enabled to mediate between the two. What greater challenge could there be to a theological conflict-resolver than the Hegel/Kierkegaard clash? Yet the Taylorian strategy serves to dissolve even this conflict, straight away, with the greatest of ease. It does so by the simple expedient of *a priori* devaluing all that gives real passion to the struggle. Taylor sets out, in effect, to convert both Hegel and Kierkegaard into 'beautiful souls' – so that in his presentation their opposing world-views will flow together just like two 'shapeless vapours'.

As a result of which, he has abandoned not only Hegel's passionate political seriousness but also all the anti-Hegelian passion that goes into Kierkegaard's humour. After all, no matter how witty Taylor may be, he can never be as genuinely humorous as Kierkegaard – for lack of that passion. In this peaceable co-existence of two 'beautiful souls' that he proffers us the true greatness of both thinkers is simply left to drift away. For what true philosophical greatness can there ever be that does not grow out of some sort of sublated rage? Whereas the 'beauty' of the 'beautiful soul' is very much the beauty of a purely rage-less equanimity.

11 A new covenant?

In discussing the thought of Oliver O'Donovan in the preceding chapter, I drew a contrast between two basic different approaches to political theology: one approach, ideally framed as guidance to rulers, prioritizes the problematics of authority; the other approach, framed as guidance for the grassroots activist, prioritizes the problematics of solidarity-building. Since the former approach is the prevailing one in Christian Scripture, and was always predominant in the thinking of Christian first modernity, O'Donovan urges a systematic return to it – yet it seems to me that he ignores the very good practical reasons why the latter approach should nowadays increasingly be supplanting it. And it is at all events quite clear that any theology of *third* modernity must be of the solidarity-prioritizing type.

But this is by no means to say that a solidarity-prioritizing political theology will be an authority-*denying* one, in the manner of Mark C. Taylor. For then it would not really be a political theology any longer.

Rather, one needs to distinguish two contrasting modes in which properly religious authority may be made publicly manifest. There is, on the one hand, its direct manifestation in a system of rule: religious authority, so to speak, directly translated into political authority. But then, on the other hand, there is also its indirect manifestation – as that which guides the consciences of those engaged in solidarity-building initiatives.

The founding of such indirectly operative religious authority is represented, in the Jewish and Christian traditions, first and foremost by the symbolism of the '*covenant*' between God and humanity.

Here and there in the Hebrew Scriptures, it is true, one finds the notion of the covenant applied to the establishment of a specific license to rule: so it is in the case of Yahweh's special covenant with King David (2 Samuel 23: 5; Psalms 89: 34); and with the Aaronites, conferring on them the privilege of perpetual priesthood (Numbers 25: 5–13). These, though, are the exceptions. For the most part, the covenant is between God and the people as a whole. It becomes the basis for extensive sacred legislation. But *in itself*, from the people's point of view, it is just a solidarity-building recollection of certain key shared memories; a solidarity-building affirmation of shared trust in the God decisively revealed by those remembered events; a solidarity-building expression of shared hopes, for their future collective relationship with that God.

In explicitly turning his back on modernity, Taylor at the same time tacitly abandons any sort of covenant-thinking. What we have here, in my view, is very much the same sort of short-sightedness that also characterizes the thought of secular postmodernists such as Lyotard, only now applied to a systematic dismembering of Christian theology. And against Taylor I basically want to argue that, just as the bankruptcy of earlier forms of modernity does not necessarily mean the wholesale ruination of all modernist hope as such, so it is with this broader concept of the covenant as well. True healing for the lingering after-effects of Christendom's original trauma surely demands not the mere abandonment of covenant-thinking, but, on the contrary, its radical reappropriation. It requires the opening up of our theology to the possibility, now, of a new covenant – new because, for the first time, post-metaphysical. Precisely, a pure covenantal sealing of the solidarity of the shaken.

Salvation history

In Letter to the Hebrews 12: 25–9, the experience of the early church is compared to the experience of the people of Israel, in the awesome moment of Moses' encounter with God to receive the covenant on Mount Sinai:

> See that you do not refuse him who is speaking. For if they [the ancient Israelites] did not escape when they refused him who warned them on earth [not to touch the mountain, Exodus 19: 12], much less shall we escape if we reject him who warns from heaven. His voice then shook the earth; but now he has promised, 'Yet once more I will shake not only the earth but also the heaven' [Haggai 2: 6]. This phrase, 'yet once more', indicates the removal of what is shaken, as of what has been made, in order that what cannot be shaken may remain. Therefore let us be grateful for receiving a kingdom that cannot be shaken, and thus let us offer to God acceptable worship, with reverence and awe; for our God is a consuming fire.

A voice with mighty shaking-power warns the people not even to touch the mountain on whose summit the covenant is being made. The shaking-power of this voice has a double symbolic significance: it represents both the sheer authority of the covenant and its radical testing quality. For only the testing experience of being shaken reveals what is truly unshakeable – and the essence of *any* covenant surely consists in that revelation. The more emphatic and repeated the shaking ('yet once more …') the better.

So what if that which 'cannot be shaken' in this sense – or the one thing which the 'consuming fire' of the true God leaves intact – were to be recognized, simply, as the ethos of the solidarity of the shaken?

It is clear that such a covenantal sealing of post-metaphysical insight would require a decisive reinterpretation of the whole history of covenant-making. In the work of Wilfred Cantwell Smith we have already seen a paradigmatically post-metaphysical interpretation of the concept of 'faith'. But this might also be expressed in Heideggerian terms: true faith, one might say, is a mode of the *Ereignis*, 'the event of appropriation'. It is nothing other than the appropriation of shakenness – in a certain mode. In which mode? Precisely, in the *covenantal* mode. It is the appropriation, by each individual member within a covenant-founded community, of that founding covenant. A post-metaphysical notion of faith demands an equivalently post-metaphysical notion of covenant; and hence of the covenanting God.

The covenant of Israel with Yahweh, sealed on Mount Sinai, is the covenant of a particular tribal people with their tribal god. Yet at the same time it serves as a symbol for the whole Axial Period transformation originating within Semitic culture. It is, as we have received it, a story constructed in the Axial Period, in which that transformation is symbolically compressed into a single event, and then back-projected into the distant past.[1]

This actual symbolization process is a unique feature of the Semitic Axial Period. But, in post-metaphysical terms, one would have to acknowledge that there is an at least implicitly covenantal quality to *all* the great Axial transformations, and not only the Semitic one: just as there may be authentic faith in all the great post-Axial traditions, so they all have their own covenants.

Within the originally Semitic corpus of religious traditions, on the other hand, one can observe the following progression beyond its initial tribal particularism. First, in the book of Genesis 9: 1–17 there appears the story of the covenant with Noah after the flood, whose sign is the rainbow. (This belongs to the later 'priestly' stratum of the text, probably composed in the context of the Babylonian exile in the mid-sixth century BCE.) Here by contrast the covenanting God is the Creator, and the covenant is with the forefather of all humanity. Noah's descendants are commanded to 'be fruitful and multiply, and fill the earth'. And it is also ordained that 'whoever sheds the blood of man, by man his blood shall be shed; for God made man in his own image'. The Noachic covenant, in short, functions as a symbolic representation of the covenantal element inherent in all civilized social life, pre-Axial as well as post-Axial, as developed in the face of the shaking-potential both of natural disaster and, by extension, of war. It represents, so to speak, the covenantal aspect of what in political philosophy has traditionally been called 'the social contract'.

Then, in the prophecy of Deutero-Isaiah (originally delivered in the period around 540 BCE, again in the context of the exile) the whole background to the Sinai covenant is reinterpreted: the covenanting God is now understood as the one and only God, besides whom there is none other. Which, at length, sets the scene for the covenants of first modernity as registered in the New Testament and the Qur'an. Thus, the covenants of modernity essentially originate as the translation of monotheist theory into cosmopolitan practice: a practical, missionary affirmation of the oneness of humanity.

The covenant-making of second modernity seeks to liberate that primary cosmopolitan impulse from the ideologization of confessional identity. One finds 'covenant' language most explicitly applied to the projects of second modernity among the Americans, as they appropriate the Sinai story, by analogy, to themselves. For was not the Sinai covenant the polity-founding covenant of an exodus-people, and were not the early immigrant Americans, as they sought to found their own new polity, also an exodus-people, having departed from the 'Egypt' of despotic Europe, for their promised land? In the use of this metaphor, American Protestant first modernity flows straight into American civil religious second modernity. Robert Bellah, as the chief theologian of 'American civil religion', prophetically laments what he sees as the 'breaking' of that primal covenant, and seeks to reaffirm it – his major essay in civil theology is entitled *The Broken Covenant*.[2] But in a sense, whether its actual protagonists speak of it in covenant terms or not, the actual religious practice of second modernity – as the sacralizing of the secularization-process – is always essentially covenantal, just as much as that of first modernity.

And the new invitation that I would see opening up before us now is very much an invitation to move on, one stage further, along the same trajectory: towards an ever more authentically religious cosmopolitanism.

The Joachimist tradition

This movement onwards would be in the direction of a covenant that has not yet been sealed. Compare the prophecy of Jeremiah 31: 31–4:

> Behold, the days are coming, says Yahweh, when I will make a new covenant with the house of Israel and the house of Judah, not like the covenant which I made with their fathers when I took them by the hand to bring them out of the land of Egypt, my covenant which they broke, though I was their husband, says Yahweh. But this is the covenant which I will make with the house of Israel after those days, says Yahweh: I will put my law within them, and I will write it upon their hearts; and I will be their God, and they shall be my people. And no longer shall each man teach his neighbour and each his brother, saying, 'Know Yahweh', for they shall all know me, from the least of them to the greatest, says Yahweh; for I will forgive their iniquity, and I will remember their sin no more.

Traditional Christian theology has, of course, always sought to appropriate this prophecy as a reference to the founding of the church. But what interests me far more is the historic re-emergence, within Christendom, of the same sort of hope which Jeremiah himself originally entertained: the notion of a new covenant which is still to come.

In fact, such hope first bubbles up quite suddenly towards the end of the twelfth century – in the work of *Joachim of Fiore* (1145–1202). And something quite remarkable, I think, has happened here. Joachim may not have been all that sophisticated a theologian. Yet it nevertheless seems to me that, in a sense, he is the first Christian thinker since the apocalyptic upheavals of the apostolic period to have been really serious about history.

To take history seriously: I repeat that by this I mean to allow historical consciousness genuine shaking-power – or, in other words, positively to cultivate the very sharpest possible awareness of historical transience, even as regards what one's own community most automatically takes for granted when it comes to moral values and practice. To be sure, all explicitly covenant-founded religious thinking implies a certain shaken sense of history; and Christianity affirms a definitive incarnation, no less, of the eternal within history. Yet O'Donovan's polemic against 'historicism' actually has a very long and distinguished pedigree. Christian theologians have seldom been ready to think altogether incarnationally. Time and again, they have sought to maintain at least a little bit of a reserve.

Compare Joachim with Thomas Aquinas for example. (It is not that he is an especially bad offender – rather, I choose him just because of his exceptional greatness as a classic mediaeval representative of the tradition.) Faithful to biblical authority, Aquinas considers faith to be the very highest mode of thought. And yet consider how he defines 'faith'.

The basic error of Thomist theology seems to me to be succinctly encapsulated in one inconspicuous little article of the *Summa Theologiae*: 2a2ae Question 5, Article 1, where 'faith' is defined as that orientation towards God which redeemed humanity has in common with Adam and Eve before the Fall, and with the angels in their original condition. For the trouble is, this lifts 'faith', in its essence, right out of its original setting in community life as an historical phenomenon. Humanity before the Fall is humanity before history, and outside community. And neither do angels, as Aquinas conceives of them, have any community – inasmuch as each of them is a species apart from all the rest.[3] If such creatures may also be said to have 'faith' (and indeed, in his view, they have a higher form of faith than is possible for us)[4] then 'faith' would seem to be, in the first instance, a private affair; in our case, feeding into the historic life of the church – but not *primarily* determined as a critical reflection on the historicity of that life.

My objection, in short, is to what confessional theologians like Aquinas have in common with trans-confessional theologians like John Hick, discussed above. Both categories of thinker, in their opposing ways, present salvation as the ideal appropriation, not so much of one's historically shaken identity, but rather of truths which are supposed to transcend history. This is perhaps a partly justifiable reaction against the often quite destructive self-assurance of prophetic movements claiming special insight into the secrets of history. However, it is surely an overreaction. For such movements (it seems to me) are destructive only insofar as their hopes are linked to coercive power-claims. The problem lies in the coerciveness, not in the openness to historical novelty, as such.

Some three-quarters of a century after Joachim, Aquinas simply rejects the Joachimist hope for a new covenant still to come in favour of a more conventional view, allowing only an indefinite continuation of the present dispensation until the end of time.[5] This was also a far safer view from the perspective of the established church authorities, inasmuch as the present dispensation was of course just what their authority was based on. Not that Aquinas was a mere church-ideologist, far from it – Wilfred Cantwell Smith actually discusses the Thomist concept of faith at some length, to show just how different it is from later, more ideologized notions of faith-as-'belief'.[6] And yet it is clear that, in general, the more timeless – and therefore the more purely metaphysical – a theological vision is, the less likely it is to help stir up troublesome discontent with the way things presently are.

The Joachimist tradition, by contrast, has always been a troubling one.[7] Unlike the faith of which Thomist doctrine speaks, Joachimist faith is a virtue, necessarily, of historical beings. For it is not just the internalized acknowledgement of a past revelation of the eternal in history; at the same time, it also involves active public involvement in an ongoing historic revelation process.

This process is conceived by Joachim as being essentially threefold.[8] Thus, he sees world history as being divided up into three 'conditions' ('*status*'): three levels of revelation. In other words, three 'times' or 'ages' – corresponding to three covenants. The first age comprises everything represented by the Old Testament, the covenant-founded history of Israel; the second is inaugurated by the resurrection of the crucified. We speak of the 'New Testament', but 'testament' is just another translation for '*diathéké*', 'covenant'. The idea echoes through the letters of Paul, as well as Letter to the Hebrews; it is central to Christian worship: 'this is my blood of the new covenant'. But if there can be one such 'new covenant', why not another in turn? If God is Trinity, Joachim reasons, then surely the first age belongs pre-eminently to God the Father, the second to God the Son. And are we not therefore to expect yet a third age, also, belonging to God the Holy Spirit? In Joachim's view, everything depends upon our rightly discerning the advent of this new covenant which is still on its way.

Indeed, he thinks the forerunner has already come: St Benedict, in his role as the great original rule-giver for Western monasticism.[9] For the carrier-community of Joachim's grand narrative is to be the world of the religious orders; he himself was after all a reforming abbot.[10] And the third age, as he envisages it, will essentially consist of the global triumph of the monastic ethos, at its purest. Two new religious orders will be its harbingers:

an ideal order of hermits and an ideal order of preachers. The time, he suspects, is drawing near.

In many ways Joachim and Aquinas belong either side of a great cultural watershed. Aquinas's world was one of seething urban life, the university and the Inquisition. Joachim is a thinker shaped by a completely different environment – I am inclined to say a much more benign one, although also one which is much more alien to us. It is true that towns were growing in his day – but he was a monk in rural Calabria. Nor could anything be more different from Aquinas's new-fangled university style of thinking than Joachim's old-fashioned monastic style. In complete contrast to Aquinas, Joachim shows no sign of being influenced, in any way, by the challenge of classical philosophy. He argues, instead, in terms of an elaborate typological interpretation of the Bible: looking everywhere for what might be seen as allegorical anticipations of future events, and thereby constructing a great network of (more or less bizarre) symbolic associations. Much of his work consists of mnemonic diagrams and their interpretations – he loved tree-symbols for instance, where each branch represents a different historic figure or phenomenon. All in all, he inhabits a thought-world so remote from us today as to be virtually impenetrable.

Yet the sheer elemental power of his basic idea nevertheless radically transcends its original context, giving rise to a long history of subsequent developments and adaptations. And there is no doubt a certain sense – as I am happy to acknowledge – in which my own argument, here, also represents just one more twist to that same old tradition.

Joachim was in his own day a widely respected figure, receiving encouragement as a prophet from no less than three popes.[11] Some of his posthumous followers, however, were much wilder. The real turning point in 'official' attitudes to Joachimism came in 1255 when a certain Gerard of Borgo San Donnino produced an introduction to a selection of Joachim's writings, presenting them – in terms that would have horrified Joachim himself – as a new holy scripture for the imminent third age; the 'Eternal Evangel', superseding the New Testament. Others were especially interested in the role that Joachim had allotted to future religious orders.[12] Despite Aquinas's authoritative repudiation of Joachimism, there were at least some others among the early Dominicans who sought to apply his prophecies to their order, for instance. Certain Augustinian hermits made similar claims for themselves. So too, later on, did certain Jesuits. But the new order whose ethos could be seen as embodying the most dramatic break from the ways of the older church establishment was that of St Francis. And of all the orders, therefore, the Franciscans were perhaps the most natural candidates for the role of Joachimist pioneers. Joachimist ideas became a major inspiration to the Franciscan radicals, the 'Spirituals', in their long struggle against the 'Conventual' moderates. The struggle was, in the first instance, over the issue of how rigorously the community was to implement St Francis's original ideal of poverty: whether it should simply entail a lack of actual ownership, or a highly restricted use of goods as well. But Joachimist theology transformed this into a matter of the most urgent world-historical significance. By 1318 the Spirituals were defeated, and from that year onwards many were martyred for their extravagant hopes; yet in Italy the movement survived, outside the official order, well into the fifteenth century, as a continuing form of Joachimist organization.

Furthermore, Joachim's three-age scheme also acquired other non-monastic devotees. Among the social revolutionary Taborites of early fifteenth-century Bohemia, for example, there appears to have been a ferment of apocalyptic thinking, at least partly drawing on the Joachimist tradition. A similar ferment accompanied the beginnings of the Reformation. Thomas Müntzer, although he denied being a Joachimist, had read and admired at any rate the most influential of the various mediaeval forgeries attributed to Joachim, the *Super Hieremiam*.[13] Indeed, in one way or another, such interests appear to have been shared by all the more radical Reformers. And then, in the very different circumstances of the later eighteenth century, Lessing sought to appropriate the Joachimist scheme for the hopes of second modernity. The third age which Lessing looks forward to would be one where humanity had at long last learnt to love the rationality of Christian virtue for its own sake, independently of the confessional faith and church-loyalties hitherto associated with it as a guarantee of heavenly rewards. He attributes the same hope to the mediaeval Joachimists; and criticizes them only for the impatience of their 'enthusiasm'.[14] Joachimist ideas also thrived in the nineteenth century. The later thought of Schelling provides one notable example, as he sought to hitch the Joachimist tradition to the general cause of a new philosophically-transfigured post-Enlightenment religiousness.[15] Another, this time from the *milieu* of early Christian Socialism, is George Sand's exploration of Joachimist ideas in her novel *Spiridion*.[16] Whilst, in the twentieth century, one finds Ernst Bloch for instance seeking to integrate Joachim as an authoritative figure into the larger prehistory of Marxism.[17]

Towards a post-metaphysical Trinitarianism

Some of these adaptations are more convincing than others. But what of Joachim's own theory? Its most fundamental weakness, I think, lies in its Trinitarian aspect. The direct correlation here of the three persons of the Trinity to three successive ages is surely far too hasty. Thus, given that this appears to be what essentially determines the distinctness of each divine person for Joachim – and that the second and third age are understood entirely to subsume, as well as to extend, the truth of what precedes them – then it becomes very hard to see in what sense the three persons can possibly be said to be co-equal. Joachim still affirms their 'immanent', transhistorical equality in theory; but only, apparently, out of formal deference to authority. And the result is not just a major implicit break with orthodoxy.

It also seems, in effect, to empty the dogma of too much of its traditional meaning.

Joachim's theory arises out of a context in which the dogma of the Trinity had, in effect, been almost entirely reduced to the level of a metaphysical conundrum; and it is certainly a bold attempt to rediscover some more than merely metaphysical meaning here. But what would a post-metaphysical response to the Trinity look like, which actually held fast to the original *pre*-metaphysical meaning of the dogma?

At all events, if one considers how the early church first arrived at its perception of God's fundamental three-in-oneness, the threeness in that context was not the threeness of three ages. It seems to me, in fact, far more accurate to say that – besides registering three aspects of the divine presence within biblical narrative – it also corresponded to the threeness of the following three quite distinct areas of urgently shaken theological conversation in the early church:

(a) As a missionary movement spreading Hebrew monotheism especially among Greek-speaking pagans, early Christianity found itself situated at a point of tectonic collision between two completely different post-Axial cultures – so that Christian theology rears up like a sort of intellectual Himalayas from the resulting problematics. The early Christian theologians of the post-apostolic period were men who had been trained in the traditions of Greek philosophy, and who therefore now needed to reconcile those traditions with those of the Bible. Hence they were caught up into conversations about the latent identity of the God of the Bible with the Platonist 'Idea of the Good', the Aristotelian 'unmoved mover', the Stoic 'seminal logos'. And in such conversations the idea of God's universal 'fatherhood', embracing the peoples of all different intellectual cultures, naturally had a special resonance.

(b) Christian converts' experience of conflict with the surrounding world, whose ways they had so controversially rejected, also required talking through. They were dissidents who needed to justify their dissent, whether in conversation with one another or with their pagan relatives and neighbours. These conversations were all about the demands of following the paradigmatic way of the cross, as pioneered by the incarnate Son of God.

(c) The early Christian church was a new religious movement. In breaking loose from the binding authority of Jewish religious law, as such, it was left largely without any definitive precedents to determine its practice. Much of its theological conversation, accordingly, revolved around problems of organizational improvization. Here, God was invoked above all as the encourager ('the Paraclete'), the inspirer of wise decision-making, the Holy Spirit.

Christian theology emerges as a Trinitarian enterprise, in the first instance, by virtue of its being a single over-arching shaken conversation-process in which each of these primary areas of discussion are equally involved; herein surely lies its original pre-metaphysical rationale.

But the lessons of this specific historical experience may also be generalized in trans-confessional terms. As a general rule, one might well argue, there are three key types of possible stimuli that give rise to shaken conversation: the experience of encounter with other cultures which are both alien and yet attractive; the experience of being confronted by a fundamentally hostile ruling order; and the experience of having startlingly unprecedented opportunities open up before one. The first two are opposing ways of experiencing the otherness of other already existing ways of life; the third involves an intuition of the potential otherness of the future. Conversation responsive to the first stimulus has as its presiding ideal the virtue of culture-transcendent intellectual generosity; the essential demand of the second is for the virtue of a robust free-spiritedness; the third demands an ideal sort of flair for tradition as a creative enterprise.[18] And when the traditional dogma speaks of three divine 'Persons', each 'Person' is surely best understood as that living truth which appears in and through the animation of one of these virtues – the primary virtues of the solidarity of the shaken.[19]

For, after all, what is it that *internally* constitutes a 'person'? A person is precisely a conversation-process. Or a contained set of conversations. In the case of the individual human being, one's personality may be said to emerge out of the conversations between the voice or voices of conscience, the voice or voices of ambition, the voice or voices of sensual desire; or between the internalized voices of one's parents, one's peers, society at large, and the sometimes resistant voice of the ego. So too in the case of corporate persons, a category which I take to include not only what in Roman law are called '*universitates*', that is, 'persons' in the formal sense of being potential corporate litigants – states and other political institutions, business enterprises, educational, charitable or religious organizations – but also, more informally, nations, clans, distinctive cultural groupings of every kind. A corporate person becomes a 'person' by virtue of representing a certain clearly bounded framework for public conversation, of a particular character. And is it not the same with the Trinity?

However, to speak of a conversation as constituting a 'person' is not only to register its distinctiveness; it is, at the same time, immediately, to relativize that distinctiveness. A person becomes a person only in relation to other persons. So Hegel, for instance, speaks of the distinctiveness of persons as their 'abstract personality'. But, as he remarks, 'in friendship and love I give up my abstract personality and thereby win it back as concrete. The truth of personality is found precisely in winning it back through this immersion, this being immersed in the other.'[20] Each of the conversation-processes in question here is at once 'immersed' in the other two; there is no polemical opposition between them. It is just that in each case the configuration is different, with a different overall agenda, suggesting different emphases.

The three Persons of the Trinity cannot in this case be crudely correlated, as Joachim would correlate them, to three successive ages. For they are made manifest in three qualities of shaken conversation which are equally a potential feature of every age. A proper post-metaphysical interpretation here would need to get back behind the pattern of three ages, to encounter the three Persons rather as three perennially re-emergent agencies of cultural shake-up – of strictly incommensurable complementary significance.

And yet, even so, it still seems to me that Joachim's proclamation of an impending new age of the Holy Spirit does represent quite a momentous theological advance. For it has indeed often been remarked that the theology of the Third Person remained relatively underdeveloped in patristic thinking. By far the greater emphasis was placed on determining the proper interrelationship of the First and Second Persons.[21] This is because the initial impulse to Third-Person theology soon started to lose its urgency. As the church began to develop its own authoritative tradition, the need for charismatic improvization correspondingly dwindled; the more precedents there were to follow the less problematic the question seemed, how to discern the Holy Spirit's fresh guidance. But Joachim's thought served, in the most dramatic fashion, to reopen that issue all over again.

In its essence, Third-Person theology is all about reading the signs of the times, on the understanding that this may also entail all manner of revisionary reinterpretation of the past. And that is the task which Joachim, so to speak, rediscovers.

There are, so far as I can see, two great pioneers in the history of Third-Person theology. The first is Joachim. And the second is Hegel. Of course, Hegel is an incomparably more sophisticated thinker, as well as being a much more cautious one. He needs to be more sophisticated, not least because he is so much more cautious – whilst nevertheless being driven by such an intrinsically subversive underlying critical impulse. Hegel is a prophet half hidden within a philosopher. But what else after all does he mean by 'absolute knowing', if not the philosophic sealing of a new covenant which has still to be implemented in public practice?[22]

What I want to affirm of new social movements, as agencies of the solidarity of the shaken, is at least loosely analogous to what Joachim, in the world of first modernity, wanted to affirm of shaken monks; or what Hegel, as a protagonist of second modernity, implicitly wanted to affirm of shaken religious secularizers.

Primarily a concept proper to Third-Person theology, third modernity – with its radical trans-confessionalism, its infinite thirst for social transformation, its loose-structured openness to organizational and therefore also to intellectual experimentation – is indeed a profoundly Trinitarian prospect. In the deepest sense, it is perhaps more truly Trinitarian than any form of first or second modernity can be; the most decisive sublation, thus, of Joachimist hope.

12 The other matrix: Islamic civil society

New social movements are an intrinsically trans-confessional type of phenomenon; therefore, only a trans-confessional approach can ultimately do full theological justice to their distinctive promise. And yet, it might be objected, so far my whole concern has been to try and situate such a project in relation to the Christian tradition, and to legitimate it in specifically Christian terms.

This is, first of all, just because I am myself a Christian. It is the Christian confessional tradition with which I am most familiar, and in relation to which my thinking has most immediately been formed.

But, at the same time, another reason is that my argument is also a modernist one – and Christendom was the original matrix of modernity. The ideal of a third modernity is relatively easy to reconcile with *non*-modern religious traditions. Theirs, after all, is another order of truth altogether. They have not already been identified with a directly rival, earlier mode of grand narrative, as is the case with Christianity. As a result, one does not have the same opportunity to find direct precedents within their confessional inheritance for what now needs doing trans-confessionally. Neither, however – in relation to them – does one have quite the same urgent apologetic *need* to locate and uphold such precedents, so as to keep alive a mutually beneficial conversation between trans-confessional and confessional thought. For there is no real equivalent, within these other traditions, to the sort of systematic resistance which derives from Christian recoil-theology.

Nevertheless, it is true that Christianity is not the only religious matrix of modernity: for there is also *Islam*.

If Christianity has a special, difficult relationship to the ongoing processes of world-history, as such, so too does Islam. And clearly, therefore, my argument would not be complete without at least some parallel consideration of the Islamic problematics as well.

Fresh traumas

Christian theology, I have suggested, has a peculiar liability to ideologization due to the original traumas of church history. Nietzsche, notoriously, declared that Christian ethics was in essence 'slave morality': an expression of sublimated *resentment* on the part of the lower orders, as one-sided in its social bias as the older 'master morality' which it overthrew – only more vindictively and less honestly so. This is of course a caricature. But let us at any rate concede that – human nature being what it is – a culture shaped, or still haunted, by the experiences of being persecuted is indeed somewhat unlikely to have much energy to spare for the more searching and strenuous forms of intellectual honesty. Fanaticism is the more likely outcome. And if one is persecuted it is, after all, not unnatural that one's ethical thinking should become just a little soured in consequence.

The Islamic tradition, on the other hand, was almost entirely spared such experiences in its originally formative years, because from the very beginning it was spread by conquest.

Both traditions possess powerful symbolic resources for the articulation of the solidarity of the shaken, but in two sharply contrasting emotional registers, with I think complementary truth-potential. Thus, the chief obligatory practice with which Christians directly commemorate the origins of their tradition, by the ritual re-enactment of one of its primal events, is the Eucharist. The closest Islamic equivalent, in this particular regard, is the *hajj*, the pilgrimage to Mecca; and the associated *'id al-adha* – the feast, observed world-wide, which coincides with the offering of the pilgrim sacrifice.

The Eucharist is all about paradox: the paradoxical transformation of the most apparently mundane or dismal of worldly realities into a manifestation of the heavenly. Bread and wine are transformed into the body and blood of Christ; the bitter worldly memory of Christ's last supper with his disciples is transformed into a memory of impending heavenly triumph. Yet that triumph still depends, for its meaningfulness, upon the bitterness. To put it in Hegelian terms, Christ symbolizes the ideal antithesis to the unhappiness of the mentally servile 'unhappy consciousness' essentially by virtue of his willingness to embrace even the utter misery of death on the cross as the price of escaping it. The Eucharist symbolically represents the solidarity of the shaken at its most embattled and darkest.

But the symbolism of the *hajj*, by contrast, represents it in the most altogether cheerful and festive of guises. There is no paradox here; no need for paradox. This great cosmopolitan throng is the most straightforward possible embodiment and representation of Islamic solidarity generally. The pilgrimage is for everyone. Distinctions of tribe and race or social class drop away. Every pilgrim wears the same simple white robes, and performs the same rites in the same sequence together with all the others, as the Prophet once did: processing round the Ka'ba; hurrying seven times back and forth between the hills of Safaa and Marwa to remember Hagar and Ishmael; standing in meditation from noon until sunset on Mount Arafat, before settling down to sleep at Muzdalifa; recalling Abraham's resistance to temptation by throwing pebbles at the pillars in Mina; and then offering the sacrifice of sheep and camels nearby. The whole heady experience is designed to shake the pilgrims right out of their everyday existence, and to bond them together in that shakenness, delightfully.

Of course, Christianity may also be exuberant, and Muslims may also be ascetic. Only, it is a question of what most decisively sets the tone: the truth of Christianity lies in a memory of torture, transfigured; the truth of Islam lies in a jubilant actual experience of cultural barriers coming down. Granted, Christianity also has its pilgrimages. But they have never had the same significance. They could not have. It is a basic precondition for the radical significance of the *hajj* that the Islamic *umma* was from the beginning a religious community in political control of its key sacred sites. Since it did not in its formative period suffer persecution by religiously alien rulers, it never grew into anything like a church; it did not need all those defence mechanisms. And without the disruptive presence of any equivalent to a church, the political society of Islamic first modernity was always far more unified in its basic structure than that of Christendom. The dynastic disputes and tribal feuds of the first Islamic century did generate two ongoing dissident communities, the Kharijites and the Shi'ites, and it is true that the latter have ever since remained a substantial minority, bitterly recalling their early defeats and sometimes – especially in the Islamic thirteenth century, the Christian nineteenth century – experiencing some harassment on their way to Mecca. Yet this was only sometimes; and they were never altogether excluded. In terms of the internal life of its great empires, mainstream traditional Sunni Islam mostly tended to be a rather peaceable sort of establishment religion. It was, in short, the very last place that one would expect to find the sort of covertly resentful and vindictive 'slave morality' at work which Nietzsche diagnosed as the all too typical disease of Christianity.[1]

But, clearly, with the more recent rise of Islamic 'fundamentalism' something else has now emerged. The spirit of these new movements – so radically inimical to the ethos of third modernity – is also a very far cry from that of the earlier Muslim centuries.

This is surely all to do with the shock of second modernity. That shock served to bring some healing to the Christian psyche; but second modernity arrived in the Muslim world very much as an alien imposition, imported from Christendom. In Christendom it had arisen, in the first instance, as a liberating protest against the grosser corruptions of Christian first modernity: the religious wars and the coercive thought-control. Islamic first modernity, however, had never been seriously subject to such corruptions. The allure of 'Western' secularism to Muslim rulers lay rather in its close association with the sheer political might of Europe and the USA. They

sought to 'modernize' in order to compete. The promotion of secular education, the development of secular political parties and secular bureaucracies,
the demand for legal reform to reflect the unprecedented newness of a new
age rather than the authority of sacred tradition – all of these characteristic
projects of second modernity have for the most part been presented in terms
of the reproduction of already existing Western models. Their Muslim advocates have been people deeply impressed by Western military and economic
superiority, who have seen the technological sophistication of the West as
deriving from the 'progressiveness' of its social mores in other respects as
well, and have wanted their world to catch up.

The whole process was thus intimately bound up with the great trauma of
Islam's global encounter with Western imperialism. And Islamic 'fundamentalism' arises largely as an alternative, more defiant response to the perceived
humiliation of that same encounter. Spared any equivalent to the original
traumas of Christendom, and the attendant consequences, the Muslim
world has now for the first time been hit by major traumas of its own. As a
result of which, substantial sections of the *umma* appear, for the time being,
to have caught the old Christian disease – in quite a feverish form.

The half-forgotten heritage

There are naturally some individuals within the Muslim world who have
appropriated aspects of the new social movement ethos: feminists in particular, defenders of endangered civil liberty, and campaigners for the poor. In
places they are also well organized. But the thriving of new social movements, in general, very much depends upon the thriving of a larger
independent civil society as their host environment. And, on the whole,
Islamic civil society tends nowadays to be at a rather low ebb.

Meanwhile, all that is most poisonous in the legacy of 'Western' second
modernity increasingly takes shape as Islamophobia; which in turn helps
generate a reaction in the Islamic world against all things perceived as
Western – including unfortunately the pioneering Western developments
towards third modernity. Which then reinforces the Islamophobia ...

There can be no denying the gravity of the problem. This syndrome is
indeed one of the main reasons for not confusing a hope for third modernity
with any very immediate actual expectation of its triumph, anywhere.

The most one can aim to show, in response, is that at any rate there is
nothing in Islamic tradition which *necessarily* prevents the development of a
vigorous civil society.

But, as it happens, it is quite easy to demonstrate the aberrance of the
present situation in that regard: one has only to consider the past. The great
Islamic empires of the past were, after all, home to a very vigorous and free-
spirited civil society. It is just that people forget.

During the mid-1970s I spent two of the happiest years of my life
working as a teacher in the small provincial town of Qena in Upper Egypt.

(It was a small town then, much larger now.) My home at first was a little hut on the roof of a block of flats in the centre of town; but, since it almost never rains, I used to sleep outside – so much cooler than indoors – under a mosquito net and the stars. After the evening traffic had subsided, the night air would be filled with a low murmur of voices, a clatter of dominoes and backgammon, the croaking of frogs. And then, sometimes, in the distance one could hear the flutes of a Sufi (or dervish) *dhikr*.

It was a time of intense religious revival in Egypt: a quest for consolation, or some deeper, more reliable source of hope than the secular world could provide, after the terrible shock of defeat by Israel in the war of 1967. Every type of local religious tradition was flourishing, including Sufism – with the government's blessing. And Qena was a major Sufi centre. Every Friday there would be one or two groups of dervishes gathered outside the mosque of the town's great Sufi saint, Sidi 'Abd ar-Raheem al-Qenawi, rhythmically swaying together, swinging their arms and chanting the name of Allah, to the accompaniment of a flautist and a hymn-singer equipped with crackling microphones. The fringes of the desert nearby were dotted with the shrines of saints, little mausoleums with flags fluttering; occasionally, too, a procession would pass down the street, with a gaily decorated camel and braying fifes, to celebrate a saint's birthday. The dervishes themselves, however, appeared to be drawn mostly from the poorest classes: men clothed in rather threadbare gallabiyas, with now and then an ill-fitting military uniform in amongst them. Certainly the people I got to know, that is to say, the people who could speak English – my colleagues and students – did not have much good to say about this tradition. They tended to see it as something irredeemably 'superstitious', vulgar and old-fashioned. Nor did they appear to have any knowledge of its history.

In fact, though, for many centuries the Sufi religious orders were the chief large-scale structures of Islamic civil society – along with the artisan and trade guilds, with which they were in many instances closely linked. And it seems to me that, at least in some periods of their history, they did actually represent a most remarkable Islamic anticipation of the solidarity of the shaken in organized form.

The evolution of the orders represents a classic case of a charismatic movement being progressively routinized in the process of achieving missionary success.[2] From its second/eighth-century origins, Sufi culture arose out of the informal communities of often itinerant devotees, which then began spontaneously to crystallize around particular holy men. From the fourth/tenth century these started to attract financial sponsorship from the government or from wealthy members of the ruling class, in the form of endowments for Sufi hostels (*khanaqahs*). The period between the sixth/twelfth and eighth/fourteenth centuries saw for the first time the formal development of traditions or 'chains' of transmitted authority, constituting distinctive associations, each with their own doctrine, rule of community life and methods of communal prayer. This was also when much of the finest

Sufi literature was produced: for example, the work of Suhrawardi al-Maqtal (d. 587/1191), al-'Attar (d. 627/1230), Ibn al-Farid (d. 631/1234), Ibn al-'Arabi (d. 638/1240), al-Rumi (d. 672/1273), Ibn 'Ata' Allah (d. 709/1309) and Yunus Emre (d. 720/1320). In the ninth/fifteenth century the literature largely dries up. And yet the orders continued to thrive thereafter – now as mass-membership organizations, devoted to the cult of their saints, increasingly with hereditary leadership, and indeed with strong family traditions of membership. In Christendom the monastic orders were from the beginning caught up in the church's struggle to establish its own institutional loyalty-claims as taking precedence over those of family and tribe; hence their fundamental insistence on celibacy. But for the Sufi orders it was not so. Instead, they achieved an easy symbiosis with local family and tribal culture wherever they spread.

The Sufi orders promoted Islam as a religious culture for civil society; the *'ulama*, meanwhile, represented the legal-religious aspect of Islamic political society. There was, no doubt, always a certain element of tension in this relationship. And yet it is, by and large, remarkable how seldom it actually erupted into serious conflict. The Sufi tradition counts two celebrated martyrs, who died as victims to the hostility of the *'ulama*: al-Hallaj in the fourth/tenth century and Suhrawardi al-Maqtal in the sixth/twelfth. Prior to Ibn 'Abd al-Wahhab in the twelfth/eighteenth century, however, no major Sunni leader ever went so far as to denounce Sufism in itself.[3] Criticism was always restricted to what were seen as particular excesses. Not even that admittedly formidable critic, and especial hero both to the Wahhabis and to the radicals of today, Ibn Taymiyya (d. 728/1328), could imagine Islam altogether without Sufism.

On the other hand, it was not only the literature of mysticism that dried up. The same thing had also happened to Islamic philosophy. Despite the promising foundations laid, in particular, by al-Farabi (d. 340/950) and Ibn Sina (d. 429/1037), the practice of philosophy never managed to take enduring hold in Islamic culture. Ibn Rushd (d. 575/1198) was the last original thinker of the tradition. Why were there no more? What was it that made Christian Europe, eventually, so much more productive in this regard? It seems to me, in fact, to be very largely just another consequence of the far greater degree of underlying structural harmony in Islamic society. Both philosophy and the literature of mysticism thrive best in the context of unresolved struggles for cultural hegemony, to which such writings partly contribute. The ceaseless struggle within Christendom between the upholders of the church-institution and its critics, at first dissident clerical defenders of the laity, then independent lay philosophers, created the ideal climate for such creativity. Islamic culture was intellectually less productive, in the end – because it was happier.[4]

There are two particular areas where the Sufi orders continue to constitute the dominant form of Islam today: sub-Saharan Africa and the successor-states to the former Soviet Union. Especially in Chechnya and elsewhere in the northern Caucasus, but also in the Central Asian republics and in Azerbaijan, they represented perhaps the most resilient of all the various forms of civil society under Soviet rule. In the circumstances, it is indeed a remarkable record. Whereas active participant membership in most Christian churches was, from the late 1920s onwards, effectively confined to the less educated classes, to the elderly, and to women, the Sufis in their strongholds went on recruiting from all the main categories of the population alike; and, despite being officially banned, managed to remain genuine mass organizations.[5] They survived six decades of at times quite savage persecution – which left the official Islamic establishment, the community's representatives at the level of political society, decimated.[6] The price of that establishment's attenuated survival was its total public compliance with the regime. But the Sufi orders, by contrast, were never regulated. The 'progressive' *'ulama*, the natural agents of such regulation on the state's behalf, no longer had the capacity to undertake the task even if they wanted to.

Everywhere else, though – and Egypt in this respect is quite typical – the prevailing trend over the past several decades has been in the exact opposite direction. Islamic political society has been transformed by the emergence of two new movements, both highly ideologized and unprecedentedly aggressive in their reforming ambitions. The first of these is secularizing party-political Nationalism. The second is what, in its more militant forms, is commonly known as 'fundamentalism'. But I prefer the term 'Salafism': from the Arabic *salafiyya*, meaning 'fidelity to the earliest origins of the tradition' – which, unlike 'fundamentalism', has the fundamental merit of being readily acceptable to those it is meant to designate.[7]

The element of commonality between secularizers and Salafists

The secularizing impulse of second modernity has only ever made much headway in the Muslim world where it has hitched itself onto an ideological Nationalism. But this option for Nationalism is already in itself a basic act of rebellion against the older Islamic ethos. Nationalism, after all, is fundamentally a product of Christian culture, in which linguistic difference is given free play both religiously and politically. It may be said to originate in Western Europe (perhaps first of all in England) at the same time as the translation of holy Scripture, out of the universal language of Latin, into the vernacular.[8] Such a development could never have spontaneously emerged out of Islamic culture, in which the sacred authority of the Qur'an is so closely identified with its original Arabic text, as such. Moreover, it seems to pull directly away from the essential symbolism of the *hajj* – as a celebratory ritual enactment, precisely, of pan-Islamic internationalism.

The pre-eminent protagonist of secular Nationalism in an Islamic context is Mustafa Kemal Atatürk. When Atatürk decreed the abolition of the Ottoman caliphate in 1924, this was partly just a recognition of the inevitable: insofar as the Ottoman sultans had been able to lay effective claim to the proper global moral authority of caliphs, it was because they were the rulers of the one and only surviving Sunni empire; with the demise of that empire at the end of the First World War the claim could scarcely any longer be maintained. But, at the same time, Atatürk's move was also a decisive affirmation of Turkish Nationalism – as something radically opposed to the older Ottoman ideology of pan-Islam, promoted especially by Sultan Abdülhamid II (1876–1909). This ideologization of the pan-Islamic ideal served (like pan-Slavism in Tsarist Russia for instance) to invest what would otherwise have been a rather humdrum form of authoritarian conservatism with all the glamour and excitement of a full-scale world-historical movement.[9] But Atatürk, for his part, repudiated this particular ideologized version of pan-Islamism only in order to replace it with an equally ideologized form of 'modernization'.[10]

Atatürk's primary aim was to break the power of the conservative *ulema* as an establishment within political society. But this then issued in an all-encompassing process of cultural revolution which also brought the regime into irreconcilable conflict with the Sufi orders. Islamic law was repealed, and replaced with European civil and penal codes; religious education under the control of the *ulema* was first restricted, then banned; the traditional Arabic script was replaced by a version of the Latin alphabet; it was decreed that the muezzin's call to prayer should henceforth be in Turkish rather than Arabic; and a new dress code was imposed, including the symbolic replacement of the fez by European hats. For such a far-reaching project to be pushed through, despite widespread popular resistance, the regime clearly needed to place quite drastic restrictions on the autonomy of civil society. In the period leading up to the First World War a number of prominent figures within the Sufi orders had been active in the progressive movement of the Young Turks; and, in the same spirit, there had actually been strong dervish involvement in the earlier stages of Atatürk's own movement, from 1918–20. Nevertheless, in November 1925 his government also – at a stroke – dissolved the orders, nationalized all their very considerable assets, and banned them from any future corporate activity whatsoever.

It is true, none of the other Nationalist movements in the Muslim world have ever gone quite as far as Atatürk did in Turkey. And yet, even where the conflict has been less extreme, the fact is the ethos of such movements has always been fundamentally alien to that of Sufism – whilst the new party-political organizations naturally function as a rival mode of popular social bonding. So that it is, at any rate, surely no coincidence that wherever Muslim-majority nationalistic political parties have gained power and put down roots the Sufi orders have at the same time tended to decline.

The hostility of the radical Salafists to Sufism, meanwhile, is still more emphatic. For Salafism is an appeal to the authority of the earliest origins of Islamic tradition; and therefore to that which pre-dates the emergence of Sufism. From the pure Salafist's perspective it is as though everything that happened later – including the development of the Sufi orders – merely amounts to a steady process of decline, culminating in the eventual lamentable vulnerability of Islamic civilization to the violence of Western imperialism.

Sufism seeks to build up Islamic religious community-life from below, for its own sake as a testimony to divine love; mature Salafism by contrast aims at the governmental imposition of 'pure' Islamic law, from above. Its community-building is strictly incidental to that strategic goal. Salafists and conservative Sufis are at one in their rejection of second modernity; yet they are two entirely different modes of rejection. The pioneering Egyptian Salafist Hasan al-Banna ran the two together when he defined the Muslim Brotherhood, which he founded in 1928, as 'a Salafist call and Sunni order, a Sufi reality ...'.[11] He was speaking here as a populist, seeking to maximize the appeal of this first Salafist mass movement. And the formula also encapsulates a certain ambivalence in the early identity of the Brotherhood: as regards the extent to which they were to be, like the Sufi orders, primarily a consciousness-raising pressure group within civil society, or else a Salafist party within political society. But from the late 1930s onwards, once they had become well established, the second option clearly began to prevail. And so it was that, shortly thereafter, they started to develop their own paramilitary organization and even to engage in the politics of terror.

There is indeed a sense in which Salafism, generally, began as a rival movement aiming to displace Sufism within civil society,[12] and only later developed into a project aiming positively to repel the political inroads of second modernity. Al-Banna derived his Salafist ideology largely from the Syrian Rashid Rida, who was in turn a disciple of Muhammad 'Abdu, perhaps the real founder of the Salafist tradition. Under 'Abdu's leadership a new Islamic reform movement had emerged amongst Egyptian intellectuals from the 1880s onwards. This movement was Salafist in the sense of arguing for a return to the sources of the faith, purging it of the accretions to which the Sufis, and their allies amongst the *'ulama*, were attached. Yet his relationship to the secular rationalism of second modernity was on the whole quite respectfully apologetic. Nor did Rida for instance, who continued the same struggle, have any difficulty in combining it with his own brand of pan-Arab/Syrian Nationalism.

Salafism only began to become primarily anti-secularist when faced with the secularism of new post-colonial Nationalist governments. And then the struggle against these rivals within political, rather than civil, society rapidly escalated. The two key figures in this development are the Pakistani Abu'l-A'la Mawdudi and the Egyptian Sayyid Qutb. Mawdudi founded the Jama'at-i Islami in 1941 as a Salafist political party to rival the nationalistic Muslim League, as the League manœuvred to assume power once the British had left. And in his denunciations of the League he pioneered a decisive escalation in Salafist rhetoric: he argued that the secularizing impulse was plunging the Muslim world back into a new *jahiliyya* – that is to say a new 'age of ignorance', a new 'barbarism'. *Jahiliyya* is primarily a term for the polytheistic culture of pre-Islamic Arabia. Second modernity, in Mawdudi's judgement, is as bad as that, or as un-Islamic as polytheistic Hinduism. The Rida and al-Banna had seen their secularizing enemies as decadent Muslims; but Mawdudi, fighting against essentially the same forces, saw it as a battle against outright apostasy. For him a secularizing 'Muslim' government, like that of the Muslim League, is no longer really Muslim at all.

Qutb (who was later to be martyred under the Nasser regime in 1966) then went one step further: by seeking to appropriate the concept of *jihad*, the sacred duty of holy warfare, for the anti-secularist struggle. Insofar as it refers to actual armed conflict, *jihad* had hitherto almost exclusively been applied to warfare against professed non-Muslims. There was just one exception to which Qutb was able to appeal as a precedent: the mediaeval rigorist Ibn Taymiyya and his disciple Ibn Kathir had urged armed resistance to the Mongols as a form of *jihad* even after the Mongol regime had professedly converted to Islam, justifying this use of the category on the grounds that the Mongols' conversion had only been nominal. In the same way, Qutb argued, *jihad* must also be waged against 'nominally' Muslim rulers today, who pursue secularizing policies.[13]

These are indeed extraordinary innovations – which are, one might think, rather hard to reconcile with the all-inclusive reconciliatory symbolism of the *hajj*. This sort of fanatical intolerance has of course been a recurrent feature of Christian history. But in the Muslim world it is really quite odd, and new.

For the Salafist radicals, the great Westernizer Atatürk has become a prime symbol of evil. Nothing could more eloquently express Qutb's abhorrence of the Nasser regime, for instance, than his identification of Nasser with Atatürk. Let us note, however, the clear element of Western influence also on Salafism itself. Much of the Salafists' party-political organization and propaganda-strategy is derived from Western models – both al-Banna and Mawdudi, in the 1920s and 1930s, were admirers from afar of the European Fascist and Nazi movements, in particular.

The two sides, Salafists and Nationalists, feed off each other's fury, each pointing to the undoubted menace of the other in order to justify their own excesses. And, unfortunately, neither side in the heat of the struggle feels secure enough to show any very serious respect for the liberties of civil society.

Perhaps though, in a world of new propaganda-technologies and vast bureaucracies, a culture can only in the end be immunized against the concomitant dangers of totalitarianism by itself having some actual experience of the misery it brings. In post-revolutionary Iran a liberalizing, chastened neo-Salafist movement has at length arisen, explicitly speaking of the need for a resurgence of civil society, after so many years of its having been suppressed in the immediate wake of the revolution. Nor is there any reason to suppose that Islamic culture is for ever condemned to be locked into its current conflicts. Inasmuch as these essentially seem to derive from two contradictory responses to the shock of temporary defeat by Western imperialism – and not from anything more deep-rooted in the tradition – the long-term future is surely still wide open. Muslim tradition, after all, contains so much else which entirely transcends the narrow terms of this particular struggle.

13 'Holy, Catholic and Apostolic'

So much, then, for the claims of third modernity in relation to the major already existing traditions of modernist religion, both Christian and Islamic.

But now let us spin the argument, briefly, around. Let us also ask: *what of the general claims of religion – in relation to third modernity?*

Of course, the new social movements which are the potential carrier-communities of third modernity have a great many adherents who remain quite irreligious. So – how might one try to vindicate the sort of sustained and sympathetic conversation with religious traditions which I am advocating, specifically to such sceptics? This cannot be a matter of metaphysical apologetics. Metaphysics is concerned with the criticism and defence of particular belief-systems; but what I am concerned with here is not any particular belief-system. It is, precisely, a species of conversation.

What does religion – *as such* – have to offer at that level?

I am inclined to answer, two main things:

(a) a vigorous spiritual community of intellectuals with non-intellectuals; and
(b) a thought-provoking spiritual communion of the progressively-minded with the past.

By 'spiritual' I mean grounded in shaken thoughtfulness. The community of intellectual with non-intellectual in a religious context is thus, in principle, quite different from their more immediate emotional community in a shared national or ethnic identity. And true religious rootedness differs radically from the rootedness that finds expression in a xenophobic ideology. It depends, rather, on that which is unique to religion: namely, its sheer poetic power. For the simple fact is that no other form of communication has such power to speak – of the most disturbing things – direct to the hearts of people from every social class, so as to create a community in which each class is enabled to hold the others critically to account; or such power to bring the disturbing testimony of the past vividly back to mind, in a living community context.

Admittedly, to be the adherent of a new social movement and at the same time also to be the follower of a confessional religious tradition is to have two loyalties which are more or less bound to come into some conflict with one another. The virtue of this situation, however, lies in the provocation to thought it produces, as each loyalty becomes the potential basis for a critique of the other.

Of course, the contradictions of mixed loyalty are often frustrating. And campaigning temperaments, above all, are no doubt always somewhat liable to yearn for an ideal community of the like-minded. But let us note the potential destructiveness of the resulting *sectarian impulse* – as one surely has to call it – even in the very purest of new social movement contexts.

Deadly Innocence

Thus, by way of vivid illustration, consider for example Angela West's theological reflections, in her book *Deadly Innocence*, on the story of the Greenham Common peace camp.[1]

The Greenham story does indeed seem to be a rather striking cautionary tale. For, to begin with, the peace camp was so extraordinarily successful in its symbolic fusing together of two of the most powerful new social movements active in the Britain of the 1980s: the anti-nuclear peace movement and the feminist movement.

It all started in the summer of 1981, shortly after NATO medium-range nuclear cruise missiles had been installed at the local USAF/RAF base. That summer, following a protest march from Cardiff, a group called Women for Life on Earth settled down to camp outside the various gates of the base, to give urgent expression to their sense of the sheer insanity of this NATO policy. And there they stayed, as an ongoing focus for protest.

The camp had always been primarily a women's initiative, and from February 1983 onwards it became a women-only space. So it came to represent a challenge not just to NATO nuclear-terrorist militarism in itself but, by extension, to the whole underlying patriarchal ethos of that militarism – as a systematic institutional channelling of male aggression. The Greenham protest was directed against the deployment of genocidal technology, essentially, as so many 'toys for the boys'. West herself was not one of the camp-members, but an active supporter. And she records both the camp's rise and its fall.

In December 1982 some 30,000 women came together at Greenham to 'embrace the base':

> To pause over this snapshot of ourselves embracing the base is for many women no doubt to open the floodgates of nostalgia for the early days. Here we are as we like to remember ourselves – thousands of women publicly taking strong 'womanly' action for peace; women creating their own space and at the same time reclaiming the common space that had been misappropriated by the men with their military machine. It was a

time of wonderful imagery and disarming tactics as women pioneered new forms of non-violent direct action like embracing the base of male power, besieging it with women's bodies, rocking their fences until they collapsed, snipping holes in the chain mail of male armour (the perimeter fence), hanging out the nappies on their defences, keeping watch on those appointed to be our protectors ...

Then, however, over the following years the sectarian impulse began to take hold:

The camp continued to survive and endure in gruelling conditions, against all expectations, and to attract support from a wide spectrum of women. But as time went on, it also began to change. The new mode of women's sexuality and freedom that had marked its early days lost something of the playful quality it had possessed even amid the utter seriousness of the women's intention to defend the planet against the imminent threat of its destruction. Contact with men that was not confrontational became seriously polluting, and a fierce new puritanism began to undermine the relations of women who lived in or supported the camps. Women's space now became territory that had to be defended – even eventually from other women, those who did not measure up to the ideal of gender purity that Greenham had come to stand for. What began as a movement of women loving women and making space for each other ended up with women tearing each other apart in the name of sisterhood. By a sad and telling irony, the latter days of the camp at Greenham Common became a spectacle of peace women split into two hostile camps and locked in bitter strife with one another.[2]

In the end, there developed a virtual cold war between the women at one gate and those at the others. So West describes a situation in which one woman, refusing to accept the new sectarian party line of the community at the gate where she was settled, found herself ostracized:

Groups fell silent as she approached, no one would sit near her. On one occasion, when friends came to visit her, and felt the chill of this treatment, they decided to move away a little and make a new fire. The other women responded to this by moving in, in the manner of the bailiffs [deployed against the camp by the hostile local authority], and stamping out the fire.[3]

There could not be a more dramatic illustration of the final decay of the Greenham ideal than this little incident.

The specific issues at the heart of the conflict here, which erupted in 1987, largely concerned the leadership claims of two black women, who were quite ruthless in their manipulation of white middle-class guilt.[4] However, for West the real moral of the story lies in what it shows us about the sectarian impulse in general – as that impulse encroached upon what had begun as such a profoundly shaken and creative movement. The conflicts arose out of the intrinsic incompatibility of the sectarian impulse with that shakenness. (Where there is no shakenness sectarianism has no problem in imposing uniformity.) This is what makes it such an instructive story. And, as a theologian, West then goes on to apply the resulting lesson, above all, to a critique of the more 'post-Christian' forms of feminist theology.

Now, it is true that post-Christian feminist theology comes in many forms, some of them no doubt also quite deeply shaken, and by no means sectarian in a crude sense. But the crucial point at issue is the notion of *intellectual integrity* at work in such thinking. For, when faced with all the accumulated corruption of the Christian tradition, these thinkers are all too quick to identify true intellectual integrity with, as West puts it, 'walking out'.[5] Which is very much the sectarian instinct, again. West, by contrast, remains a loyal Roman Catholic, not because she in any way denies the difficulty of reconciling her Roman Catholicism with her feminism, but just because she places altogether more weight than the post-Christians do on the need to try, wherever possible – and in the fullest sense – to hold conversation open.

'Walking out' is typically vindicated by a 'myth of innocence'. The way that post-Christian feminist theology tends to present it, in the relationship between the sexes men are the corrupters, women the corrupted – to the extent that salvation for women is essentially identified with withdrawal from the world of men. Orthodox church tradition teaches that the primary sin for all humanity is self-assertive pride. Not so, it is argued: *that* is the primary sin only of the male. The primary sin of the female is the moral sloth of self-effacing servility.[6] Separation is therefore necessary for women in order to create new spaces for healing experiments in self-assertion.

West does not entirely reject this analysis. What she rejects is just its conversion into an ideological justification for 'walking out', sectarian fashion. The feminist 'myth of innocence' reverses the old patriarchal reading of the story of the Fall, according to which Eve was the corrupter, Adam the corrupted. But in doing so it unfortunately misses the deeper potential meaning of that story – for, at the deeper level, the story of the Fall is nothing other than a symbolic warning against sectarian idealism. We are fallen creatures: this means that – without despairing of reform – wisdom largely consists in our nevertheless learning to live with the inevitable imperfection of our given communities. Sectarianism is the impatient desire for a perfect community; perfectly like-minded, perfectly innocent. But the story of the Fall is saying, in the form of a myth, what the Greenham Common story for example also seems to confirm historically: that outside the Garden of Eden such impatience is futile, self-defeating. The apple having once been eaten, there is no longer any going back.[7]

Or so, at any rate, West argues. And one might surely also go on to develop this same argument somewhat further – in trans-confessional terms.

The sectarian impulse, one might say, is definable as an unbalanced bid for *'holiness'*. But 'holy' in this context is, essentially, a religious term for that aspect of religiousness in general which is also to be found in any reforming social movement.

When a confessional religious community claims to be 'holy', this first of all means that it has broken with the surrounding world, rejecting that world's prevailing values, customs and conventions, just as a trans-confessional reforming social movement does. The impulse to holiness operates within a religious community as a continual drive to spiritual renewal – without which the community would sink into the merest lethargy and preoccupation with outward forms. Yet at the same time it carries with it the perpetual risk that it may be ideologized into the sectarian impulse. Confessional religious traditions, of every sort, have a long history of dealing with this risk. Nor is it only the biblical tradition which is therefore rich in potential resources to be deployed for that remedial purpose. There are various such resources in different traditions, from all of which it may well be highly desirable for trans-confessional movements to learn.

In the words of the Nicene Creed, the Christian church identifies itself as 'holy, catholic and apostolic' – which I take to mean that it aspires to a holiness which is essentially *balanced* by catholicity and apostolicity. But, in a certain sense, 'catholicity' and 'apostolicity' are surely just the Christian terms for qualities which in any healthy religious community must serve to balance that community's commitment to holiness. Namely: a proper refinement of the two basic virtues of religion referred to at the beginning of this chapter.

The term 'catholic' originates as an antithesis to the self-professed intellectual élitist sectarianism of the Gnostics.[8] At least to some extent, it has always meant a basic transcendence of the sort of pre-existing social divisions which may help create the constituency to which a sectarian movement can appeal. Etymologically, 'catholic' carries connotations of inclusiveness and universality; true 'catholicism', strictly speaking, depends upon a spirit of radical *classlessness*, the pure antithesis to any mere sectarian contempt for the unenlightened masses. And at least part of the traditional meaning of 'apostolicity' is a fundamental respect for the challenging otherness of the past. That is to say, it may be taken as a term for *honest rootedness* in the sense of owning the whole of one's community history, taking responsibility for both the good and the bad alike; the exact opposite, in short, of the sectarian's desire for a 'deadly innocence'.

Hence, the Christian church's confessional aspiration to be 'holy, catholic and apostolic' corresponds, in trans-confessional terms, to the universal need for a proper balance between reforming intransigence, classlessness and honest rootedness.[9]

True religion, one might say, is nothing other than what is constituted by this balance. Ideology, in general, is just the opposite. Ideology may equally be conservative in form, snuffing out the critical demands of 'holiness', or else sectarian, snuffing out the critical demands of 'catholicism' and 'apostolicity'. But in either case alike it is always fundamentally self-protecting of its unthinking, *mono-perspectival* sense of self-interestedness.

Sub specie aeternitatis

Stepping back here for just a moment to another level of reflection, compare John Rawls's classic approach to the question of 'justice' …

Rawls imagines a group of people who are, so to speak, condemned to the most purely impartial *multi*-perspectivalism by being placed in what he calls the 'original position', behind a 'veil of ignorance': deliberating upon the ideal arrangements for society without any knowledge of the actual place which they themselves will occupy within it.[10]

This heavenly citizens' jury, in other words, consists of people hypothetically liberated – for the time being – from what Buddhists speak of as the illusion of selfhood. The 'original position' is really nothing other than an Anglo-Saxon philosopher's equivalent to nirvana. And, for Rawls, the true political ideal is whatever people placed in such circumstances might be supposed rationally to agree to for the world that, when the 'veil' is lifted, will once again be their home.

This seems to me to be a theologically very intriguing notion. Not that Rawls himself uses it for any sort of theological purpose. He is solely concerned with issues concerning the just distribution of material goods, not issues of religion. And yet – why should we not also ask what such a jury might consider to be *the ideal communitarian structuring of public ethical debate*, in the just society?

Since the participants in the 'original position' by definition remain ignorant of which particular communities they belong to, they are completely free from any sort of mono-perspectival prejudice. Herein lies their special claim to theological wisdom, for the answering of that question. They are uniquely well placed to consider the requirements of good public conversation *in itself*, as distinct from the narrower ideologized self-interest of any of its participants. Theirs is thus the supernatural judgement – exposed as they are, unlike us, to all the shaking-power of historical relativity without any reserve, as they flit experimentally from one perspective to another – which most fundamentally defines what transcends such relativity; the true 'meaning', in that sense, of history.

And so what would these hypothetical sages want to see, in this regard? I think it would be two things above all.

In the first place, they would certainly wish to affirm the underlying ethos of third modernity, as a uniquely direct testimony to the infinite demands of true 'holiness' in the trans-confessional sense. But then, at the same time, they would surely also wish to see this same ethos carefully incorporated (by theological means) into a larger 'catholic' and 'apostolic' context, for the sake of critical balance.

They would on reflection demand both, equally: that, in a nutshell, is my basic contention

14 Discourse ethics and religion

As a set of missionary enterprises, modernity in all its forms naturally appeals first and foremost to the disaffected, those who feel most oppressed under the old order which is to be superseded. Yet these are missionary enterprises which make universal claims.

Their promises are for all, in principle decisively transcending any form of mono-perspectivalism; it can never be enough for them only to replace one oppressive system of domination by another, which oppresses other groups. And to judge them on their own terms must therefore primarily mean asking how far they succeed in confronting *domination of every sort*.

Indeed, from a philosophical point of view, it seems to me that one might very well correlate what I have called the three stages of modernity with three levels of argument, in response to this sort of enquiry.

Augustine/Kant/Habermas

Thus, it seems to me that Augustine is the first great philosophico-theological defender of first modernity specifically in its aspect as a form of modernity.

He merits the title simply by virtue of the way he upholds the Christian gospel in *The City of God* as a systematic counter-blast to the *libido dominandi*, the addictive lust for domination, in all its works. This actual phrase, '*libido dominandi*', comes originally from the work of the pagan historian Sallust (86–35 BCE). As Sallust presents it, the history of Rome appears to be a story mostly of disastrous moral decline, from the good times immediately following the overthrow of the monarchy onwards; a decline whose chief symptom was endless conflict between patricians and plebeians. And one of his key formulations for what had gone wrong is just that there had been a terrible running wild of the *libido dominandi*.[1]

Sallust is one of Augustine's main sources for Roman history. And Augustine adopts the Sallustian argument for Christian apologetic purposes. He accepts that there have been fluctuations in the power of the *libido dominandi* within pagan culture. But what actually held it in check, for example during the good old days at the very beginning of the Roman republic?

Sallust himself, Augustine notes, attributes this in the first instance to the continuing military threat then posed by the exiled king Tarquin and his Etruscan allies, which demanded that the Roman people stuck close together as a matter of collective life or death.[2] In the same way, according to Sallust's account, for a brief period following the Second Punic War (202 BCE) morality was restored as people saw the need for unity against the new military threat from Carthage – but after the final destruction of Carthage (146 BCE) things had once again gone from bad to worse. In short, he concludes, the only remedy against the *libido dominandi* in a pagan culture appears to be the remedy of *fear*.

Properly understood, however, the Christian gospel offers an altogether more reliable remedy. This is because, unlike paganism, Christianity does not found its morality on a pursuit of earthly praise and glory but, on the contrary, involves a positive cultivation of humility.[3] The pursuit of earthly praise and glory may on occasion serve to check certain greater vices, yet is itself a vice – already closely akin, at least, to the *libido dominandi* in the most destructive sense.[4] That is not how Sallust sees it – as his own glorification of Julius Caesar, especially, demonstrates. Yet for Augustine the connection here is quite obvious: after all, are not those who dominate others for ever being flattered with praise from their underlings?

The missionary impulse inherent within any modernist movement necessarily inclines it to a certain populism. Hence such movements typically differ from pre-modern classical philosophy – when it comes to their distinctive notion of the highest wisdom – in the relatively low significance they accord the claims of any particular sort of acquired intellectual sophistication. That is to say: they tend to be much more concerned with wisdom as a quality of *will* – as distinct from a quality of *intellect*. What concerns them, above all, is a certain turning of the will; which, in itself, precedes its proper intellectual interpretation.

It has often been remarked that in classical philosophy one scarcely finds any concept of 'the will' in this sense.[5] There was no need for it. For such philosophy was very much the self-assertive activity of a dominant educational élite – simply assuming the dependence of the highest wisdom on the greatest possible intellectual sophistication. Augustine was the first true philosopher of modernity because he was the first philosopher preoccupied with a problematics of the will. This is expressed not only in his theoretical writings on psychology, but also in the whole project of his *Confessions* as a pioneering work of spiritual autobiography – inasmuch as the *Confessions* are essentially an account of the pre-theoretical, existential process of the turning of his own will towards faith. For classical philosophy, truth and error are two opposing levels of theoretical insight; for Augustine they are, before that, two opposing orientations of the will. And truth in its *primordial* character, as a right turning of the will, is actually just as accessible to the uneducated as it is to the educated.[6]

These two opposing orientations of the will then become for him, in pragmatic terms, the founding principles of two 'cities':

> We see then that the two cities were created by two kinds of love: the earthly city was created by self-love reaching the point of contempt for God, the heavenly city by the love of God carried as far as contempt of self. In fact, the earthly city glories in itself, the heavenly city glories in the Lord. The former looks to its glory from men, the latter finds its highest glory in God, the witness of a good conscience. The earthly lifts up its head in its own glory, the heavenly city says to its God: 'My glory; you lift up my head'. In the former the *libido dominandi* lords it over its princes as over the nations it subjugates; in the other both those put in authority and those subject to them serve one another in love, the rulers by their counsel, the subjects by obedience. The one city loves its own strength shown in powerful leaders; the other says to its God, 'I will love you, my Lord, my strength'.[7]

As regards its pragmatic implications, the love of God which founds the 'heavenly city' is effectively *defined* by its radical opposition to the *libido dominandi* which founds the 'earthly city'.

Pagan Rome is, for Augustine, the prime embodiment of the 'earthly city'. But, of course, the struggle between the two principles runs right through history. The universality of the *libido dominandi* is symbolized by Cain; the universal counter-operation of divine grace is symbolized by Cain's brother Abel, whom he kills. Cain is also said (in Genesis 4: 17) to have built a city. The heirs of Abel, by contrast, are a pilgrim-people on earth, seeking a city above, 'not made by hands'. And so forth. A large part of *The City of God*, in fact, consists of a great ramble through the Scriptures in search of allegorical foreshadowings of the two cities; in the course of which Augustine also considers all sorts of other more naïvely literalistic questions of interpretation, in the manner of his age.

The fundamental weakness of Augustine's doctrine, however (or so it seems to me), emerges most clearly when it is juxtaposed to the great second-modernity ideology-critique of *Kant*.

But then the fundamental weakness of Kant's doctrine, in turn, is high-lighted by being compared above all with the twentieth-century ideology-critique of Jürgen Habermas, precisely as a pioneering precursor of third modernity. These three thinkers each have a fundamental interest in the strategic overcoming of the *libido dominandi* ...

The basic trouble, I think, is that when Augustine speaks of a 'city' what he essentially has in mind is always a hierarchy of rulers. For him, what I have called 'ideology' – in his terms, adherence to the earthly city – is first and foremost a matter of submitting oneself to the wrong rulers: to demons and their representatives, rather than to God. The heavenly city includes the redeemed of all generations, and only those present-day members of the church who have attained salvation. But it also needs symbolic representation here on earth. Its symbolic representative is the church, very much in its character as a hierarchical order; in Augustinian thinking, therefore, the difference between freedom and domination largely melts into the rather different difference between rule in accordance with valid, church-traditionally legitimated authority and rule without it. The 'love of God' which Augustine envisages as the founding principle of the heavenly city does indeed have many of the traits of the solidarity of the shaken. Yet his advocacy of such solidarity nevertheless remains awkwardly entangled with his concomitant advocacy of obedience to orthodox church order. Which, even at its most genuinely desirable, is surely quite another sort of good – not to mention its all too obvious corruptibility.

As a philosopher of second modernity, Kant by contrast adopts a completely opposite approach: he is much less interested in the objective difference between two types of ruler, distinguishing freedom from domination rather in terms of the subjective difference between two attitudes to decision-making. Again, these are two basic opposing orientations of the will. But for Kant the key question is whether one just uncritically surrenders oneself to the dictates of other persons, the prevailing cultural ethos and one's own emotional impulses, or else systematically submits those dictates to the proper jurisdiction of 'practical reason', as autonomous moral legislator.

When Augustine thinks of divine law, he does so as an interpreter of the Pauline epistles. So he envisages it as an objective datum of historic revelation, whose whole truth lies in its character as a constraint on egoism; strictly subordinated, on the other hand, to faith – inasmuch as it is faith alone which saves. The Kantian 'moral law' is also divine. But of course it is the exact opposite of this. Subjectively arrived at by each individual alone – as an ideally rational code for self-government – its rationality is not merely a constraint on egoism, but also possesses an authority absolutely outranking that of any historic tradition; to be appealed to, not least, *against* the 'irrational' claims of faith in the Pauline sense.

Such a notion of the 'moral law' fits its historic moment perfectly. For, after all, Kant lived in an age when 'progress' in the public domain also primarily signified an extension of the secular rule of law, as a defence against the threat of ecclesiastical thought-control. Augustine's chief concern was that we should have, and be loyal to, the right rulers: good Catholic Christians, fully emancipated from the *libido dominandi* typical of pagan rule. Kant's concern is that we should, each of us, maintain a sufficient self-protective mental reserve, with regard to the ideological pretensions of *any* ruler – inner defences against unreason, as it were, to supplement the external defences provided by secularizing legislation. His primary political loyalty is not, as in Augustine's case, to a particular regime; it is simply to the general principle that rulers should not also be thought-controllers. Herein lies the absolutely decisive difference between the rival critical impulses of first and second modernity.

Habermas, however, reflects quite another world again.

This is a world where the cause of progress has in fact ceased to be so immediately or so exclusively identified with actual legislative projects, in themselves – and is increasingly bound up, instead, with larger *consciousness-raising* projects, aiming at altogether more wholesale cultural reform.

The Habermasian approach to ethics involves setting out to rethink everything in terms of a comprehensive philosophico-sociological analysis of that which makes for undistorted communication *in general*. And this, I think, has major intrinsic advantages over both the Augustinian and the Kantian approaches. By comparison, both Augustinian objectivism and Kantian subjectivism alike are oversimplifying abstractions from the actual concrete inter-subjectivity of the ethical with which Habermas deals.

Thus, each of these two doctrines in a different way correlates to a political preoccupation with the relationship between rulers and those they rule: Augustine conceives of freedom from domination in terms of the authority-claims of the rulers; Kant conceives of it in terms of the inner moral disposition of the ruled, in the sense of their intellectual methodology when it comes to ethical decision-making. (Of course, the moral law applies to everyone, both ruled and rulers – but it liberates us insofar as we submit to it as a system of rule.) But where Habermas differs is just in his having larger concerns than either of these: for what really determines the rationality or irrationality of the individual conscience is surely the *overall* quality of public debate. And the relationship between the rulers and the ruled is, in the end, only one factor in determining that overall quality; it is by no means the whole story.

From a Habermasian point of view, the point is: freedom from domination has to be understood as involving a certain quality of conversation *both* within political society, between rulers and ruled, *and* within civil society, as a space for mutual support. Much, in other words, also depends upon the sort of creative solidarity-building initiatives which contribute to enhanced conversation horizontally, as well as vertically. Beyond the limitations of the Augustinian metaphor of ethics as submission to an ideal civic hierarchy and the Kantian metaphor of ethics as submission to an ideal law, Habermas's theory holds open this other aspect of the matter: the fact that ethics is also a quality of creative civil-society *imaginativeness*, with regard to solidarity-building among equals. His thinking, at one level, is simply a classic exploration of this perennial truth.

At another level, though, it is also a direct response to the unique, eye-opening new opportunities for organizational experimentation, in horizontal terms, which characterize the historic emergence of the possibility of third modernity. (Were it not for this, he would simply be writing footnotes to Hegel.) The potential carrier-communities of third modernity resemble those of second modernity in their trans-confessionalism, but they also seek to do far more than simply rationalize the law in a secularist spirit as second modernity does. They are communications-reformers of all sorts, constituted, as a matter of principle, precisely in order to provide a voice for those otherwise silenced by those who dominate them, and to raise awkward issues which the dominant powers would rather have left unraised.

A doctrine like Habermas's, which effectively celebrates that sort of vocation as representing the very highest form of ethics, is perhaps only possible in such an environment. At all events it is certainly notable that avowed Habermasians have been amongst the most vigorous theoretical partisans of third modernity.[8] Just as in the case of Kant and second modernity, so also here: there is a natural fit.

Augustine affirms the solidarity of the shaken as citizenship in the city of God, or the solidarity of shaken Christians; Kant affirms it as 'religion within the limits of pure reason alone', or the solidarity of shaken secularizers. Only with Habermas do we (in effect) have an equivalently systematic affirmation of the solidarity of the shaken *as such*.

Theological critique

And yet Habermas is no theologian. He approaches religion only as a sociologically-minded philosopher.

His wide-ranging critique of sociological and philosophical traditions is based on an elementary analysis of 'speech-acts': for him, everything, in the first place, depends upon maintaining a radical distinction between 'communicative' and 'strategic' action. A speech-act is communicative to the extent that its guiding intention is just to gain, or to promote, an improved understanding – whether of the world, of oneself or of others. It is strategic to the extent that it is intended to affect the world, or to influence the behaviour of others, according to some predetermined understanding, not subject to revision. And the central task of ethical theory, as the antithesis to the *libido dominandi*, is then formally definable as a systematic calling into question of the purposes of strategic action.

Authentically communicative action, on the other hand, is further analysed in this theory into its three 'pure' constituent elements: 'constative speech acts', 'normatively regulated action' and 'dramaturgical action'.[9] These are distinguished by their differing validity-claims. Thus, 'constative speech-acts' aim at the objective theoretical truth, arrived at by way of accurate observation and explanation; 'normatively regulated action' aims at rightness, in accordance with a traditionally-given moral-practical ideal; and 'dramaturgical action' aims at truthfulness, in the sense of the most honest and eloquent form of self-expression.

In Habermasian terms, theology is a 'constative' commentary on sacred ritual. But by 'sacred ritual' here I mean, precisely, *any* sort of corporate action insofar as it combines both 'normatively regulated' and 'dramaturgical' features – intermingling, in equilibrium, and with real intensity. In principle, at least, this is clearly a category full of the most diverse possibilities. But the basic trouble is, Habermas himself does not consider them. He nowhere discusses how that particular combination may most fruitfully realize its potential to be authentically communicative. On the contrary; quite explicitly in his major work, *The Theory of Communicative Action*, he holds fast to the dogmatic view that with the development of the most sophisticated 'forms of mutual understanding' sacred ritual must tend to wither away.[10] Why? Because, it seems, he cannot envisage any other role for sacred ritual apart from that of affirming, and so reinforcing, fundamentally *arbitrary* limits on what it is legitimate to say and do.[11]

But what if all other taboos were to fall away, except one: the primary taboo by which religion, in a strict sense, is differentiated from both magic and ideology, the taboo banning the *libido dominandi*? And what if it were just *an ideal communicativeness as such* – in its ultimate absolute otherness from the strategic quality of strategic action – which was defined as the very essence of the sacred?

After all, why not?

First modernity has no problem in developing appropriate ritual forms for itself. The protagonists of second and third modernity, in general, have a much more difficult task. For they find the ground already occupied by another, rival form of modernity; and their ideals forbid them to oppose it in the straightforward fashion of one confessional tradition competing with another. It certainly makes life easier, in this situation, if one therefore simply abandons the whole business of religious ritual – easier, inasmuch as then one does not have to think so hard. Habermas represents that labour-saving option in non-theistic form. Kant's 'religion within the limits of pure reason alone' does the same thing theistically; for it is, of course, a form of 'religion' entirely devoid of the sort of narrative resources which ritual requires. Habermas is the non-theistic Kant of third modernity.

Responding to his theological critics in 1989 he does, it is true, partially retract the polemically anti-theological tone of some of his earlier remarks.[12] He is even quite warmly appreciative, in particular, of the 'Christian atheist' theology of Jens Glebe-Möller – the professed 'atheism' of which is really nothing more than an aspiration to purge the idea of 'God' in the most thorough way of all ideological content, whilst nevertheless preserving as much of it as possible from the rest of the tradition.[13] And yet, at the same time, he confesses his continuing 'embarrassment' when it comes to this whole sort of discussion. He would, he says, prefer to remain silent on the matter. That he responds at all is only because it is a point of principle for him always to respond when challenged – and not to be like Heidegger, striking a 'reactionary' pose of lofty inscrutability.

There are in fact quite a number of theologians, especially among the Roman Catholics, who have sought to incorporate something of the Habermasian doctrine into their work. To the Catholics, his doctrine represents a valuable resource in the ongoing process of theologically carrying forward the *aggiornamento* of the Second Vatican Council. And perhaps the most notable of them has been Helmut Peukert.[14] For it is Peukert above all who has sought to merge the doctrine into a straightforwardly apologetic argument for orthodox faith. On the one hand, Peukert is a radical Habermasian in his theology: he sets out to interpret the whole history of divine revelation essentially in terms of its drive towards what Habermas has called 'the ideal speech situation'. Yet, on the other hand, he is also a critic of Habermas, attempting to show, against Habermas, that the intrinsic logic of that ideal already points towards the necessity of Christian theology.

So Peukert's argument runs somewhat as follows. The ideal speech situation would first and foremost be one in which no potentially relevant voice, on any topic, was ever excluded. But what, then, of those whose voices are silenced by *death*? What, in particular, of those who die as victims of human wrong: how are we most authentically to hear their cries of protest – or perhaps their testimony to alternative ways of life, crushed by the oppressor? Is there any way – other than as the source of mere communications-shrivelling despair, or a communications-destroying lust for revenge – for their memory to be kept alive amongst the living? Herein, Peukert suggests, lies the ultimate truth of the orthodox dogma of the resurrection. It lies in the absolute urgency with which that dogma, in principle, symbolically presses the claims of the dead to be heard, in a context of hope and forgiveness; proclaiming, as it does, that they are not just dead and gone. The rightness and truthfulness of Christian worship, founded on a faith in the resurrection, fundamentally consists in its ritual embodiment of solidaristic relationships with the dead – as a vital contribution to the infinite all-inclusiveness of the ideal speech situation. Without the contribution of such ritual, the ideal can never be complete. At this level, the irreligiousness of Habermas' own doctrine may actually be seen to be self-contradictory.[15]

Habermas however – whilst he registers the argument – is still unpersuaded.[16] For, after all, what he is looking for is a strictly post-metaphysical basis for solidarity. And from his point of view Peukert's theology falls short just because its Christian confessionalism, after all, renders it so entirely metaphysical in character.

In fact, I think that there are significant elements of truth on both sides of this disagreement. Peukert's engagement with Habermas clearly produces a most thought-provoking reinterpretation of the resurrection; and one may indeed well wonder how it could ever conceivably serve the cause of enhanced communication to just jettison the rich linguistic resources of religious (as opposed to magic or ideological) ritual – with all its old accumulated resonances and multi-layered expressiveness – as Habermas does, in such dismissive haste. Yet, at the same time, there surely is an inescapable cogency to Habermas's post-metaphysical trans-confessionalism – as a response to the actual trans-confessional realities of emergent third modernity.

In a sense, my whole aim here has been to try and point beyond this sort of impasse.

15 *'Wo aber Gefahr ist ...'*

In some cultures, what Habermas calls 'strategic action' protects itself from critical analysis by posing as a decree of fate, or as the will of God; in the ideologies of complex industrial societies, with which Habermas is primarily concerned, it does so rather by posing as a mere submission to the inexorable demands of, as he puts it, 'the System'.

Habermas refers to this as 'the colonization of the Lifeworld by the System'. The 'Lifeworld', before it is 'colonized', is made up of every sort of artifice that goes to render 'communicative action' possible in the first place: that is, every form of pre-reflective linguistic convention, every imagination-enriching custom, every commonly shared ethical assumption or moral reference point – everything, in short, that serves the general purposes of communication simply for mutual understanding's sake.

Industrial civilization first 'uncouples' its System from the Lifeworld, creating more and more new economic and bureaucratic organisms each with their own distinctive ethos, more concerned with success in achieving the strategic goals they have set for themselves than with gaining honest consensual understanding for what they do. Then the System, so constituted, proceeds to expand its operations imperialistically into more and more areas of life, manipulatively imposing a new consensus from above. Habermas himself sees, and welcomes, the rise of later twentieth-century new social movements primarily as a series of defensive responses to this underlying 'colonization' process.[1]

Václav Havel meanwhile, in his essay 'Politics and Conscience', seeks to capture the conflict between System and Lifeworld pictorially. So he recalls an experience from his childhood in the Czech countryside:

> I used to walk to school in a nearby village along a cart track through the fields and, on the way, see on the horizon a huge smokestack of some hurriedly built factory, in all likelihood in the service of war. It spewed dense brown smoke and scattered it across the sky. Each time I saw it, I had an intense sense of something profoundly wrong, of humans soiling the heavens.[2]

This chimney, poking filthily into the sky, becomes for Havel a symbol of the hubristic self-assertion of the industrialized System – in its full-blown totalitarian form. He imagines a mediaeval peasant out hunting in the woods, suddenly transposed into the twentieth century and confronted with the sight. No doubt, that peasant 'would think it the work of the Devil and would fall on his knees and pray that he and his kin be saved'. A child and a peasant: what they both have in common, Havel suggests, is just that they are altogether more intensely 'rooted in the Lifeworld' than most modern adults. They have not yet been recruited into the System.

One might also recall the words of Jesus: 'I tell you this: unless you turn round and become like children, you will never enter the kingdom of Heaven' (Matthew 18: 3). To enter the heavenly domain, it might be said, is precisely to recover the child's pre-reflective rootedness in the Lifeworld – only now in full reflective awareness of that world's suffering from its ideologically-minded 'colonizers' in every generation.

The chimney soiling the heavens represents, for Havel, a twofold hubris. In the first place, quite directly, it represents the general hubris of reckless technological experimentation, endangering the physical environment. The northern part of the Czech Republic became, under Communist rule, one of the most polluted areas in Europe. And then he thinks, for example, of the disastrous Communist experiment with collectivized agriculture.

But, second, the chimney also stands for the way in which the Czech *political* environment had been ravaged – by an analogous hubris. And not only the Czech political environment; nor, indeed, only where there were Communist or other totalitarian (or 'post-totalitarian') regimes. For what Havel deplores is a trend which he sees as stretching back not just to Marx, but all the way to Machiavelli. The process begins with the removal of moral scruples even from the ideal theory of politics. It ends in the systematic 'anonymisation and depersonalisation of power and its reduction to a mere technology of rule and manipulation'. The secularity of second modernity, therapy for an older disease, does nothing to hinder this one – but may actually contribute to it, by undermining traditional moral authorities.

> The rulers and leaders [he writes] were once personalities in their own right ... still in some sense responsible for their deeds, good and ill, whether they had been installed by dynastic tradition, by the will of the people, by a victorious battle or by intrigue. But they have been replaced ... by the manager, the bureaucrat, the *apparatchik* – a professional ... expert in the techniques of management, manipulation and obfuscation, filling a depersonalized intersection of functional relations, a cog in the machinery of state caught up in a predetermined role. This professional ruler is an 'innocent' tool of an 'innocent' anonymous power, legitimized by science, cybernetics, ideology, law, abstraction and objectivity – that is, by everything except personal responsibility to human beings as persons and neighbours ... Power [in such an environment] is a priori

innocent because it does not grow from a world in which words like guilt and innocence retain their meaning.[3]

Totalitarian regimes exhibit the syndrome with an especial starkness. For they have more or less abandoned all inhibitions. But, Havel urges,

> the totalitarian systems warn of something far more serious than Western rationalism is willing to admit. They are, most of all, a convex mirror of the inevitable consequences of rationalism, a grotesquely magnified image of its own deep tendencies, an extremist offshoot of its own development and an ominous product of its own expansion. They are a deeply informative reflection of its own crisis.[4]

And hence the particular authority of those like him who write as dissidents, from inside the totalitarian nightmare, warning of the dangers dramatically accentuated by that experience.

'*Wo aber Gefahr ist, wächst/Das Rettende auch*': 'But where danger is, there grows/Also that which saves.' Hölderlin's lines, from the opening stanza of 'Patmos', derive from a very different historic context – but they refer to the perennial *subjective* aspect of all such dangers to the free functioning of the Lifeworld, in whatever form.

Thus, the 'danger' Hölderlin means is evidently the one that faces any greatly shaken individual, in circumstances where shakenness tends to mean sheer social isolation: the danger of profound alienation and despair. (After all, we have here the words of a poet who was himself teetering on the brink of insanity.) So that – over and against this – 'that which saves' is presumably nothing other than an appropriate countervailing solidarity.

Indeed, I know of no more vividly compressed poetic invocation of the solidarity of the shaken in general than the larger passage from which these lines come – and so let me conclude with it.

The whole stanza becomes a sort of prayer, specifying the vocation of the shaken poet – as a preserver, one might say, of something not unlike the childlike spirit evoked in Havel's parable. Or, rather, the vocation of the shaken poet-theologian. For it is as a poet-theologian that Hölderlin writes.

His prayer is addressed to a God who is described as being both 'near' and yet 'elusive'. He had in his student days been a close friend of Hegel's, and this seems to me to be essentially the same vision of God as the one which Hegel seeks to articulate in philosophical terms: 'near' in the sense of transcending the servile metaphysical projection, into the remote distance, of the 'unhappy consciousness'; 'elusive' in the sense of being made manifest, first and foremost, in that infinite toil of dialectical questioning which is the shaken process of *Geist*.

It is a prayer composed in Hölderlin's abrupt yet rolling Pindaric manner, issuing in an urgent cry from the midst of the 'danger' of which he speaks –

the disorientation of the shaken individual in the face of the apparent inexorability of the System.

He is as though stranded in the high Alps: a place of shakenness, symbolized by 'flimsy bridges' slung over abysmal depths. Two things are asked for. The first is 'chaste water', representing, perhaps, a spiritual baptism – initiation into communion with kindred spirits down the ages, on 'the summits of time'. The other is the gift of 'wings', to pass like the eagles from summit to summit. For it is just the inaccessibility of those Alpine peaks which symbolizes for him the 'dangerous' solitude he seeks to escape. (And in the poem that follows he does indeed take imaginative flight, through both space and time, to the island of Patmos where the Book of Revelation was written, there to commune with the Apostle John, whom he supposes to have been its author.) The two gifts are thus, I think, in reality just two aspects of the same.

The full text runs as follows:

Nah ist
Und schwer zu fassen der Gott.
Wo aber Gefahr ist, wächst
Das Rettende auch.
Im Finstern wohnen
Die Adler und furchtlos gehn
Die Söhne der Alpen über den Abgrund weg
Auf leichtgebaueten Brücken.
Drum, da gehäuft sind rings
Die Gipfel der Zeit, und die Liebsten
Nah wohnen, ermattend auf
Getrenntesten Bergen,
So gib unschuldig Wasser,
O Fittige gib uns, treuesten Sinns
Hinüberzugehn und wiederzukehren.

Near and
Elusive is the God.
But where danger is, there grows
Also that which saves.
In the dark dwell
The eagles and fearlessly
Over flimsy bridges the sons of the Alps
Cross the torrential abyss.
There, heaped up all around stand
The summits of time, and friends dearly loved
Are in trouble, close by, but
On quite separate slopes.
So, now, give us chaste water
And wings, O give us wings for the high soaring
Loyalty needed to traverse the chasms.[5]

Notes

1 The promise of new social movements

1 Václav Havel, 'The Power of the Powerless', English translation by P. Wilson, in *Living in Truth*, edited by Jan Vladislav, London: Faber & Faber, 1987, p. 41.
2 Ibid., p. 42.
3 Ibid., p. 50.
4 Ibid., p. 45.
5 Ibid., p. 55.
6 English translation in H. Gordon Skilling, *Charter 77 and Human Rights in Czechoslovakia*, London: George Allen & Unwin, 1981, p. 209.
7 Ibid., p. 212.
8 These essays, written in the immediate aftermath of 1968, were first published in 1975. The final chapter has been translated into English, in *Telos* 30 (1976–7). The whole work has appeared in French as *Essais hérétiques sur la philosophie de l'histoire*, Lagrasse: Editions Verdier, 1981, and in German as *Ketzerische Essais zur Philosophie der Geschichte*, Stuttgart: Klett-Cotta Verlag, 1988. See also the discussion in my *Civil Society, Civil Religion*, Oxford: Blackwell, 1995, Chapter 3.
9 Jan Patočka, 'What Charter 77 Is and What It Is Not', in Skilling, *Charter 77 and Human Rights in Czechoslovakia*, p. 219.
10 See also Havel's remarks at the conclusion to 'Politics and Conscience': *Living in Truth*, p. 157.
11 See especially 'An Anatomy of Reticence', 1985: *Living in Truth*, pp. 164–95.
12 Ibid., p. 182.
13 See for example Jean Cohen and Andrew Arato, *Civil Society and Political Theory*, Cambridge, MA: MIT Press, 1992.
14 Compare the argument I develop in *Civil Society, Civil Religion*, Chapter 1.
15 Alberto Melucci claims to have initiated this, in two articles first published in Italian in 1977, translated into English as 'The New Social Movements: A Theoretical Approach', in *Social Science Information* 19, 1980, and 'Ten Hypotheses for the Analysis of New Movements', in D. Pinto, ed., *Contemporary Italian Sociology*, Cambridge: CUP, 1981. See also his later article, 'The New Social Movements Revisited: Reflections on a Sociological Misunderstanding', in L. Maheu, ed., *Social Movements and Social Classes: The Future of Collective Action*, London: Sage, 1995; and his book, *Nomads of the Present: Social Movements and Individual Needs in Contemporary Society*, London: Hutchinson, 1989.

Volume 52(4) of the journal *Social Research*, 1985, contains a number of significant articles on the topic, notably Jean L. Cohen, 'Strategy or Identity: New Theoretical Paradigms and Contemporary Social Movements'; Alain

Touraine, 'An Introduction to the Study of Social Movements'; and Claus Offe, 'New Social Movements: Challenging the Boundaries of Institutional Politics'. Other relevant texts include W.A. Gamson, *The Strategy of Social Protest*, Belmont, CA: Wadsworth, 1990; S. Tarrow, *Democracy and Disorder*, Oxford: Clarendon Press, 1989, and *Power in Movement*, Cambridge: CUP, 1994; B. Klandermans, H. Kriesi and S. Tarrow, eds, *From Structure to Action*, Greenwich, CT: JAI Press, 1988; and Jürgen Habermas, *The Theory of Communicative Action*, English translation by Thomas McCarthy, Cambridge: Polity Press, 1987, vol. 2, pp. 391–6.

16 See Joan B. Landes, *Women and the Public Sphere in the Age of the French Revolution*, Ithaca, NY: Cornell University Press, 1988.

17 See for example Christine Bolt, *The Women's Movements in the United States and Britain from the 1790s to the 1920s*, Amherst, MA: University of Massachusetts Press, 1993.

18 For a detailed account, see Martin Ceadel, *The Origins of War Prevention: The British Peace Movement and International Relations, 1730–1854*, Oxford: Clarendon Press, 1996. Also W.H. van der Linden, *The International Peace Movement 1815–1874*, Amsterdam, 1987.

19 See for example David Turley, *The Culture of English Antislavery, 1780–1860*, London: Routledge, 1991.

20 Martin Ceadel, *Pacifism in Britain, 1914–45: The Defining of a Faith*, Oxford: Clarendon Press, 1980.

3 Three stages of modernity?

1 Lyotard's two main works on 'postmodernity' are *The Postmodern Condition: A Report on Knowledge*, originally published in 1979, English translation by Geoffrey Bennington and Brian Massumi, Manchester: Manchester University Press, 1984; and *The Postmodern Explained: Correspondence 1982–1985*, English translation edited by Julian Pefanis and Morgan Thomas, Minneapolis, MN: University of Minnesota Press, 1993. But related critical themes run right through his writings, in diverse styles.

2 As Lyotard himself puts it, 'Modernity is constitutionally and ceaselessly pregnant with its postmodernity', in *The Inhuman: Reflections on Time*, English translation by Geoffrey Bennington and Rachel Bowlby, Cambridge: Polity Press, 1991, p. 25. As an age of civilization, what Lyotard calls 'modernity' has just one immediate opposite: the classical. 'Postmodernity' belongs entirely to the modern age – but it is modernity 'rewritten'.

3 Lyotard himself uses the metaphor of 'shakenness': notably, in the title of his book of fiction, *Récits tremblants*, Paris: Galilée, 1977.

4 Lyotard actually refers to St Augustine as 'the first modern': *Political Writings*, London: UCL Press, 1993, p. 25. But, if the definitve criterion is the presence of grand narrative, why stop at Augustine?

5 What Christianity and Islam crucially have in common, from this point of view, is their mix of missionary zeal with worldly, as well as other-worldly, hope. Buddhism has equal missionary zeal. So, once upon a time, did Epicureanism. But, of course, for both Buddhists and Epicureans it nevertheless remains the individual's highest vocation to be released from all 'mere' worldliness. Hence, their narratives are not grand narratives. They do not meet the third of the three definitive criteria for grand narrative set out above: they lack the properly modern commitment to the worldliness of the carrier-community's own historic hopes.

6 Lyotard introduces this terminology in his first major work: *Discours, figure*, Paris: Klinksieck, 1971. Cf. Bill Reading's interpretative formulation, in his *Introducing Lyotard: Art and Politics*, London: Routledge, 1991, pp. xxxi–xxxii:

> The figural is an unspeakable other necessarily at work within and against discourse, disrupting the rule of representation. It is not opposed to discourse, but is the point at which the oppositions by which discourse works are opened to a radical heterogeneity or singularity. As such, the figural is the resistant or irreconcilable trace of a space or time that is radically incommensurable with that of discursive meaning: variously evoked throughout Lyotard's writing as the visible (figure/ground), the rhetorical (figural/literal), work, the Unconscious, the event, postmodern anachronism, the sublime affect or the thing.

7 Lyotard, *The Postmodern Explained*, p. 56.
8 Lyotard, *Heidegger and 'the jews'*, English translation by Andreas Michel and Mark Roberts, Minneapolis, MN: University of Minnesota Press, 1990.
9 Freud's article, 'Erinnern, Wiederholung und Durcharbeiten', is to be found in vol. 10 of his *Gesammelte Schriften*, Frankfurt am Main: S. Fischer Verlag, 1946. It deals only with clinical psychoanalytic practice.
   For Lyotard's cultural-political meditations on the theme, see 'Rewriting Modernity' and 'Logos and Techne, or Telegraphy' in *The Inhuman*.
10 Lyotard presents 'repetition' in terms of neurosis and myth in 'Rewriting Modernity', and, in terms of cultural 'habit' in 'Logos and Techne, or Telegraphy'.
11 Indeed, Lyotard's calling the shaken 'the jews' already obscures the issue, in that it emphasizes only what the plight of the shaken has in common with that of the Jews. Whereas the whole *difference* between the two plights lies in the relatively unproblematic naturalness of solidarity among Jews, as a people.

4 A second Axial Period?

1 Karl Barth, *Church Dogmatics*, I: 2, §17, Edinburgh: T. & T. Clark, 1956.
2 Dietrich Bonhoeffer, *Letters and Papers from Prison*, 3rd English edn, London: SCM Press, 1971, pp. 279–82, 285–6, 328, 359–61, 380–3.
3 Karl Jaspers, *The Origin and Goal of History*, London: Routledge & Kegan Paul, 1953, Chapters 1 and 5.
   Cf. also Shmuel N. Eisenstadt, 'The Axial Age: The Emergence of Transcendental Visions and the Rise of Clerics', in *Archives européennes de sociologie*, 23, 1982, pp. 294–314.
4 I use the Latin phrase as a means of recalling Augustine's usage of it in *The City of God* XIV, 28 and elsewhere: where he defines the essential difference between the heavenly and the earthly city in terms of the opposition between their two rival foundational principles, true love of God versus *libido dominandi*. See Chapter 14, this volume.
5 This is not to deny that there is something especially interesting about the interactions which have taken place: see for example Wilfred Cantwell Smith, *Towards a World Theology: Faith and the Comparative History of Religion*, London: Macmillan, 1981, Chapter 1.
6 Jaspers, *The Origin and Goal of History*, pp. 25, 71–4, 96–7, 139–40.

5 Arguments for calendar-reform

1 Jean-Jacques Rousseau, *The Social Contract*, translated by Maurice Cranston, Harmondsworth: Penguin, 1968, IV, 8.
2 Bellah's seminal article, 'Civil Religion in America' – which first introduced the concept in this context – was originally published in the winter 1967 issue of *Daedalus*. It is reproduced in Russel E. Richey and Donald G. Jones, eds, *American Civil Religion*, New York: Harper & Row, 1974. His main development of his argument is in *The Broken Covenant*, 2nd edn, Chicago: University of Chicago Press, 1992. (Eventually, in fact, the ambiguities associated with the actual term 'American civil religion' led Bellah to abandon it: see his Introduction to the second edition of *The Broken Covenant*. But by this time a whole academic industry had already grown up around the idea.)

6 Beyond 'metaphysics'

1 Although compare his remarks in *Identity and Difference*, translated by Joan Stambaugh, New York: Harper & Row, 1969, pp. 54, 120. Here he does at least acknowledge the older Greek sense of the term which, as it is pre-Christian, is pre-confessional. (And which is then taken up into the Latin of thinkers like Varro, with his systematic 'tri-partite theology'.)

For a further discussion of 'theology' by Heidegger, see especially the essays translated by James G. Hart and John C. Maraldo under the title *The Piety of Thinking*, Bloomington, IN: Indiana University Press, 1976.
2 *Ereignis* is just the ordinary German word for 'event'. Its association with 'owning' (*eigen*) is in fact more of a pun than a real etymological link. (Its actual etymological origins, as Heidegger acknowledges, are from the archaic *er-äugnen*, 'to bring before one's eyes, to bring into sight'.) But the pun nevertheless does its job.
3 Søren Kierkegaard, *Concluding Unscientific Postscript*, translated by David F. Swenson and Walter Lowrie, Princeton, NJ: Princeton University Press, 1941, p. 182.
4 Kierkegaard's primary work on '*Angst*' is *The Concept of Anxiety*, translated by Walter Lowrie, 2nd edn, Princeton, NJ: Princeton University Press, 1957. But this also stands in a special dialectical relationship with his study of 'despair' in *The Sickness Unto Death*, translated into English by Alastair Hannay, Harmondsworth: Penguin, 1989; inasmuch as despair is *Angst* already at a certain level of intensification. The formula 'truth is subjectivity' plays a central role especially in his *Concluding Unscientific Postscript*.
5 See especially, for instance, the musings of Johannes Climacus in the Frederiksberg Garden: *Concluding Unscientific Postscript*, pp. 164–7.
6 The theologian who has most directly challenged Heidegger's view of 'theology' as being intrinsically metaphysical is Jean-Luc Marion, in his book *Dieu sans l'être*, Paris: Fayard, 1982. Thus, in Marion's theology God (or rather 'G̶o̶d̶') is conceived in terms directly analogous to Heidegger's notion of Being – as the inspirer of a quite different set of cultural loyalties and rhetorical strategies from those that belong to the thinking of Being, but nevertheless no less radically transcendent of metaphysics. The polemical thrust of Marion's book title, 'God without being', is just that God is, after all, not an entity – any more than Being is a particular entity; since it is of the essence of entities to be thinkable. Entities are what thought either actually or at least potentially recognizes in the flow of experience. However, the true God is that infinite reality which is for ever shaking us into fresh thought, by being infinitely compelling, yet at the same time –

intrinsically – for ever beyond recognition; and by no means, therefore, just the 'supreme being' of metaphysics.

Marion remains a confessional theologian, albeit without making any sort of apologetic claim as regards the uniqueness of Christian truth. But otherwise, I think, my notion of 'theology' is just the same as his.

7   On the *Ge-stell*, in relation to the *Ereignis*, see in particular the two essays, 'The Question Concerning Technology' and 'The Turning', in Heidegger, *The Question Concerning Technology and Other Essays*, translated by William Lovitt, New York: Harper & Row, 1977. (These two essays both originated as lectures, delivered in 1949.)

8   Heidegger speaks of both 'the leap' and 'the step back' in *Identity and Difference*, translated by Joan Stambaugh, New York: Harper & Row, 1969. 'The leap' appears in the first of the two essays here, 'The Principle of Identity', pp. 32, 96. 'The step back' appears in the second essay, 'The Onto-theo-logical Constitution of Metaphysics', pp. 49–52, 115–18.

For 'the leap', see also for example *What is Called Thinking?*, translated by Fred D. Wieck and J. Glenn Gray, New York: Harper & Row, 1968, pp. 7–8, 12, 18.

9   In German: *Beiträge zur Philosophie: Vom Ereignis*, vol. 65 of Heidegger's Gesamtausgabe, edited by Friedrich-Wilhelm von Herrmann, Frankfurt am Main: Klostermann, 1989, Part 7. Although written in 1936–8, and a key document for understanding the 'turn' in Heidegger's thought during that period, this work was never published in Heidegger's own lifetime.

10   *Hölderlins Hymnen 'Germanien' und 'Der Rhein'* (lecture course at Freiburg, winter semester, 1934–5), Gesamtausgabe vol. 39, edited by Susanne Ziegler, Frankfurt am Main: Klostermann, 1980; *Erläuterungen zu Hölderlins Dichtung* (1936–68), Gesamtausgabe vol. 4, Frankfurt am Main: Klostermann, 1981; *Hölderlins Hymne 'Andenken'* (lecture course at Freiburg, winter semester, 1941–2), Gesamtausgabe vol. 52, edited by Curd Ochwadt, Frankfurt am Main: Klostermann, 1982; *Hölderlins Hymne 'Der Ister'* (lecture course at Freiburg, summer semester, 1942), Gesamtausgabe vol. 53, edited by Walter Biemel, Frankfurt am Main: Klostermann, 1984.

Hölderlin's gods are, first and foremost, the spirits of poetic inspiration. His work is largely a lament over the imaginative impoverishment of contemporary culture (he lived from 1770 to 1843, although his major works were all written before 1804, when he fell into insanity). The gods, according to his private mythology, are now absent. In the days of Ancient Greece they were present, communing with humankind; but then they departed. Christ was the last of them. Hölderlin's poetry – framed as an expression of yearning for their return – is itself an anticipatory sacrament of that return. And Heidegger's 'last God' is the divine principle, glimpsed far off, belonging to the last stage of this Hölderlinian cycle of departure and return.

On the general background, in his work as a whole – see for example George Kovacs, *The Question of God in Heidegger's Phenomenology*, Evanston, IL: Northwestern University Press, 1990.

11   *Gelassenheit*, Pfullingen: Günther Neske Verlag, 1959; translated into English by John M. Anderson and E. Hans Freund as *Discourse on Thinking*, New York: Harper & Row, 1966.

(The second part of this short work is entitled 'Conversation on a Country Path about Thinking': a dream-like, indeed rather spooky conversation between three featureless figures, a 'scientist', a 'scholar' and a 'teacher' – chiming in, one after the other, without any dialectical tension between them – which is dated in a footnote to the ghastly winter of 1944–5. And yet there is no further allusion to the actual events occurring in the background. It is almost as if the sheer enormity of those traumatic events precluded any more direct reference. Is this wisdom – or just a form of intellectual anaesthesia? The setting of the conversation is said to be, symbolically, 'far from human habitation'. Nothing could be further from the lively urbanity of Socratic dialogue. It is really the most unconversational of conversations – is 'releasement', I wonder, an intrinsically conversation-inhibiting ideal?)

12 *Der Spiegel*, 1976, no. 23. In view of the nature of the *Spiegel* as a current affairs magazine, this is naturally an issue on which the interviewers press him – but if you want to see the practical 'effectiveness' of a thinking like his, he answers, first wait three hundred years or so!

7 Post-metaphysical faith

1 John Hick, *An Interpretation of Religion: Human Responses to the Transcendent*, Basingstoke: Macmillan, 1989, pp. 236–46. He also makes the identical move in his essay 'A Philosophy of Religious Pluralism', first published in Frank Whaling, ed., *The World's Religious Traditions: Essays in Honour of Wilfred Cantwell Smith*, Edinburgh: T. & T. Clark, 1984, and then reprinted in Hick, *Problems of Religious Pluralism*, Basingstoke: Macmillan, 1985.

2 Hick's most extended discussion of Christology is in his book, *The Metaphor of God Incarnate*, London: SCM, 1993.

3 Hegel, *Lectures on the History of Philosophy*, translated into English by E.S. Haldane, London: Kegan Paul, Trench, Trübner & Co, 1892, vol. 3, pp. 476–7.

4 Hick does defend his Kantian 'realism' against various other forms of 'anti-realism', in *An Interpretation of Religion*, Chapters 11–12. But the basic notion of 'non-realism' in question is one according to which 'that "God exists" [simply] means that there are human beings who use the concept of God and for whom it is the presiding idea in their form of life' (p. 199). And I would certainly agree that such a view (if anyone actually holds it) is quite inadequate.

Surely, that 'God exists' means not only the above, but also (at the very least) that the use of the concept, by the faithful, potentially helps enhance their capacity to articulate the morally most significant levels of their own life's reality – without in any way thereby necessarily inhibiting their learning from all sorts of others.

5 Wilfred Cantwell Smith, *Towards a World Theology: Faith and the Comparative History of Religion*, London & Basingstoke: Macmillan, 1981, Part 3.

6 Ibid., p. 193.

7 John B. Cobb, *Beyond Dialogue: Toward a Mutual Transformation of Christianity and Buddhism*, Philadelphia, PA: Fortress Press, 1982. This book, as a whole, is an admirable instantiation of what it thus advocates.

8 John Milbank, 'The End of Dialogue', in Gavin D'Costa, ed., *Christian Uniqueness Reconsidered: The Myth of a Pluralistic Theology of Religions*, Maryknoll, NY: Orbis, 1990, p. 190.

9 Smith, *Towards a World Theology*, pp. 52–3. And see also his article, 'Philosophia, as One of the Religious Traditions of Humankind: the Greek Legacy in Western Civilization, viewed by a Comparativist', in Jean-Claude Galley, ed., *Différences, valeurs, hiérarchie*, Paris: Éditions de l'École des Hautes Études en Sciences Sociales, 1984, pp. 253–79.

10 See Smith's debate with Hans Penner in Robert D. Baird, ed., *Methodological Issues in Religious Studies*, Chico, CA: New Horizons Press, 1975, especially p. 99.

11 Smith, *Towards a World Theology*, p. 82.

12 This includes dead cultures, too. See his discussion of ancient Egyptian religion – and in particular the ancient Egyptians' mysterious identification of the sky as a cow – in his book *Belief and History*, Charlottesville: University Press of Virginia, 1977, pp. 11–14.

13 Smith, *Towards a World Theology*, p. 59.

14 Ibid., p. 97.

15 On Smith's 'personalism', see for instance ibid., p. 62:

> In Western understanding of, let us say, India, there has been a clear advance through successive stages: first, ignorance; secondly, impressionistic awareness of random parts of the culture (an outside subjective stage); thirdly, a growingly systematic and accurate yet insensitive and externalist knowledge of facts (an objective stage); and, more recently, and richly promising, the beginnings of serious and even profound humane understanding of the role and meaning of those facts in the lives and the culture of the persons involved. (This last carries strikingly forward, in some cases almost transforms, India's own self-awareness, the erstwhile insider's subjective knowledge.)
> I call this last stage personalist.

Also see his article 'Thinking About Persons', in *Humanitas* 15, 1979, pp. 147–52.

On his view of Buber, as both personalist philosopher and model missionary, see in particular the article 'Participation: The Changing Christian Role in Other Cultures', reprinted in the collection of his writings, *Religious Diversity*, edited by Willard G. Oxtoby, New York and London: Harper & Row, 1976, pp. 131–3. Also, his book *Faith and Belief*, Princeton, NJ: Princeton University Press, 1979, pp. 325–6.

16 Smith, 'Methodology and the Study of Religion: Some Misgivings', in Baird, ed., *Methodological Issues in Religious Studies*, p. 2.

17 Ibid., p. 21.

18 Smith's early work, *Modern Islam in India: A Social Analysis*, Lahore: Minerva, 1943, is distinctly Marxist in outlook.

19 Smith, *The Meaning and End of Religion*, New York, Toronto and London: Mentor, 1964, pp. 47–8.

20 Ibid., p. 175.

21 See ibid., Chapter 2, for a comprehensive history of the evolution of the word.

22 At the same time, Smith also detects a parallel development in the meaning of 'philosophy':

> In 1500 if one asked about a person, 'ejusne philosophia vera est?' this would have meant, 'Is his love of wisdom genuine?' With the Enlightenment it meant (and means) 'Is his philosophy true?'
>
> (ibid., p. 40)

23 Ibid., Chapter 3.

'Judaism' was the first faith-tradition with such a name: one finds it already in II Maccabees 2: 21, 8: 1, 14: 38; also in the New Testament, Galatians 1: 13–14. 'Christianity' appears to have acquired its name very early on: Acts 11: 26. 'Islam' is unique in that its name is actually given in its founding revelation, although it is still not the name for a 'religion' among 'religions'. As one sees, for example, when one tries translating the sentence 'I am not a Muslim' directly back into Arabic – and finds one is saying, rather, 'I do not submit to God'.

24 'Shinto', by contrast, *is* an indigenous Japanese term. But, as such, it means 'the way of the gods'. Whereas, Smith remarks, when converted into the name of a 'religion' it becomes – very differently – 'the way of the Japanese vis à vis the gods'.

25 Smith, *Towards a World Theology*, pp. 154–7.

26 Ibid., p. 176.

27 Smith also cites Ranke's dictum here, that every generation is equidistant from eternity. There is a sense in which I think this overstates the matter: surely, in any community there will have been some generations whose experience of history was more spiritually distressing – and to that extent more thought-provoking – than the experience of others. And are not such generations thereby brought closer to the eternal – inasmuch as they find themselves, with special urgency, once again compelled to reopen the great questions of life, the ones which most significantly always abide?

Yet the point remains. Not all such shake-up events are of the sort that inaugurate a whole new confessional strand in religious history.

28 Smith, *Faith and Belief*, Princeton, NJ: Princeton University Press, 1979, Chapter 6; *Belief and History*, Charlottesville, VA: University Press of Virginia, 1977, Chapter 2.

29 As he further remarks, the same basic vowel variation occurs both in English and in modern German. In English: love/believe; in German (the other way round): *sich verlieben*, 'to fall in love with'/*(sich) verloben*, 'to betroth, engage'. The latter belongs with *geloben*, 'to promise' – and hence also with *Glaube*, 'faith', *glauben*, 'to have faith', and *loben*, 'to praise'. See *Faith and Belief*, p. 106.

30 *Credo* derives from *cor, cordis*, 'heart', and **-do, *-dere*, 'to put'.

31 Smith, *Belief and History*, p. 44.

32 Smith traces the history of *credo*, in Roman Catholic tradition, in *Faith and Belief*, Chapter 5. From the point of view of mediaeval Scholastic theology, one might say that 'I believe' has degenerated from an expression of *fides* to an expression of mere *opinio*; or that it has come to express *fides* only in the limited sense recognized by Aristotle (where Aristotle speaks of *pistis*), not the properly Christian sense.

33 Smith, *Belief and History*, p. 52.

34 Ibid., pp. 60–7.

35 Ibid., p. 46; and see also pp. 73–80.

36 Smith (ibid., pp. 47–8) sees Hobbes as a transitional figure. Thus, Hobbes argues that for people to 'believe in God' is essentially for them 'to hold all for truth they heare him say': *Leviathan*, I, vii. And, more generally, he distinguishes 'belief' from 'opinion', as being the admittance of an opinion 'out of trust to other men': *Human Nature*, Chapter 6, §§ 7, 9. Here 'belief' in persons is halfway to becoming 'belief' in propositions; but only halfway.

For, by contrast, as Smith remarks:

> 'To believe a person' has with us come to mean, to accept as true what he is saying, and usually only that; without regard, any longer, to what he does, or feels, or is, or even to trusting him. 'I believe his statement, but I do not trust him' is in our century not a contradiction in terms – as it would have been for Hobbes.

37 John Stuart Mill, *A System of Logic*, London: Parker, 1843, Chapter 1, § 2, p. 21.

38 Smith, *Belief and History*, p. 51.

39 Ibid. Quotation from A.J. Ayer, *The Central Questions of Philosophy*, London: Weidenfeld & Nicolson, 1973, p. 211.

40 *Mark Twain's Notebook*, ed. Albert Bigelow Paine, New York and London: Harper, 1935, p. 237. Cited in Smith, *Belief and History*, p. 66.

41 Smith, *Towards a World Theology*, p. 178.

42 See for example his remarks in *Introduction to Metaphysics*, translated by Ralph Mannheim, New Haven, CT: Yale University Press, 1959, pp. 6–7, where, in a somewhat mischievous way, he in effect reverses St Paul's description of gospel faith, in 1 Corinthians 1: 22–5, as 'foolishness to the [philosophically minded] Greeks' – and speaks of his sort of philosophy as being, necessarily, 'foolishness to faith'.

43 Again, one might compare Kierkegaard's formula for authentic faith, cited above. The essential differences are twofold: unlike Kiekergaard, Smith is a genuine theologian, inasmuch as he is centrally concerned with the conversational preconditions for effective solidarity-building; and, unlike Smith's, Kierkegaard's thinking – insofar as it nevertheless remains at any rate parasitic on pre-existing solidarity-bonds – still quite unquestioningly presupposes an absolute confessionalism. But otherwise they are no doubt in perfect agreement.

44 Hugo Meynell, 'The Idea of a World Theology', in *Modern Theology* 1 (2), 1985, p. 154.

45 William J. Wainwright, 'Wilfred Cantwell Smith on Faith and Belief', in *Religious Studies* 20, 1984, in particular pp. 364–6. The quotation is from Smith, *Towards a World Theology*, p. 97.

46 Wainwright, ibid. p. 363, finds another problematic aspect of Smith's doctrine to be his contention 'that any attempt to articulate transcendence in a set of propositions involves objectifying it'. But this is Wainwright's own formulation, and it is much too general – he himself has here imported the element of exaggeration which he then goes on to call into question. What Smith is against is, more specifically, a second-order doctrine of 'salvation'. It is not, in itself, the articulation of a propositional belief-system regarding transcendence which 'objectifies' it, according to Smith; but it is the attribution – in any degree – of positively *salvific* significance to 'correct' belief, at that propositional level. That is, its being thought to convey not merely intellectual advantages, but also somehow moral ones.

47 John Cobb, 'Christian Witness in a Plural World', in John Hick and Hasan Askari, eds, *The Experience of Religious Diversity*, Aldershot: Gower Publishing Co, 1985, p. 153.
    As examples of 'Vedantist imperialism' affecting Western thinkers, Cobb cites the theological writings of Aldous Huxley, Arnold Toynbee, Frithjof Schuon and Huston Smith in particular. Its chief Indian exponent, on the other hand, is perhaps Radhakrishnan.

48 Cobb, *Beyond Dialogue*, pp. 123–8. And when Shinran, for instance, speaks of *shinjin* in relation to Amida, *shinjin* is not so very far removed from 'faith'.

49 In the same way, one might argue that it is quite inappropriate to speak of non-fideist traditions as offering doctrines of 'salvation'. See for example J.A. Di Noia, 'Varieties of Religious Aims: Beyond Exclusivism, Inclusivism and Pluralism', in Bruce D. Marshall, ed., *Theology and Dialogue*, Notre Dame, IN: University of Notre Dame Press, 1990.

50 See for example Aquinas, *Summa Theologiae* 2, 1: Q. 62 art. 2. The 'intellectual virtues', for Aquinas, are just those of which Aristotle wrote in the *Nicomachean Ethics*, Book 6.

51 Compare for example Gavin D'Costa's lament, 'The End of "Theology" and "Religious Studies"', in *Theology* 99 (791), 1996, pp. 338–51. D'Costa's solution

to the resulting problems is a system of free-market competition between a range of much more overtly confessional Theology Departments. I agree that this might in some ways be an improvement over the present situation – even though I also want to argue for more.

52 It was not for nothing that the liberal Harnack should have accused Barth of being a 'despiser of academic theology' – urging, against him, that the 'professorial chair should not be turned into a pulpit'. (This was just after Barth's appointment to the chair of theology at Göttingen in 1921). Barth naturally rejected the charge, in that form. But he also made it quite clear that the new concerns he shared with people like Eduard Thurneysen 'arose simply out of what we felt to be "*the need and promise of Christian preaching*"': see Barth, *The Word of God and the Word of Man*, Grand Rapids, MI: Eerdmans, 1935, p. 100.

He expresses deep respect for Schleiermacher, as a liberal apologetic theologian who was nevertheless a dedicated preacher; but regrets that Schleiermacher's main concern nevertheless appears to have been with the requirements of preaching, specifically, to the most cultivated sort of congregation – those capable of appreciating the 'virtuosity' of the true 'religious virtuoso'. And – as he complains in his combative preface to the second edition of his commentary, *The Epistle to the Romans*, in 1921, translated into English by Edwyn C. Hoskyns, Oxford: OUP, 1933 – the whole tendency of later liberal thinking was for biblical scholarship and church history to become increasingly divorced from the demands of preaching. In a letter to Thurneysen, again dating from his early days at Göttingen, he therefore expresses his determination to come back, in his lectures, again and again 'with stubborn persistence and from all directions to the situation of the preacher in the pulpit'. Both in those lectures and in the later *Church Dogmatics* one sees the results: it is not that these works are intended to provide direct source material for sermons – but their whole orientation is towards the training of preachers.

See in particular *The Göttingen Dogmatics: Instruction in the Christian Religion*, edited by Hannelotte Reiffen and translated into English by Geoffrey W. Bromiley, Grand Rapids, MI: Eerdmans, 1991, Introduction, § 2, 'Preaching as the Starting Point and Goal of Dogmatics', and *passim*; *Church Dogmatics*, 1:1, translated into English by Geoffrey W. Bromiley, Edinburgh: T. & T. Clark, 1975, § 3, 'Church Proclamation as the Material of Dogmatics', and *passim*.

To this extent I am entirely in agreement with Barth. It is just that I am also concerned with the task of the preacher in somewhat less conventional contexts than those that he envisages.

53 Karl Barth, *Church Dogmatics*, 4: 3, 1, translated into English by G.W. Bromiley, Edinburgh: T. & T. Clark, 1961, p. 86.

54 Ibid., p. 87.

55 He immediately refers, in the passage cited here, to the *Theological Declaration* of the 1934 Synod of Barmen; drafted by him as an anathematization of the German Christians.

56 Ibid., pp. 92–6.

57 Barth himself is simply blind to this basic distinction. All he sees is a multitude of reified 'religions'.

8 Expressivism and individuality in new social movements

1 Translated into English by Theodore M. Greene and Hoyt H. Hudson, New York: Harper & Row, 2nd edn, 1960. It was also translated, more recently, by George di Giovanni, in the Cambridge edition of the *Works of Immanuel Kant*, the volume entitled *Religion and Rational Theology*, Cambridge: CUP, 1996 –

    although here the German *Die Religion innerhalb der Grenzen der bloßen Vernunft* is actually rendered as 'Religion Within the Boundaries of Mere Reason'.

2   English translation by H.B. Nisbet in Kant, *Political Writings*, edited by Hans Reiss, 2nd edn, Cambridge: CUP, 1991.

3   Ibid., p. 50.

4   'What Is Enlightenment?', ibid., p. 54.

5   English translation by June Barraclough, London: Weidenfeld & Nicolson, 1955.

6   In Germany, one finds a rather similar development in the thought of Fichte, albeit further complicated, in his case, by a messianic anti-Napoleonic nationalism. Fichte begins as a Kantian.

7   'Journal of My Voyage in the Year 1769', partially translated by F. M. Barnard in his *J. G. Herder on Social and Political Culture*, Cambridge: CUP, 1969.

8   Partially translated into English in Barnard, op. cit.

9   See especially his *Metakritik zur Kritik der reinen Vernunft*, in *Sämmtliche Werke*, edited by B. Suphan, vol. 21, Berlin: Weidmannsche Buchhandlung, 1881.

10 Barnard, *J. G. Herder on Social and Political Culture*, p. 309.

11 On Herder's influence generally, see F.M. Barnard, *Herder's Social and Political Thought*, Oxford: Clarendon Press, 1965, Chapter 9.

12 Charles Taylor, *Hegel*, Cambridge: CUP, 1975, Chapter 1; *Sources of the Self*, Cambridge: CUP, 1989, Chapter 21. And cf. also Isaiah Berlin, *Vico and Herder: Two Studies in the History of Ideas*, London: Hogarth Press, 1976 – Berlin for his part speaks of Herder's 'expressionism'.

13 This wave of enthusiasm originated in the mid-eighteenth century, with the aesthetic writings of Winckelmann, and lasted well into the nineteenth century. Hölderlin, referred to above, was only a particularly extreme example.

     It is indeed a rather striking fact about Kant that he – quite exceptionally – appears to have remained immune to it.

14 Translation as in Taylor, *Hegel*, p. 55.

15 See H.S. Harris, *Hegel's Development: Towards the Sunlight, 1770–1801*, Oxford: Clarendon Press, 1972, pp. 271–2. 'Of all the major influences on the young Hegel', Harris writes, 'Herder's is the hardest to estimate reliably, but I suspect that it was great.' The only direct evidence of his reading of Herder comes in a letter from Hölderlin, in January 1795, and a passing reference in the notable fragment (dating from 1796), 'Jedes Volk hat ihm eigene Gegenstände', translated in T.M. Knox, *Hegel's Early Theological Writings*, Philadelphia, PA: University of Pennsylvania Press, 1971, p. 150. But if the notion of 'folk religion', which pervades these early texts, comes from any external source, it surely would be Herder.

16 This is, admittedly, not the actual terminology of the eighteenth or early nineteeth centuries. Nevertheless, I think it will serve.

17 *Lectures on the Philosophy of Religion*, English translation edited by Peter C. Hodgson, in 3 vols, Berkeley & Los Angeles: University of California Press, 1984, 1985, 1987.

18 English translation by A.V. Miller, Oxford: Clarendon Press, 1977. The *Phenomenology of Spirit* was originally published in 1807, the first of Hegel's properly 'systematic' writings.

19 *Phenomenology of Spirit*, paras 599–631.

20 Ibid., para. 670. Every 'action' is in some sense 'evil', so the argument runs – if only because of the impossibility of controlling the consequences, and the inevitable conflict between different duties (ibid., paras. 642–3). But the point is to get beyond good and evil, in this regard, as a falsely absolute opposition (paras 660 ff.).

21 For the most extreme version of this, see the maverick Alexander Kojève's all too influential *Introduction to the Reading of Hegel*, New York: Basic Books, 1969, pp. 34–5, 69–70, 72–3, 282.
22 *Phenomenology of Spirit*, para. 665.
23 Ibid., paras 648–58.
24 Ibid., paras 444–76.
25 I owe this particular point to a paper by professor Jay Bernstein, 'Conscience and Transgression: On the Persistence of Misrecognition', read at the 1993 annual conference of the Hegel Society of Great Britain.
26 See especially the commentary to para. 140: English translation by T.M. Knox, *Hegel's Philosophy of Right*, Oxford: Clarendon Press, 1952, pp. 94–103.
27 It is in this sense, for example, that he declares 'the divine principle in the state is the Idea made manifest on earth', *Lectures on the Philosophy of World History: Introduction: Reason in History*, translated by H.B. Nisbet, Cambridge: CUP, 1975, p. 95.
28 For a more extended version of the following argument, see my *Hegel's Political Theology*, Cambridge: CUP, 1991.
29 That is, in Hegelian jargon, 'the Idea' – as a generic term.
30 *Phenomenology of Spirit*, paras 206–30, 751–3. The Christological argument in Hegel's various lecture-series on the 'philosophy of religion' is rather differently framed: only in the 1827 series does he explicitly return to this particular way of putting things, and then only quite briefly. But it is in the *Phenomenology* that he seems to me to be at his theologically most profound.
31 *Phenomenology of Spirit*, para. 209, p. 127.
32 *Philosophy of Right*, para. 260, p. 161.
33 'Secularization' is a post-Hegelian term, but this is the chief polemic thrust of his remarks on church–state relations. See in particular: *Philosophy of Right*, commentary on para. 270; *Lectures on the Philosophy of Religion*, vol. 3, pp. 237–47, 339–47.
34 Hegel, *The Philosophy of History*, English translation by J. Sibree, New York: Dover Publications, 1956, pp. 412–24. He writes:

> In the Lutheran church the subjective feeling and the conviction of the individual is regarded as equally necessary with the objective side of Truth. Truth with Lutherans is not a finished and completed thing; the subject himself must be imbued with truth, surrendering his particular being in exchange for the substantial Truth, and making that Truth his own … In the proclamation of these principles is unfurled the new, the latest standard round which the peoples rally – the banner of *Free Spirit*, independent, though finding its life in the Truth, and enjoying independence only in it. This is the banner under which we serve, and which we bear. Time, since that epoch, has had no other work to do than the formal imbuing of the world with this principle
>
> (p. 416)

And see also p. 438, where he refers to 'the principle of subjectivity' as being that which Protestantism has' 'introduced' – in its liberating clarification of the underlying truth of the gospel.
35 Emil Fackenheim, *The Religious Dimension in Hegel's Thought*, Bloomington, IA: Indiana University Press, 1967, p. 224.
36 *Lectures on the Philosophy of World History: Introduction: Reason in History*, p. 27 (Sibree's translation, p. 9).

37 The concept of 'reason' actually figures in Hegel's thought in two basic sorts of context. The other is the contrast he draws between the two types of mental faculty: reason and 'understanding' (*Verstand*). By the faculty of 'understanding' he means a thinking solely concerned with questions of propositional correctness – fine for an analysis of the finite phenomena of nature, but ultimately useless when it comes to theology.

Here, reason is that which goes beyond mere understanding, in the sense of being the pursuit of truth – not just as a quality of propositions abstractly considered in themselves, but, rather, as the validity of any valid process of communication, in its concrete actual consequences.

38 *Philosophy of Right*, Preface, p. 10; *Hegel's Logic*, translated by William Wallace, Oxford: Clarendon Press, 1975, Introduction, p. 9.

39 See also *Lectures on the Philosophy of World History: Introduction: Reason in History*, pp. 27–9 (Sibree's translation, pp. 9–10). Here, Hegel further defines his project as a study of historical 'necessity': thus, he remarks, 'the sole aim of philosophical enquiry is *to eliminate the contingent*'. But not in the 'natural' sense of 'necessity', as in a doctrine of determinism – he is no determinist. No, the philosophy of world-history, as he understands it, 'eliminates the contingent' by definition, in that it deals with everything which is historically necessary for the full clarification of the meaning of 'reason', in all its implications, and nothing besides. Reason, in short, 'governs' the world of world-history, as perceived by philosophy, in the sense of being philosophical world-historiography's governing concern.

The whole project, in the first instance, 'presupposes' that 'reason ... is *substance* and *infinite power* ... the *infinite material* of all natural and spiritual life, and the *infinite form* which activates this material content'. This is Hegel's philosophical act of faith: that reason is the 'substance' of reality, in the sense that there is nothing whatsoever in human experience which is to be regarded as irreducibly alien to rationality, so setting limits on reason's 'infinite power' to question; that it connotes an invitation, in other words, to infinite enquiry into both the potential of human life (the 'infinite material') and its actuality (the 'infinite form'); that our rationality is of the essence of the divine dwelling within us.

And yet – 'these provisional remarks ... are not, even within our own discipline, to be regarded simply as prior assumptions, but as a preliminary *survey* of the whole, as the *result* of the ensuing enquiry'. The presupposition is also the result. Indeed, Hegel even, provocatively, speaks of his argument as 'proving' what it has already presupposed. It is 'proved' true in the sense that what was at first just abstractly posited is now concretely thought through. And – taste and see. The validity of the enterprise is demonstrated in its pragmatic capacity to reinforce the ethos it essentially celebrates, feeding into a new religious sensibility. This is no merely intellectual exercise. Reason is more than 'understanding' (note 37, above).

40 Francis Fukuyama, *The End of History and the Last Man*, Harmondsworth: Penguin, 1992.

41 The actual passage in the *Phenomenology* he does focus on is Chapter 4, A: the discussion of 'lordship and bondage'. In this he follows the emphasis of Alexandre Kojève, on whose reading of Hegel he is in fact largely dependent.

42 *Lectures on the Philosophy of World History: Introduction: Reason in History*, p. 54 (Sibree's translation, p. 18).

43 The key period for the decline of slavery in Western Europe was from the second half of the seventh century to the early eleventh century; prior to that, the institution continued to flourish with undiminished vigour under Christian rule. The

church's attitude was consistently ambivalent. Augustine justified slavery; other church fathers, such as Gregory the Great in the sixth century and Isidore of Seville in the seventh, argued forcibly and at length in its defence. The church itself was a major slave-owner: in Visigothic Spain, for instance, the sixteenth Council of Toledo (693) specified that each rural church needed at least ten slaves in order to support a full-time priest. Most would presumably have had far more.

Slavery eventually declined, it seems, above all because the class of city-dwellers for whom slaves were a luxury-possession had dwindled; and because of changing patterns in land usage. There ceased to be so many large estates. It was the smaller estates which flourished, and they needed well-motivated tenant-farmers rather than slaves. New technological developments – the introduction of water mills, the frontal yoke for oxen and the horse-harness – meant that there was less need for brute human labour. The general trend was for economic growth, and as a result there was no lack of work available for runaway slaves.

See for example Pierre Bonassie, 'The survival and extinction of the slave system in the early medieval West (fourth to eleventh centuries)', in idem., *From Slavery to Feudalism in South-Western Europe*, Cambridge: CUP, 1991; and, for a wide-ranging sociological approach, Orlando Patterson, *Slavery and Social Death: A Comparative Approach*, Cambridge, MA: Harvard University Press, 1982.

44 Hegel does not speak of 'shakenness'. But he does speak of 'revealed religion' passing over into 'absolute knowing' by virtue of letting its 'actual self-consciousness' become 'the object of its consciousness': *Phenomenology of Spirit*, para. 788. By the 'object' of revealed religious consciousness is meant what it regards as divine. And the 'actual self-consciousness' of revealed religion – insofar as *Vorstellen* has given way to authentic *Denken* – is its participant's experience of shakenness.

9 Against 'recoil-theology'

1 Dietrich Bonhoeffer, *Letters and Papers from Prison*, edited by Eberhard Bethge, translated by Reginald Fuller, Frank Clarke and others, enlarged edn, London: SCM Press, 1971, p. 382.

2 O'Donovan, *The Desire of the Nations*, Cambridge: CUP, 1996.

3 Theodor Adorno, Else Frenkel-Brunswick, Daniel Levinson, Nevitt Sanford, *The Authoritarian Personality*, New York: Harper & Row, 1950. This famous study, based on survey work in the United States done in the immediate aftermath of the Second World War, originated as an attempt to understand the psychological appeal of totalitarian movements. 'Authoritarianism' here, therefore, is intended to signify that whole constellation of pre-political attitudes most likely to predispose people to sympathize with totalitarian politics. But it was perhaps a rather unfortunate choice of terminology – in O'Donovan's terms, quite a revealing indication of the 'late modern liberal' prejudices of the authors themselves. As if the very notion of proper 'authority' were suspect in this regard!

4 He is a 'liberal' in the same strictly political sense that Karl Barth, for instance – that great scourge of 'liberalism' as a matter of theological methodology – might nevertheless also be called one.

5 O'Donovan does have a number of other objections to the background intellectual culture of 'late modern liberalism': a marked distaste for its politics shaped by mass-culture; an unease with the way it has tended to counterpoise a shallow-rooted 'revolutionary' progressivism, on the one hand, with social-scientific fatalism on the other; and a general worry about the spiritual implications of its

largely utilitarian and social-contractarian ethos. But then a great many of those he would call 'late modern liberal' theologians would also want to criticize *these* features of their environment, in their own way, just as much as he.

6 O'Donovan, *The Desire of the Nations*, p. 16.

7 Ibid.

8 Ibid., p. 18.

9 Ibid., p. 16.

10 John Milbank, '"Postmodern Critical Augustinianism": A Short Summa in Forty Two Responses to Unasked Questions', in *Modern Theology* 7 (3), April 1991, p. 235.

11 Milbank, *Theology and Social Theory: Beyond Secular Reason*, Oxford: Blackwell, 1990, p. 278.

12 Milbank, 'The Midwinter Sacrifice', in *Studies in Christian Ethics*, 10 (2), 1997.

13 *Theology and Social Theory: Beyond Secular Reason*, Part 2.

14 Ibid., Chapter 6.

15 Ibid., Chapter 8.

16 Ibid., p. 196. (And he also refers here to his article 'Were the Christian Socialists Socialists?' in Jack Forstman and Joseph Pickle, eds, *Papers of the Nineteenth Century Working Group*, AAR 1988 Annual Meeting, vol. 14, pp. 86–95.)

17 Milbank, *The Word Made Strange*, Oxford: Blackwell, 1997, Chapter 12.

18 Ibid.

19 O'Donovan, *Resurrection and Moral Order: An Outline for Evangelical Ethics*, Leicester: Inter-Varsity Press, 1986, p. 58.

20 O'Donovan nowhere speaks much of 'solidarity'. He speaks rather of 'community' – as that which emerges from a response, of 'praise', to authentic authority.

21 *Resurrection and Moral Order*, p. 74.

10 The healing of Christendom's original trauma

1 This, it seems to me, is the essential truth of the saying of Jesus recorded in Matthew 5: 18–19, Luke 16: 17.

2 See 1 and 2 Timothy, Titus, Jude, *2 Peter* and Colossians. (But Gnosticism was nevertheless intermingled with Catholicism in church-life right up until the late second century.)

3 These are the aspects of Gnostic thought on which Elaine Pagels focuses, for instance, in *The Gnostic Gospels*, London: Weidenfeld & Nicolson, 1980.

4 Cf. R.I. Moore, *The Formation of a Persecuting Society: Power and Deviance in Western Europe, 950–1250*, Oxford: Blackwell, 1987; John Boswell, *Christianity, Social Tolerance, and Homosexuality: Gay People in Western Europe from the Beginning of the Christian Era to the Fourteenth Century*, Chicago, IL: 1980; Norman Cohn, *Europe's Inner Demons*, revised edn, London: Pimlico, 1993.

As Moore notes, the growth of towns in the twelfth and thirteenth centuries also resulted in the rise of new privileged classes, whose power was entirely money-based. There were, he argues, two basic ecclesiastical responses to this. The more critical response took the form of a renewed affirmation of God's concern for the poor, firstly in sermons and then more especially in the emergence of the mendicant religious orders. But wherever the church took the other way – and sought, on the contrary, to uphold the new secular regimes – the result was, more or less inevitably, for it to get caught up in the diversionary politics of persecution.

5 I put the word in inverted commas in order to indicate the uncertainty of the actual medical diagnosis appropriate to the victims: see Moore, op. cit., pp. 73–80.

6   Boswell notes this with particular reference to the persecution of homosexuals, for instance – which may, indeed, often have had a certain anti-clerical impetus to it: op. cit., p. 278.

7   Mark C. Taylor, *Deconstructing Theology*, New York: Crossroad, 1982, p. xii. This is actually something of a show of modesty on Altizer's part – since these are all the things he himself was already attempting to be, in his own earlier work.

Taylor is indeed to some extent a representative figure. Besides Altizer, there are several also others who might perhaps be cited, more or less, as allies: Robert P. Scharlemann, Charles Winquist, David Ray Griffin, Don Cupitt. Cf. Graham Ward, 'Postmodern Theology', in David Ford, ed., *The Modern Theologians*, 2nd edn, Oxford: Blackwell, 1997, who groups all these various figures together under the general heading of 'liberal postmodern theologians'.

8   Taylor, *Erring: A Postmodern A/theology*, Chicago, IL: University of Chicago Press, 1984. And see also *Altarity*, Chicago, IL: University of Chicago Press, 1987.

9   See especially *Journeys to Selfhood: Hegel and Kierkegaard*, Berkeley, CA: University of California Press, 1980.

10 Hegel, *Lectures on the Philosophy of Religion*, vol. 3, English translation edited by Peter C. Hodgson, Berkeley: University of California Press, 1987, p. 162.

11 Hegel, *Phenomenology of Spirit*, para. 658, p. 400.

11   A new covenant?

1   It is in fact back-projected into three different stories. Besides the covenant sealed by Moses on Mount Sinai, there is also the covenant sealed by Joshua at Shechem: Joshua 24: 1–27. (Shechem had in pre-Israelite times contained the sanctuary of a Canaanite god called Baalberith or El-berith, 'Baal of the covenant' or 'El of the covenant'; see Judges 8: 33, 9: 4, 46. And it has been controversially suggested that the Israelite notion of the covenant may have orig-inated as a borrowing from that cult.) And there is the much briefer story of the covenant with Abram, in Genesis 15: 17–18.

2   See Chapter 5, note 2, above.

3   St Thomas Aquinas, *Summa Theologiae*, Ia, 50, 4.

The New Testament notion of angels and demonic powers appears to be rather different. Aquinas finds direct scriptural backing for the attribution of 'faith' to the demons, in James 2: 19: 'You believe that God is one; you do well. Even the demons believe – and shudder.' Wilfred Cantwell Smith's comment on this verse (*Belief and History*, p. 74) is that it is the one place in the Bible where the verb *pisteuô* (translated as 'believe') does *not* refer to 'faith'. Aquinas, on the other hand, distinguishes 'formed faith' from 'unformed faith': what the demons have is a type of 'unformed faith', without love. And if the demons, the fallen angels, have 'faith' – he then argues – how could the unfallen angels not have it, in its fuller version?

Well, it may be that the authority of James does indeed compel us to talk in such terms. But even in that case the question still remains: are *these* demons the same as those of Aquinas? Are they not, rather, just metaphorical aspects of historic human community? It was the Neo-Platonist metaphysics of the Pseudo-Dionysius which decisively tended to dehistoricize the notion of demons and angels for Christian theology, in the early sixth century.

4   It was, in each case, a higher form of faith inasmuch as it was closer to 'knowl-edge'. And the first two objections to the proposition that 'faith' is attributable to unfallen humanity and to the angels, considered and refuted by Aquinas in

2a2ae, 5, 1, are both arguments to the effect that it was not 'faith' because it was really 'knowledge'. (However, he replies that 'knowledge' of God is only properly attributable to the beatific vision, to which the angels did not attain until after their primal faith-inspired option for obedience to God, and which humanity still awaits.)

The third objection is, I think, more to the present point. It is based on Romans 10: 17: 'faith comes by hearing and hearing by the word of God'. But, so the argument runs, 'this has no application to the original angelic or human condition, wherein there was no way of hearing from someone else. Therefore in neither case did faith exist.' And I agree: faith depends on being historically situated! Aquinas however, in his refutation, simply brushes this aside with the observation that 'hearing came in the original state, not from a man speaking from without, but from God inspiring from within'. Which is all very well – only, how then does it help to use the same term, 'faith', for what follows from two such totally different experiences of 'hearing'?

5 *Summa Theologiae*, Ia, 206, 4. Augustine is the great primary authority for this view. In biblical terms the struggle was, in the first instance, over the interpretation of Revelation 20: 1–10. Here we read of a 'binding' of Satan, followed by a period of a 'thousand years' in which Christ reigns in the company of the martyrs, before the final end of time. But how are we to understand this: as a prophecy of the future – or as a veiled description of the present age? For Augustine, the binding of Satan is simply a symbol of the already accomplished resurrection of Christ. Joachim, by contrast, insists on seeing it as something more.

6 Smith, *Faith and Belief*, pp. 78–91, 274–304. Thus:

(i) Smith claims that mediaeval theology in general, including Aquinas's, largely anticipates his own distinction between 'faith' and 'belief' with its own distinction between *fides* and *opinio* or *aestimatio*: *fides* being understood here as a response to direct personal experience, and hence to that which is certain; whereas *opinio/aestimatio* is always a thinking at some remove from direct experience, and uncertain. In Thomist terminology, even the most perfectly correct *opinio* about God, insofar as it remains at the level of mere *opinio*, only amounts to a sort of 'unformed faith' (*fides informis*) – which, unlike true, or 'formed' faith, is entirely devoid of any *saving* significance. (There are two sorts of 'unformed faith': the other is that of the demons in James 2: 19, who by contrast see with certainty. See note 3, above.)

(ii) Basing his argument on the authority of Augustine, Aquinas also clearly implies that saving faith can in fact co-exist with all manner of false *opinio* – just so long as the false *opinio* is not held 'obstinately'. For heresy – that which excludes saving faith – consists in a sort of obstinacy. Just as much as faith, it resides primarily in the will, and only secondarily in the beliefs to which the perverted will then clings.

(iii) In *Summa Theologiae* 2a2ae, 1, 2 he explicitly remarks upon the somewhat ambivalent relationship which faith therefore has to its own propositional expression, in whatever form that may take. On the one hand, the expression is necessary inasmuch as faith is, subjectively, a dynamic of the human intellect. But on the other hand it inevitably distorts what it represents: propositions, by their nature, represent reality in composite terms, yet 'the first truth' – God, the proper object of faith – is an intrinsically *non*-composite, or 'simple' reality.

7 On Joachimism generally, see for example: Marjories Reeves, *The Influence of Prophecy in the Later Middle Ages: A Study in Joachimism*, Oxford: OUP, 1969 and *Joachim of Fiore and the Prophetic Future*, London: SPCK, 1976; Bernard

McGinn, *The Calabrian Abbot: Joachim of Fiore in the History of Western Thought*, New York: Macmillan, 1985.

8 Essentially, but not exclusively: he also made some play with a sevenfold scheme, looking forward to the seventh age (*aetas*), the 'great Sabbath' ...

9 To be more precise, the third *status* actually grows from two roots for Joachim, corresponding to the double procession of the Holy Spirit (in the Western tradition) from both the Father and the Son. Its first root stems from the prophets Elijah, Elisha and their followers – understood as the remote predecessors of Christian monasticism.

10 Originally a Cistercian, he left to establish his own order, the Florensians – although this new order never spread very far. See Stephen Wessley, *Joachim of Fiore and Monastic Reform*, New York: Peter Lang, 1990.

11 These were Lucius III, Urban III and Clement III. And King Richard of England, on his way as a crusader to the Holy Land, also came to consult with Joachim.

12 See Reeves, *The Influence of Prophecy*, Part 2.

13 Letter 46, in Peter Matheson, ed., *The Collected Works of Thomas Müntzer*, Edinburgh: T. & T. Clark, 1988, pp. 71–2.

14 Gotthold Ephraim Lessing, *The Education of the Human Race*, §§ 85–90, first published in 1780. English translation in Henry Chadwick, ed., *Lessing's Theological Writings*, London: A. & C. Black, 1956. Lessing's chief source on Joachimism appears to have been J.L. von Mosheim, *Institutiones historiae ecclesiasticae*, 1st edn 1737–41, 2nd edn 1755, XIII Saeculum, II, 2, §§ 33–4: a very sketchy account of Joachimist ideas among the Spiritual Franciscans. Mosheim is, in fact, unsure whether Joachim was a real historical figure.

15 F.W.J. Schelling, *Philosophie der Offenbarung*, lecture 36, in *Sämmtliche Werke*, II, 4, Stuttgart & Augsburg: J.G. Cotta, 1858.

16 George Sand, *Spiridion*, Paris: Félix Bonnaire, 1839. The two main influences on the thinking in this Gothic novel of ideas are the Abbé Lamennais and, still more directly, Pierre Leroux, to whom it is dedicated: both key figures in the movement.

17 See for instance Bloch, *The Principle of Hope*, English translation by Neville Plaice and Paul Knight, Cambridge, MA: MIT Press, 1986, vol. 2, pp. 509–15. But there are eulogistic references to Joachim throughout Bloch's writings.

18 Cf. my *Civil Society, Civil Religion*, Oxford: Blackwell, 1995, Chapter 4.

19 By a 'post-metaphysical' doctrine of the Trinity I simply mean one which focuses on the conversational contexts and necessary virtues bound up with the solidarity of the shaken throughout history. Metaphysical doctrines, by contrast, tend to jump straight from biblical narrative to the dialectics of eternity, in celebration of the eternal significance of the church's confessional identity.

20 Hegel, *Lectures on the Philosophy of Religion*, vol. 3, p. 286.

My chief criticism of Hegel's Trinitarian doctrine, however, would be that in a sense he still conceives of the 'abstract personality' of the three Persons all too abstractly. For he does not consider the concrete church-origins of the doctrine at all – the only early Trinitarianism he discusses is that of the pagan Neo-Platonists! But, instead, he correlates the threeness of the three Persons to the three poles of a syllogism: universality, particularity, singularity. So we have three 'elements' or 'realms' of thought. The element of universality, correlated to the First Person, is constituted by a thinking radically detached from the particularity of particular historic or mythic events, seeking to grasp the underlying logical structure common to all validly systematic reflection. (Hence, his discussion of this element is also the context for his analysis of the 'immanent Trinity'; that is, the interplay between divine universality, particularity and singularity, conceived in the most general terms.) The element of particularity, correlated to the Second Person, is the exact opposite: so it encompasses a thinking entirely immersed in the narrative detail of salvation history. Whilst the element of singularity, correlated to the Third Person, is just what mediates between these two poles at the level of actual religious practice.

This is neat. And, no doubt, First-Person theology in the sense of friendly inter-cultural encounter will indeed tend towards a certain reconciliatory universalism of thought; Second-Person theology in the sense of a reflection on struggle will tend to base itself on the particularity of particular exemplary moments of conflict; Third-Person theology in the sense of an opening to the future will also tend to mediate between the other two.

But, as Hegel himself presents it, the connection of his doctrine to the original tradition is not spelt out at all.

21 The major adjustments had to do with the establishing of the equality of the Persons. Origen for example, writing in the first half of the third century, takes it to be quite uncontroversially axiomatic that there is a hierarchy within the Trinity, with the First Person the highest. But in the course of the fourth century, after much bitter conflict, the opposite view eventually prevailed. It seems to me that this development needs to be considered, at least in part, sociologically. Thus, the problematics giving rise to First-Person theology were primarily an issue for the philosophically-educated élite within the church; the problematics, in particular, of Second-Person theology were an issue for all Christians, inasmuch as all were affected by the world's hostility. One did not need to be able to think in abstract conceptual terms to relate to the incarnate Son; stories sufficed. But to relate to God the Father was in this regard more difficult. Hence, subliminally, God the Father appeared to have a special relationship to the élite; and was assumed to have a pre-eminent status within the Trinity, in effect corresponding to theirs within the church.

Note, however, that in Origen's day this élite drew its prestige essentially from its educational qualifications, not ecclesiastical rank. Many of the leading early theologians were laymen: Justin Martyr, Tatian, Tertullian, Clement and Origen himself for much of his career. (And all of these were also Binitarian or Trinitarian subordinationists.) Later on, this changed. In the fourth century the task of theology was becoming increasingly reserved for bishops, more interested in the authority deriving from their rank than in that which came from a philosophical education. In this context – where the prestige of a philosophical education, specially associated with First-Person theology, mattered less – the intrinsic egalitarianism of the gospel was able to reassert itself, and was projected into a transformed Trinitarianism.

22 On the relationship between Joachimism and Hegel, see Cyril O'Regan, *The Heterodox Hegel*, Albany, NY: SUNY Press, 1994, pp. 263–5, 270–9. O'Regan follows Henri de Lubac in linking Hegel to a supposed tradition of 'Joachimite Lutheranism'. And perhaps there is some truth in this. On the other hand, the evidence for such a tradition is somewhat tenuous; Hegel nowhere refers to Joachim, and Schelling, who came from the identical intellectual background to Hegel, professes only to have discovered about Joachim quite late on in his career, after Hegel's death. If there was any actual influence, it was probably therefore only very indirect. The one passage in Hegel's writing which does seem to fit quite closely with the Joachimist scheme is in fact the 'unhappy consciousness' passage in the *Phenomenology*, with its three stages: the unchallenged unhappy consciousness; the unhappy consciousness overcome symbolically but not yet in practice; and true 'freedom of self-consciousness'. But this

correspondence could just be coincidental. On the whole, I think, the Hegelian doctrine has to be seen as another completely fresh start.

12 The other matrix: Islamic civil society

1 Just to consider the very grossest and most obvious symptoms of this mentality: whilst it may not have been quite the paradise of religious toleration which some Muslim apologists like to claim, the fact remains that there was in this world never any Inquisition of the sort the Dominicans ran in contemporary Christendom, far less institutionalized homophobia; there were no persecution of 'lepers' and no great witch-scares.

As for the Jews, they like the Christians may have been second-class citizens, and sometimes brutally repressed. But at any rate – up until the traumas of the nineteenth century – Islam remained immune to the paranoid fantasy of the blood-libel; that is, the lethal charge that Jews used Gentile blood for ritual purposes. From the fifteenth century CE onwards there is evidence of this notion spreading from Christendom into the Ottoman Empire. See Bernard Lewis, *The Jews of Islam*, Princeton University Press, 1984, pp. 147, 156–9. The sultans issued several decrees requiring that such cases should be brought to trial before the Imperial Divan in Istanbul – 'where', as Lewis remarks, 'presumably, the high officers of state would be less subject to bigotry and superstition and less open to local pressures'. But the accusers, here, seem to have been Christians. Similarly in the nineteenth century, when such cases proliferated, it was the Christians who took the lead – even though in the end Muslim minds were also infected.

2 On the history of Sufism generally, see J. Spencer Trimingham, *The Sufi Orders in Islam*, Oxford: Clarendon Press, 1971; Seyyed Hossein Nasr, ed., *Islamic Spirituality: Manifestations*, London: SCM Press, 1991.

3 Admittedly, in later Safavid Iran the Shi'ite *'ulama* had already turned decisively against the orders, the key instigator of this turn being Muhammad Baqir Majlisi (d. 1110/1699)

4 As Hegel puts it: 'The History of the World is not the theatre of happiness. Periods of happiness are blank pages in it', *The Philosophy of History*, translated by J. Sibree, New York: Dover Publications, 1956, p. 26.

5 See Alexandre Bennigsen, 'Official Islam and Sufi Brotherhoods in the Soviet Union Today', in A.S. Cudsi and A.E. Hillal Dessouki, eds, *Islam and Power*, London: Croom Helm, 1981; Alexandre Bennigsen and Chantal Lemercier-Quelquejay, 'Muslim Religious Conservatism and Dissent in the USSR', in *Religion in Communist Lands*, 6, August 1978.

In the 1974 Census, 63 per cent of the Muslim population in the Chechen-Ingush ASSR declared themselves to be 'believers', as compared with just 12 per cent of all Russians; and a 1975 survey indicated that 'more than half the believers' were members of Sufi orders. This would suggest that there were over half a million Sufis in the Northern Caucasus region as a whole, far more members than the Communist Party could boast – and truly, as Bennigsen and Lemercier-Quelquejay remark, 'a fantastic number for an underground society which is banned by Soviet Law'! The two main orders there, the Naqshabandiyya and the Qadiriyya, have a long tradition of holy war against the Russians; the struggle of the 1990s was nothing new. And their holiest shrines are those of saints who were also resistance fighters. The orders had survived the mass deportations from the Northern Caucasus to Siberia and Kazakhstan in 1943; in fact, they had even prospered and put down new roots in Central Asia as a result. (There was then a great return from exile in 1957–8.) Although otherwise very conservative, they had also begun to recruit large numbers of women as adepts, even as sheikhs; and were increasingly attracting young people.

6   Where there had been 24,000 mosques in 1917, there were less than 300 officially licensed in 1978.

7   'Fundamentalism' is not only first and foremost a term of abuse, it also tends to be very imprecise. It derives originally from the description of certain Christian phenomena. Far better, I think, to use a term which immediately advertises the radical difference of what is being described from anything Christian. Nazih Ayubi, in *Political Islam*, London: Routledge, 1991, pp. 67–8, distinguishes 'salafism' from 'fundamentalism' and 'neo-fundamentalism', as three successively appearing sub-groups of 'Islamism'. But Ayubi himself acknowledges the imprecision of the distinction: all he can say is that 'fundamentalists' differ from 'salafists' in being 'generally less sympathetic to *fiqh* (jurisprudence)' – a very impressionistic sort of judgement.

8   See Adrian Hastings, *The Construction of Nationhood: Ethnicity, Religion and Nationalism*, Cambridge: CUP, 1997.

9   See Jacob M. Landau, *The Politics of Pan-Islam* , Oxford: The Clarendon Press, 1994.

10 Properly *theological* advocacy of second modernity has been rare in the Muslim context. Perhaps the most notable example is the work of the Indian poet-philosopher and advocate of a future Pakistan, Muhammad Iqbal. At all events he welcomed the Turkish revolution. See his work, *The Reconstruction of Religious Thought in Islam*, Lahore: Muhammad Ashraf, 1951, p. 162:

> The truth is that among the Muslim nations of today, Turkey alone has shaken off its dogmatic slumber, and attained to self-consciousness. She alone has claimed her right of intellectual freedom; she alone has passed from the ideal to the real – a transition which entails keen intellectual and moral struggle.

This comes from a series of lectures, first published in 1930. Iqbal goes on to compare Atatürk's work with the Protestant Reformation in Europe, as two examples of what he terms religious 'liberalism' tied to an upsurge of nationalist sentiment. He approves of the liberalism, and deplores the nationalism. It may be that the former can only ever gain adequate popular support by some measure of association with the latter; well, if so – he seems to suggest – then so be it. Only let it be done with care. Muslims need to learn a cautionary lesson, in this regard, from the errors of Christendom.

Another example is the work of the Egyptian scholar 'Ali 'Abd ar-Raziq, who in 1925 welcomed the abolition of the caliphate, arguing for a strict secularizing separation between religious and political authority on the grounds that to confuse the two is to corrupt the former: the prophet Muhammad, he argues, was never a king; the caliphs, as mere kings, are therefore by no means heirs to his authority.

See Leonard Binder, *Islamic Liberalism*, Chicago, IL and London: University of Chicago Press, 1988, Chapter 4.

11 Quoted in Ayubi, *Political Islam*, p. 132.

12 See for instance Michael Gilsenan, *Saint and Sufi in Modern Egypt*, Oxford: Clarendon Press, 1973, pp. 203–5. Gilsenan considers the rise of the Muslim Brotherhood to have been one of the most significant factors leading to the decline of the orders in Egypt. The activities of the early Brotherhood were indeed truly multifarious: they ran their own schools and youth organizations, provided clinics and social services, and set up all sorts of co-operative business

enterprise. By the early 1950s the membership was reckoned to be almost one million. In 1954, however, they fell foul of the new government under Nasser and were for a time violently repressed.

13 'Abd as-Salam Faraj, for instance, who was the leader of the group that assassinated President Sadat in 1981, actually set out his position in the form of a commentary on the theory of *jihad* in Ibn Taymiyya and Ibn Kathir. See Emmanuel Sivan, *Radical Islam: Medieval Theology and Modern Politics*, New Haven, CT and London: Yale University Press, 1985, and Gilles Kepel, *The Pharoah and the Prophet: Muslim Extremism in Egypt*, London: Al Saqi Books, 1985.

13 'Holy, Catholic and Apostolic'

1 Angela West, *Deadly Innocence: Feminist Theology and the Mythology of Sin*, London: Cassell, 1995.
2 Ibid., p. 17.
3 Ibid., p. 57.
4 A secondary factor was the disastrous trouble at the Molesworth peace camp. Molesworth was the other airbase at which cruise missiles were stationed, but the peace camp there was mixed-sex – and it was alleged that on several occasions male peace-campers had raped female peace-campers. There was a sharp polarization of attitudes over how to respond to this crisis.
5 One of the leading post-Christian feminist theologians, Mary Daly, actually signalled her own departure from Roman Catholicism by staging a symbolic walk-out from a church service.
6 This is an argument which is in fact to be found in both post-Christian and still-Christian forms. West refers to it as the 'Saiving-Plaskow hypothesis'. It is the central thesis of the article which launched the contemporary feminist theology movement: Valerie Saiving, 'The Human Situation: A Feminine View', *Journal of Religion*, vol. 40, 1960, pp. 100–12. And it is systematically developed above all by Judith Plaskow, in her book *Sex, Sin and Grace: Women's Experience and the Theologies of Reinhold Niebuhr and Paul Tillich*, Washington: University Press of America, 1980.
7 One might compare Reinhold Niebuhr on the same general theme: his doctrine largely originates, in the aftermath of the Russian Revolution, as a response to the dangers of sectarian socialism. (But of course Niebuhr's thought does not yet contain any intimations of third modernity.)
8 The actual phrase 'the Catholic Church' first appears in Ignatius of Antioch, Epistle to the Smyrnaeans, 8: 2, dated *c*. 112, an anti-Gnostic polemic. And, for early church theology, that sets the tone.
9 Again, this also fits the Trinitarian pattern: the thinking through of reforming intransigence is the central task of Second-Person theology; the culture-transcendent spirit of strict classlessness belongs above all to First-Person theology; honesty in rootedness is the determining ideal of Third-Person theology.
10 John Rawls, *A Theory of Justice*, Cambridge, MA: Harvard University Press, 1971.

14 Discourse ethics and religion

1 Sallust, *Bellum Catilinae*, vii.
2 Augustine, *The City of God*, II, 18. The reference is to Sallust, *Historiae fragmenta*, I, 11.

3 *The City of God*, V, 12–16. Of course, Augustine still approves of the conventional authority of the Roman paterfamilias over his womenfolk, children and slaves – it would be wildly anachronistic to expect anything different. But what he is primarily concerned with in this context is the proper quality of Christian peer relationships.

4 Note in particular how in *The City of God*, V, 12 he virtually identifies the two – in antithesis to the love of liberty.

5 See for example Albrecht Dihle, *The Theory of the Will in Classical Antiquity*, Berkeley, CA: University of California Press, 1982.

6 Compare Augustine, *Confessions*, VIII, 8, where just before the actual crisis of his conversion Augustine – following a conversation with a devotee of St Antony, the first Desert Father – bursts out to his friend Alipius,

> This is just too much! What? Did you hear? The uneducated rise up and storm into heaven, while we with all our learning – look at us, still wallowing in the concerns of flesh and blood! Are we ashamed to follow because it's they who have taken the lead? Or if we can't even follow them – isn't that yet more shameful?

(And then, in the book, he launches straight into a meditation on the strange recalcitrance of the will ...)

7 *The City of God*, XIV, 28; the translation by Henry Bettenson, slightly modified, is published by Harmondsworth: Penguin, 1972.

8 See in particular Jean L. Cohen and Andrew Arato, *Civil Society and Political Theory*, Cambridge, MA: MIT Press, 1992. Another example is Larry Ray, *Rethinking Critical Theory: Emancipation in the Age of Global Social Movements*, London: Sage, 1993.

9 Habermas, *The Theory of Communicative Action*, vol. I, London: Heinemann, 1984, pp. 329, 331–4.

 In an earlier passage, pp. 84–96, 'communicative action' is actually opposed to 'normatively regulated' and 'dramaturgical' action. But that is because Habermas, there, is distinguishing between, on the one hand, sociological theories with a relatively narrow interest in one of the latter two phenomena and, on the other hand, more comprehensive theories dealing with the whole range of different potential types of communication.

10 *The Theory of Communicative Action*, vol. II, pp. 190–7.

 Note, incidentally, how Robert Bellah's notion of 'civil religion' appears in this scheme of things – as designating some of the last shadowy relics of what is disappearing.

11 Cf. ibid., pp. 188–9. Also the whole of 5.3.

12 Habermas, 'Transcendence from Within, Transcendence in this World', in Don S. Browning and Francis Schüssler Fiorenza, eds, *Habermas, Modernity and Public Theology*, New York: Crossroad, 1992.

13 Jens Glebe-Möller, *A Political Dogmatic*, Philadelphia, PA: Fortress, 1987.

 Habermas also speaks of 'the atheistic core, enveloped in esoteric insight' of Hegel's thought, presumably in the same sense. But then I immediately become uneasy. For, whilst this way of putting things may help dramatize the undoubted radicalism of Hegel's questioning of the orthodox tradition, does it not equally tend to devalue the counterbalancing seriousness and cogency of his loyalty to that tradition – and so dissolve the absolutely elementary tension on which his thought depends?

14 Helmut Peukert, *Science, Action and Fundamental Theology*, Cambridge, MA: MIT Press, 1986.

15 One finds similar themes, earlier, notably in the theology of Johann-Baptist Metz; who, in turn, is partly inspired by scattered remarks made by some of the earlier protagonists of Critical Theory – Walter Benjamin, Max Horkheimer and Ernst Bloch. But it is Peukert who develops the argument most systematically.

16 Habermas, 'Transcendence from Within, Transcendence in this World', pp. 236–8.

15 *'Wo aber Gefahr ist ...'*

1 Habermas, *The Theory of Communicative Action*, vol. II, Cambridge: Polity Press, 1987, pp. 391–6. And cf. the critical comments on this by Cohen and Arato: *Civil Society and Political Theory*, pp. 527–32. They seek to correct his analysis with a counterbalancing emphasis on the potential *creativity* of these movements.

2 Václav Havel, 'Politics and Conscience', English translation by E. Kohák and R. Scruton, in *Living in Truth*, edited by Jan Vadislav, London: Faber & Faber, 1987, p. 136.

3 Ibid., pp. 143–4.

4 Ibid., p. 146.

5 The translation here is my own (but cf. Michael Hamburger's translation of the whole poem, in Friedrich Hölderin, *Selected Poems and Fragments*, Harmondsworth: Penguin, 1998, pp. 230–49).

Index